Francis Cleary

Ontario history

vol. 9-10

Francis Cleary

Ontario history
vol. 9-10

ISBN/EAN: 9783741135316

Manufactured in Europe, USA, Canada, Australia, Japa

Cover: Foto ©ninafisch / pixelio.de

Manufactured and distributed by brebook publishing software (www.brebook.com)

Francis Cleary

Ontario history

Ontario Historical Society.

PAPERS AND RECORDS.

VOL. IX.

TORONTO:
PUBLISHED BY THE SOCIETY,
1910.

CONTENTS.

		PAGE
I.	Fort Malden or Amherstburg. By FRANCIS CLEARY	5
II.	Thamesville and the Battle of the Thames. By KATHERINE B. COUTTS.	20
III.	The Highland Pioneers of the County of Middlesex.	26
IV.	Centenary of the Death of Brant. By HERBERT F. GARDINER, M.A.	33
V.	The Pioneers of Middlesex.	55
VI.	The Beginning of London. By COL. T. CAMPBELL, M.D.	61
VII.	An Episode of the War of 1812. The Story of the Schooner "Nancy"	75
VIII.	Register of Baptisms, Marriages and Deaths, at St. Thomas, U.C., commencing with the Establishment of the Mission in July, 1824	127

I.

FORT MALDEN OR AMHERSTBURG.

By Francis Cleary.

Read at the Annual Meeting of the O. H. S., at London, Ont., Sept. 11th, 1908.

At last Canadians are awakening to the importance and necessity of making an effort to preserve and restore the historical battlefields and other landmarks of this country. This is seen in the great interest taken in the recent proposal of His Excellency Earl Grey for the conversion into a park, and the restoration of the battlefields of the Plains of Abraham and of St. Foye at Quebec.

It is an opportune time to draw the attention of the Government and of others in the immediate localities to do something to reclaim and preserve the old forts and historical landmarks of lesser note in other parts of our country. These are rapidly passing away and their preservation would do much "to strengthen the tie that binds" and make those of the present day feel proud of their ancestors, and to respect and honor the men who in 1812 and again in 1838-1839 helped to defend this country and handed down to us the glorious heritage which we now possess.

In the early history of Upper Canada this western peninsula, the County of Essex, came into notice on account of the stirring events which took place on its border, second only to those which took place in the Niagara frontier.

Fort Amherstburg, or Fort Malden, as the name under which it became better known, deserves the attention of the Government and of those interested in the reclamation of historical landmarks.

For the following account of this Fort I am indebted to extracts taken from "Early Amherstburg," published in January, 1902, by Mr. C. C. James, Deputy Minister of Agriculture for Ontario, and "Fort Malden," by Rev. Thomas Nattress, B.A., of Amherstburg, published two years later. Mr. James says he found that Fort Malden did not exist in the early days, but that Fort Amherstburg did. I found that three different forts had been constructed, or partly constructed, at Amherstburg at different times, and that the first was officially known as Fort Amherstburg; the second was known both as Fort Amherstburg and as Fort Malden, and that the third, constructed subsequent to 1837, bore the name of Fort Malden.

The war of American Independence was brought to a close in 1783; Oswego, Niagara and Detroit remained as British Posts until their evacuation in 1796, Detroit being transferred in July of that year.

The late Judge Woods of Chatham, in referring to this event in "Harrison Hall and its Associations," says this may be called the "Exodus Act," as it provided for the departure of British authority from Detroit to Sandwich, ... and that from the passing of the said Act (3rd June, 1796) the Court of General Quarter Sessions of the Peace for the Western District shall be held in the Parish of Assumption (afterwards called Sandwich) in such place as may be now found most convenient to the Magistrates of said District, on the second Tuesday in the months of July, October, January and April, until such time as it shall seem expedient to the Justices or a majority of them to remove and hold the same nearer to the island called the Isle of Bois Blanc, being near the entrance of the Detroit River.

The last Court of Quarter Sessions held in Detroit was in January, 1796, and the removal took place to Sandwich that summer.

After this date no doubt many of those stationed at Detroit, officers and men, removed to Sandwich and Amherstburg.

On June 7th, 1784, the Huron and Ottawa Indians who claimed ownership or proprietary rights in the country surrounding Detroit, gave by treaty a tract of land seven miles square at the mouth of the Detroit River to the following British Officers or fighters who had been associated with them in the recent war:—Alexander McKee, William Caldwell, Charles McCormack, Robin Eurphleet, Anthony St. Martin, Matthew Elliott, Henry Bird, Thomas McKee and Simon Girty. Henry Bird was given the northern section. This would be in the northern part of the Township of Malden, and would contain what is now the northern part of Amherstburg.

In 1784 the settlement of Malden Township first began. In July of that year Lieutenant-Governor Hay of Detroit wrote to Governor Haldimand as follows:—"Several have built and improved lands who have no other pretensions, than the Indians' consent to possession. Captains Bird and Caldwell are of the number, at a place they have called 'Fredericksburg.' "

On August 14th, 1784, Governor Haldimand wrote to Lieutenant-Governor Hay that Colonel Caldwell of Colonel Butler's late corps had applied to him for sanction to settle on the land; that he could not confirm the grant, but that they should "carry on their improvements until the land could be laid out and granted according to the King's instructions." Mr. McKee was to be directed to get the Indians to make over the land to the King, but that "two thousand yards from the centre would be reserved on all sides for the purpose of establishing a fort."

Here, as Mr. James says, we have the first suggestion of the future Fort Amherstburg and the promise of the town.

On 28th August, 1788, Lord Dorchester, who had succeeded Haldimand in the Governorship in 1786, wrote to Major Matthews to encourage settlement on the east side of the River Detroit, but that no lots must be settled upon before purchase from the Crown, from the Indians, "also to report the progress made by some Loyalists in their settlement on a spot proposed for this class of men on the east side of Detroit River, and to state his ideas fully of what may be done for its further encouragement as well as for establishing a Military Post at that quarter."

In 1790 Major Matthews wrote from Plymouth Barracks, giving a summary of his investigation in 1788. He stated that he went from Quebec to Detroit in 1787 with instructions from Lord Dorchester. He said, "should this post," meaning Detroit, "be given up, and another taken, the most convenient place will be at the entrance of the river, upon a point at present occupied by some officers and men who served the war as Rangers with the Indians. The channel for ships runs between this point and Isle Aux Bois Blanc, which should also be fortified, the distance from each to mid-channel about 200 yards. There is a fine settlement running 20 miles from this point on the north side to the lake. Here in 1788 is the reference to the future post at Amherstburg. The settlement on the north side of Lake Erie refers to what was known as 'the two connected townships' (Colchester and Gosfield)."

The District of Hesse in the west had been set apart by proclamation, July 24th, 1788, and early in 1789 the Governor was authorized by Council to appoint a Land Board, and the following were appointed as the first members in 1789:—Farnham Close, Esq., Major of the 65th Regiment of Foot, or the Officer Commanding at Detroit; William Dummer Powell, Esq.; Duperon Baby, Esq.; Alexander McKee, Esq.; William Robertson, Esq.; Alexander Grant, Esq., and Ademar de St. Martin, Esq.

One of the first duties then put upon this Board was to lay out a township to be called Georgetown, but still there was delay. On August

22nd, 1789, the Land Board reported to Lord Dorchester that Mr. McNiff, the Surveyor, had not yet arrived, and that none of the lands had yet been purchased from the Indians for the Crown, and that the Indians had some years before granted these lands to private individuals. September 2nd, 1789, Lord Dorchester instructed the Board to receive applications from the occupants for grants, etc., and also to have Mr. McKee obtain from the Indians all the land west of Niagara for settlement, the cession to include all lands held by private individuals, from the Indians by private sale, and shortly after the Board reported that all the land was claimed, and asked for power to settle the claims.

May 19th, 1790, the Indians, (Ottawas, Chippewas, Pottawatomies and . . . Hurons), cede to the Crown all the land from the Chaudiere or Catfish Creek on the east to the Detroit River on the west, and from the Thames to Chenail Ecarte on the north to Lake Erie, including the grant of 1784 before referred to, but reserving a tract seven miles square north of the 1784 grant, and also a small tract at the Huron Church (Sandwich). May 3rd, 1791, Surveyor McNiff reported that two or three families live continuously on their land east of the river (Caldwell, Elliott, Lamotte, etc.), but many more resort there in the summer to raise corn and beans. He recommended that the Indians be removed to some other reserve, suggests at Chenail Ecarte; says all the land is settled from the Reserve north to Peach Island in Lake St. Clair.

The first Legislature of Upper Canada was called to meet at Newark (Niagara) on September 17th, 1792, and on January 8th, 1793, the Executive Council resolved that a township to be called Malden be laid out at the mouth of the Detroit River; thus we see that Fredericksburg gave place to Georgetown, and this in turn to Malden.

On 8th January, 1793, it was resolved that Colonel Alex. McKee, Captains Elliott and Caldwell, be the patentees of the above mentioned township, and the persons who have settled under the authority of the late Governor Hay. It was further resolved that the land lying between Captain Bird's lot and the Indian land be reserved for the Government.

We now come to the year 1796. In the Crown Lands Department at Toronto is to be found the original plan of the Township of Malden. It gives the subdivision into lots, and each lot carries the name of the original grantee. It bears the name of A. Iredell, Deputy Surveyor of the Western District, and is dated, Detroit, 17th April, 1796. The lots on the river number from the north to the south, 19 in all, 19 ending at the marsh that fronted on Lake Erie.

The following statement may be given of a few of the patents for these lots with the dates and to whom issued:—

Lots 1 & 2,	David Cowan,	East part 100 acres,	July 2nd, 1807.
" 3	William Caldwell	all 187	" April 13th, 1810.
Water Lot	"	" 1	" August 20th, 1810.
Lot 4	Alexander McKee	all	February 28th, 1797.
" 5	Matthew Elliott	all 200	" February 28th, 1797.
" 9	Archange McIntosh	½ 187	" November 25th, 1803.
" 11	Simon Girty	all 174	" March 6th, 1798.
" 14	Hon. James Baby	all 180	" July 30th, 1799.
" 15 & 16	Thomas McKee	all 325	" June 30th, 1801.

All the above names of owners of full lots are on the Iredell map of 1796 except that on the latter. Lot 1 is left vacant and Captain Bird's name appears on Lot 2. In the C.L. record the lot to the north of Lot 1, taken from the Indian Reserve, is known as Lot A.

By agreement between the Government of the United States and Great Britain, Detroit was to be evacuated in this year—hence the necessity arose of at once making provision for the troops on the east side of the river, and of having an arsenal or depot for stores—a town and fort were necessary. Lot 1 was vacant, reserved by the Crown, and to it was added Captain Bird's Lot No. 2 which was appropriated by the Crown.

The following letter now becomes important. It was written a few weeks after the troops left Detroit:—

DETROIT RIVER, Sept. 8th, 1796.

Captain Wm. Wayne, Queen's Rangers,
  Commanding on the Detroit River, opposite the Island of Bois Blanc,
    To the Military Secretary, Quebec,

Suggest the gunpowder be placed on the "Dunmore," soon expected to lay up there, pending the erection of temporary magazine. "I have reason to fear that the merchants who have already erected buildings on the ground within the line of defence of the Post under my command will not be easily reconciled to the sentiments of the Commander-in-Chief on that subject. They have not merely built temporary sheds; some of their buildings are valuable, and have cost to the amount of many hundred pounds, authorized in these their proceedings by Colonel England, who hitherto commanded this District; at the same time they were to hold the lots on limited terms."

He then states that there is no vacant ground in the vicinity of the garrison. Colonel McKee, Captain Caldwell and Captain Elliott claim the lots to the south; on the north is the vacant land of the Indian Reserve, to the rear the land beyond the 1,000 yards reserved is a perfect swamp. "I enclose for the Commander-in-Chief's inspection a plan of a town laid out by Colonel Caldwell on his own land." A reproduction of the plan accompanies the letter, showing a town laid out in lots, with streets at right angles with a vacant square in the centre; this projected town would be in what is now the southern part of Amherstburg.

The Bird lot has just been taken over by the Government, and a garrison established there with the intention of erecting the Fort.

Thus we see that in the summer of 1796 the plans are set in motion through the Military Department for the starting of a town and post opposite Bois Blanc. On January 10th, 1797, an advertisement was put up at His Majesty's Post, calling for men with teams, oxen, carts, trucks, etc. This was to complete the work begun in 1796. Early in 1797 the creation of the Post begins in earnest. Up to February 2nd, no special name had been given. On February 9th, 1797, appears a requisition for stores for Indian presents for "Fort Amherstburg." Here for the first time the name occurs in an official document, and it no doubt came from the Military Department at Quebec.

In the Crown Lands Department at Toronto is an old plan showing what was to be included that year in the Government Reservation. It is a copy made by William Chewett from the earlier plan of Iredell. On this plan it would appear that Lot No. 3 (Caldwell's) was not required, for the first town plot of Amherstburg belongs to Lot No. 2, the original Bird lot. Lot No. 1 was left vacant in the original division of the land among the first settlers. The lot to the north of that, unnumbered, was acquired from the Indians, as it on several plans is marked a well-defined "Old Indian Entrenchment."

Mr. James also gives a copy of an old plan of 1828, showing the location of Amherstburg, in reference to the Military Reserve. The town appears therein occupying part of lot 2 with a line separating it (marked Richmond street and still so named) from the Military Reserve.

In the Michigan records appear letters dated from Fort Amherstburg in June, July, and August, 1797. On page 267 appears the following: "Captain Forbes, of the R. Artillery, who was on duty at Fort Amherstburg, resided in one of the houses built by Captain Bird from July, 1797, to August, 1799."

FORT MALDEN OR AMHERSTBURG.

In Vol. XXV. is a sketch map of Fort Amherstburg, Town of Malden, etc., showing Indian Council House, Commissioner's House, dockyards, etc., taken from the Colonial Office Records, and the following memorandum:—"Captain Bird's lot was repossessed by Government in 1796, since which time Fort Amherstburg has been constructed, the town of Malden built, a dockyard and other buildings, previous to the year 1796."

It would appear from these documents that the Fort was from the first known as "Fort Amherstburg," and that by some, at least, the group of houses outside the Fort, to the south, was for a time called by some, Malden, the same name as the township; but there was no Fort Malden in those days.

In the Vol. XXV., referred to, there is a sketch given, taken from the Colonial Office Records, showing the Fort as a five-sided enclosure, the northernmost angle in a direct line east of the north end of Bois Blanc, the southernmost corner about opposite the middle of the island, and the little town of Malden extending south to the Caldwell lot, just opposite the southern limit of Bois Blanc Island.

Mr. James continues as follows:—

We pass on now to the war of 1812-1814. Barclay sailed from Amherstburg with six vessels on September 9th, 1813, and on the following day his fleet met Captain Perry with his fleet of nine vessels. We all know the result of that naval engagement.

On September 23rd, 1813, Colonel Procter, then in command of the troops at Amherstburg, decided, contrary to the advice of Tecumseh, to abandon the Fort. Under his orders the Fort and public store-houses were burned by the soldiers, and shortly after the retreat began. General Harrison, with the United States troops, followed, and the disastrous battle of the Thames took place, resulting in the death of Tecumseh.

Major Richardson, the author of "The War of 1812," "Wacousta," etc., who was captured at Moraviantown at the battle of the Thames, speaks of Amherstburg, never of Malden. Lossing, the American author, in his well-known Pictorial Field Book of the War of 1812, refers to Fort Malden, and gives the map of the Detroit River, showing Amherstburg town and Fort Malden. Lossing says:—"The army entered Amherstburg with the band playing 'Yankee Doodle.' The loyal inhabitants had fled with the army. The ruins of Fort Malden, the dockyard and the public stores were sending up huge volumes of smoke." He also says that there were two block-houses on the mainland in 1813, one near the Fort and one near Salmoni's Hotel. Several Kentucky volunteers were taken prisoners by the Indians at the battle of the River Raisin. One of them, Elias Darnell, who served under General Winchester, published in 1854 a journal of the campaign, from which the following extract may be made:—"As he took me near Fort Malden, I took as good a view of it as I could while I passed it. It stands about thirty yards from the river bank. I judged it to be about 70 or 80 yards square; the wall appeared to be built of timber and clay. The side from the river was not walled, but had double pickets and was entrenched round about four feet deep; and in the entrenchment was the second row of pickets."

Richardson, after describing the historic meeting of Proctor and Tecumseh, says on page 121:—

"It having been resolved to move without loss of time, the troops were immediately employed in razing the fortifications and committing such stores as it was found impossible to remove to the flames kindled in the various public buildings; and the ports of Detroit and Amherstburg, for some days previous to our departure, presented a scene of cruel desolation."

We now call another witness, an expert witness, a contemporary record that should settle the question, if any doubt remains. In 1799, David William Smith, Surveyor-General of Upper Canada, prepared and published, at the request of Lieutenant-Governor Simcoe, a Gazetteer of the Province. On page 49 we find the following: "Amherstburg, the military post and garrison now building at the mouth of Detroit River, in the Township of Malden."

In 1813 a second edition was published, revised by Francis Gore, Lieutenant-Governor. In this, Amherstburg is described as a post and garrison, and there is no mention of Malden as either fort or town. Thus we see officially, the settlement was known as Amherstburg from 1797 down to 1813.

In further confirmation of these facts, so ably set out by Mr. James, I may be permitted here to mention another fact which came to my knowledge during the practice of my profession at Windsor. Many years ago I had occasion to search the title to Lot No. 11, First Street, or Lot No. 3 on Dalhousie Street, in the Town of Amherstburg. This lot fronts on what is still known as Dalhousie Street, the main street in the town, and on the southeast corner of said street and Gore Street, and about   yards from the remains of the old fort. I found that this lot, or rather a portion of it, was conveyed by deed dated July 22nd, 1799, by Richard Pattinson & Co. of Sandwich, merchants, to Robert Innes & Co., also of Sandwich, merchants, and is described as "the undivided half of that certain messuage, etc., situate and being in the *Town near the Garrison of Amherstburg,* and containing 30 feet in front by 120 feet in depth, with the dwelling-house and stable erected thereon." In the deed which follows this, dated 23rd September, 1808, from Robert Innes to William Duff, "the consideration being £362 10s. 0d.".

Mr. James cites various authorities to show that Amherstburg was occupied by United States troops from about September 27th, 1813, to July 1st, 1815, when the renewal of peace placed it in the hands of the British.

Lieutenant J. E. Portlock of the Royal Engineers, in a Report of the Post of Amherstburg prepared in 1826, thus describes it: "The Fort is square, consisting of three bastions and one semi-bastion, and in its present form was constructed by Americans. The original works which had progressed very slowly and stood unfinished at the approach of the enemy during the last war were (as far as it was practicable to do so) destroyed by the British troops prior to their retreat from the western frontier. The Americans had advanced but a little way toward the completion of the present Fort."

It would appear from further extracts that the Fort, even after its re-occupation by the British, was allowed to decay, and Mr. James comes to the conclusion that the Fort Amherstburg, reconstructed by the Americans in 1813, was not exactly on the same lines as that begun in 1797 and destroyed by the British in 1813, and that by 1826 the second Fort had fallen into decay. He further states that it must have been at some date subsequent to this report of inspection that the Fort was reconstructed and renamed, for this third Fort appears to have received an official naming as Fort Malden. One authority says the rebuilding took place in 1839.

In the Crown Lands Department is a sketch entitled, "The Survey of Reserves taken by Lieutenant De Moleyns, Royal Engineer, and copied November, 1852, by Captain Moore." On this plan Fort Malden appears as a four-sided enclosure, the southern wall or face of which is in a line with the northern end of Bois Blanc. The Commanding Officer's quarters, Fort Supanto's quarters and commissariat premises all lie outside of the Fort, between it and the Town of Amherstburg. The land to the east of the Sandwich road is laid out in lots for the pensioners, and a sample pensioner's house is sketched. The old Indian entrenchment is marked on the river to the north, Richmond Street is marked as the northern limits of the town, and the open space around the Fort north of the town, and between the Sandwich road and the river is marked "Enrolled Pensioners' Grazing Ground," and this plan comes down to the recollection of many of the older residents of Amherstburg.

The Rev. Mr. Nattress, in his pamphlet before referred to, gives short accounts of the important events which took place on this western frontier and the part taken in its defence by the Military and Militia in charge of Fort Malden during the wars of 1812-1813 and again in 1837-1838. He says: "On the breaking out of the war of 1812, Fort Malden was garrisoned by 200 of the 41st, 50 of the Newfoundland Company, and 300 of the Militia, with a detachment of Royal Artillery, being 600 men in all. (Kingsford) Colonel St. George was in command of Fort Malden when on July 12th, 1812, General Hull crossed from Detroit to the Town of Sandwich at the head of 2,500 regulars of the American army. A few days later an ineffectual attempt was made under Colonel Cass to take the River Canard bridge 5 miles above Amherstburg, Fort Malden, of course, being the objective point. Manœuvring and skirmishing continued until the arrival of Colonel Proctor at Fort Malden, on August 5th. On his arrival he effected a counter movement by sending a detachment across the river, intercepting the supplies in transport from Ohio for the American forces at Detroit, that necessitated the return of Hull's large force from Sandwich to Detroit. General Brock arrived at Fort Malden, on August 13th, 1812, from York, and next morning met the Indians in Council. Tecumseh urged an immediate attack upon Detroit, and Brock at once took up the march. The small American force at Sandwich re-crossed the river on his approach, and by the following day he had planted a battery opposite Fort Detroit, and shortly after followed Hull's surrender of his post, and all his troops and stores.

Proctor assumed command at Detroit, and in a seires of engagements in which the Essex Militia took part, achieved some important results at various points on the Raisin and the Maumee against the forces of the American General Harrison. He was finally repulsed by Harrison in his attack on Fort Meigs and met with an almost crushing defeat on August 2nd, 1813, at Fort Stephenson, and immediately retreated to Fort Malden to recruit his army.

The result of the attempted capture of Amherstburg by the insurgent leader, Sutherland, with the so-called "Patriots" and their defeat and capture with the schooner "Ann" on the 9th January, 1838, is well known.

Troops from Fort Malden again on the 24th February, 1838, defeated an attempted invasion, when an expedition led by one McLeod crossed from Michigan and took possession of what has since been known as Fighting Island, a Canadian island in the Detroit River about half way between Windsor and Amherstburg. On that occasion Major Townsend, with a detachment of the 32nd Regiment from Fort Malden, arrived upon the scene in the night, and at daybreak Captain Glasgow, of the Artillery corp, drove the enemy from their lodgement.

Other attempts to invade this part of Canada and in which troops from Fort Malden displayed a conspicuous part in defending the country, need only be mentioned, as the engagement on Pelee Island in March, 1838, and the last one, viz., the attack upon Windsor, December 4th, 1838.

Mr. Nattress says that during this rebellion Fort Malden was garrisoned by a detachment of the 24th Battalion, another of the 32nd, the 34th Regiment under Colonel Eyre, a battery of Artillery, and as many of the Essex Militia as the exigencies of the situation demanded. The latter were, when embodied with the garrison, in essential particulars, considered on the same footing with the regular troops. Last of all came three companies of the Royal Canadians. These were transferred in 1851, after which date no regular garrison was stationed at the Fort. The detachment of the 34th Regiment, which had been stationed at Halifax, did not reach Amherstburg till the early part of 1838, and subsequently the bastions at the Fort were rebuilt, and the fortifications got in good repair.

The defence of the Fort in 1838 consisted of ten 24-pounders, six 6-pounders, three brass field pieces, six mortar guns, and a number of rocket tubes, besides the full complement of small arms. There is at the present time plainly visible the well-defined outline of a mortarbed in the only remaining trench, the one on the north side of the works. Another of the mortar batteries was immediately in rear of where the last of the old flagstaff still stands on the rear of the southwest bastion. The two front bastions are well preserved, the angles being as sharp as the day they were built. On the east side of the Fort there was a double defence formed by two rows of pointed pickets, one on the moat outside the trench, and the other on the inner side of the trench. The Sally-port crossed this east trench alongside the east bastion. The trenches on the east side have been filled in and the bastions levelled in the construction of a roadway.

In 1838 the buildings, etc., in connection with the Fort were all located along the river front from where the post office now is northward. Here were the Commissary department (a part of the old brick building is still standing), the dockyards, Government stores, the hospital and Officers' quarters. The space between the Officers' quarters and the southwest bastion of the Fort was protected by a row of pickets, as was also the space between the two front bastions, not otherwise protected by trench or moat. A part of the defence, not yet specified, was the block-houses on Bois Blanc Island. There were three of them, known as the North, Centre and South block-houses, or No. 1, No. 2 and No. 3. The South block-house still stands as in the old days. The one at the north end was burned some twenty-six years ago. The centre one stands on the west side of the Island, and is embodied in the Colonel Atkinson summer residence. About opposite to it, on the east side of the island, and abreast of Richmond Street, there was a picket barracks, long afterwards used as a dwelling, but not now standing.

The main site of the Fort, with a few of its old buildings still standing, is now owned by private individuals. Some years ago a petition, largely signed by the inhabitants of Amherstburg, was presented to the Government asking for its restoration and preservation as a National Park. The situation is beautiful and it is very accessible. It has been estimated that the property could be purchased for $25,000, and an additional sum of about $10,000 might be required to lay it out as a park. It is to be hoped the Government will do something to aid in such a laudable object.

The reclamation of this Fort would not only be an object lesson to the youth of the present day but would do much to promote the study of the history of the early struggles on this frontier in 1812 and in 1838. Situated on the Detroit River, no place could be better advertised. Few places are more visited during the summer season than this river, which is only 24 miles long, yet it is one of our greatest water-ways, carrying more tonnage during the season of navigation than leaves the ports of London and Liverpool during the same period. There are many freighters over 600 feet long and carrying from 10,000 to over 13,000 tons each trip, and over 100 more between 400 and 500 feet long, carrying about 10,000 tons. The passenger traffic is enormous on the steamers plying between Buffalo, Cleveland and other lake ports to Mackinac, Chicago, Port Arthur and Duluth. The new "City of Cleveland" can carry 4,000 passengers, and the Ferry Company's steamer, "Columbia," is licensed to carry 3,666, and makes two trips a day from Detroit to Amherstburg and Bois Blanc Island, loaded with excursionists, many from the interior of Michigan and from the States of Ohio, Indiana and Illinois. These boats pass almost within a stone's throw of Fort Malden.

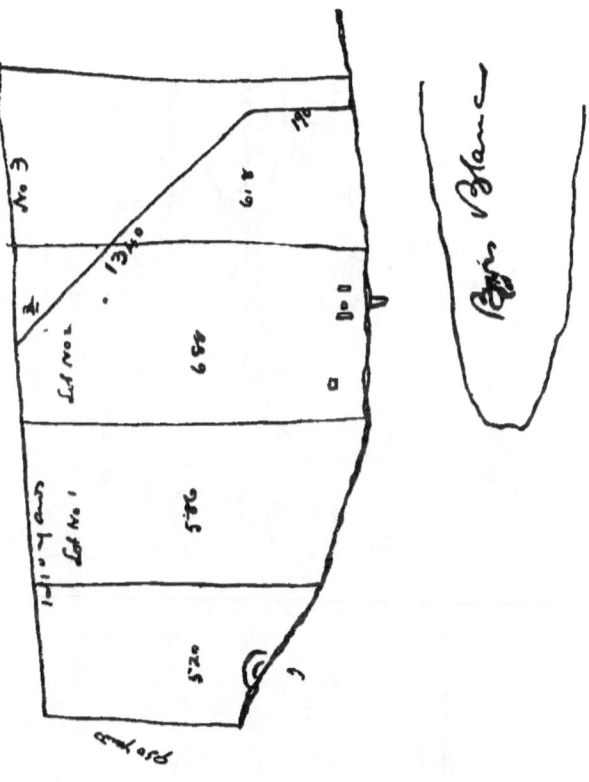

THE OLDEST MAP. JULY, 1797

Plan, dated 1797, showing the site of the Military Post of Amherstburg and the land originally reserved for Government use. The unnumbered lot, north of the present Alma Street, was acquired in 1800 from the Indians and is marked on the several old plans as a well-defined old Indian Encampment. Copy made by Wm. Chewett from original by A. Iredell. Original in Crown Lands Department, Toronto. Block D on some maps.

18   ONTARIO HISTORICAL SOCIETY.

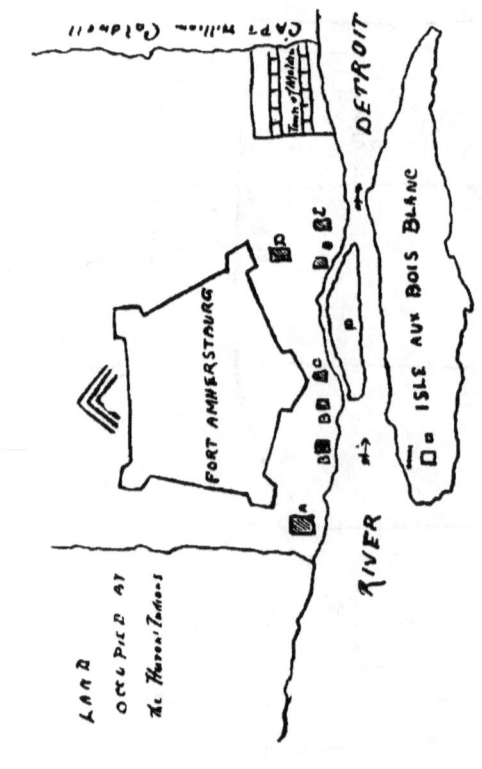

THE NEXT OLDEST MAP.

This map would go to show that the first name given to the Fort was Amherstburg. The popular name, and from a very early date the official name, was Fort Malden.

FORT MALDEN OR AMHERSTBURG.

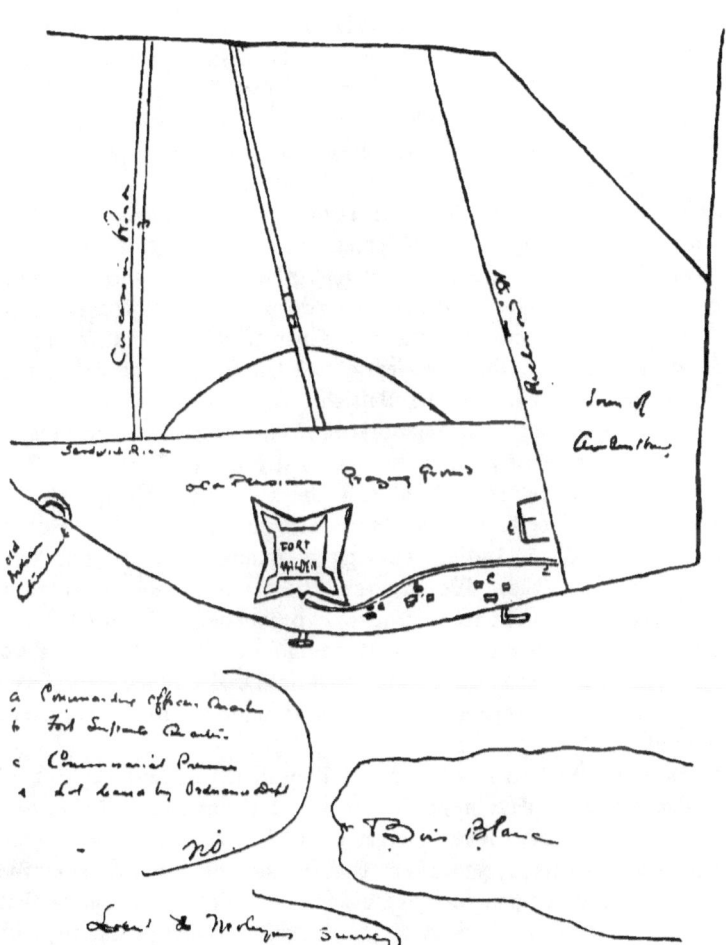

This map is more modern and true to fact in the matter of locations.
Copy of an old plan of 1828.

II.

THAMESVILLE AND THE BATTLE OF THE THAMES.

By Katherine B. Coutts.

On the outbreak of the war of 1812 General Brock, upon whom the duty of defending Upper Canada had devolved, saw the importance of securing its western frontier. Thither therefore he went; and, with a good fortune which probably exceeded his utmost expectations, he found himself by the middle of August, without a blow struck or a life lost, master of the Fort of Detroit with its supplies of ammunition and ordnance, including some interesting revolutionary trophies, and of the vast territory of Michigan, out of which five sovereign states have since been formed. It was at this time that took place the first and only meeting between Brock and Tecumseh, the two most heroic figures of the war. For Tecumseh, smarting under a sense of wrongs endured by his people at the hands of the Americans, had hastened at the first rumor of war to proffer his aid to the British. Brock soon returned to the Centre Division, leaving in command at the West General Henry Proctor, with a small number of regular troops, mostly of the Forty-first Regiment, and some companies of Kent and Essex Militia. Though all that could be spared, Proctor's force was confessedly inadequate. But he had as allies a body of Indians varying in number from time to time. He complained that these Indians were "not a disposable force" and that their zeal was too apt to be in inverse proportion to his need. These are the well known characteristics of Indian warriors. Yet there was one amongst them—Tecumseh his name—whose zeal and constancy were afterwards to form a standard by which Proctor should be tried and found wanting.

During the thirteen months that followed, the gallant Right Division and their allies gave a good account of themselves. Richardson, who was with them the whole time, says that Proctor gained from their gallantry and success a reputation that no act of his own deserved. Indeed it is borne in upon the most casual reader of his narrative that, though Proctor was at the head of the defence, Tecumseh was its soul.

After the disastrous Battle of Lake Erie—September 10th, 1813—which left Proctor denuded of his great guns and cut off from his source of supply, he held a council at which it was resolved to destroy the forts of Detroit and Amherstburg and retire via the Thames route upon the Centre Division.

This decision was bitterly opposed by Tecumseh, the mouthpiece of the Indian contingent. He accused Proctor of direct breach of trust with his people and demanded that, if the British must retreat, the forts and ammunition should be given to the Indians, who would themselves oppose the landing of the Americans. He compared Proctor to a "fat animal which slinks away, its tail between its legs," and finally hurled at him that ultimate epithet of scorn—an old squaw.

Harrison said afterwards that Proctor must have been infatuated not to make a stand as Tecumseh advised. It is certain that situations as desperate as his have been retrieved, and had there been a leader who

"When the right arm's shattered waves
The good flag with the left,"

history might have a different story to tell. Such a leader, however, Proctor was not; and I believe that his resolve to retreat has never been assailed as a normal measure. A compromise was finally arrived at which Tecumseh accepted, though unwillingly. It was to destroy the forts and retire, with such ammunition and stores as they could carry, to Moraviantown, the farthest point on the Thames to which batteaux could ascend; to fortify this village and there await the enemy. Moraviantown had been built, so far as it *was* built, by a company of Delaware Indians who, led by their missionaries, had migrated thither from the Ohio in 1792. The Moravian church abandoned its work there only about five years ago. Proctor called it half way to the Centre Division, though it is but a bare third to Ancaster,—the Centre Division's outpost. Did Proctor make this promise in good faith? I think not. He made it to escape a present perplexity. He seems to have persuaded himself that Harrison would be content with the possession of the forts and would not pursue. At all events the way he conducted his retreat shows no intention of fighting; and he did not fight. He took much pains to save the great quantity of unnecessary and forbidden personal baggage he had carried off. The safety of his little army, his honor, his reputation—these things he lost sight of. He left Sandwich September 27th and marched at the leisurely rate of nine miles a day for five days. The roads were shockingly bad, for it had been a rainy season.

Having reached Dolsen's, four miles below Chatham, he left his little army there, and, with his personal staff and baggage and the women and children, went forward to Moraviantown. He took all the guns but one, and his only officer of engineers, as if to arrange for fortifying. But he left no orders to guide Colonel Warburton, the Second in command; and at Moraviantown he took not a step towards his promised fortifications, though the place is said to have afforded facilities. Abattis could have been constructed, the houses occupied, etc.

Whilst thus tarrying by the way and knowing nothing of the general's plans, Warburton got word of the approach of the enemy. Harrison had left Sandwich on the second of October and was already, on the third, close behind them. The British retired to Chatham; and the Indians seeing what they thought a good place to make a stand where now Tecumseh Park is, clamored to fight there. Warburton was in much perplexity and consulted anxiously with the other officers. All were indignant at the General's conduct and a proposal was seriously made to deprive him of the command and confer it upon Warburton, who declined, as he very well might, so perilous an honor. However, by the arguments of Elliot, the Commissioner, the Indians consented to go on, a few remaining behind and actually disputing the progress of the Americans. A further march of six or seven miles brought the little army to Richardson's, where Proctor joined them. Leaving a rear guard here, he led the half-fed troops to Sherman's, where the night of October fourth was spent, Tecumseh, according to local tradition, having spent this, his last night on earth, in Sherman's barn. The Sherman of the day—Lemuel by name—was a member of Captain Shaw's Company of Kent Militia which in May, 1813, applied for, and seems to have got, leave to go home and till their farms. At all events it was not in the battle of the Thames, though it was in that of the Longwoods the following March, where two of Captain Shaw's sons were wounded—one mortally. The Sherman house was the first built within the limits of the present Thamesville, and probably the only one then standing. It was built on the knoll above the river now occupied by the Sherman cemetery.

On the morning of the fifth the rear guard joined the rest of the army at Sherman's, with the disheartening news that all their supplies of food and ammunition had fallen into the enemy's hands through the night, the guard as well as the sick and wounded being made prisoners. Raw meat was served for breakfast, but before that luxurious meal could be despatched news of the proximity of the enemy caused a further tramp of two muddy miles, this time to the scene of the battle. They were formed in two lines, the British in an irregular group in the woods which, having no underbrush, offered little obstacle to cavalry. The solitary gun, for which there was not a single round of ammunition, was at the left of the road. In a black ash swamp to the right, Tecumseh and his men were drawn up and here alone, according to local authority, were abattis constructed. David Sherman, the fifteen year old son of the militia man referred to, was looking for his cows that afternoon in company with a boy named Ward. Naturally they looked in the direction where something unusual was going on. An Indian, sitting on a newly-felled tree, called the boys, questioned them a little and advised them to get their cows and hurry home. He wore a scarf wound round his head in which was stuck a large white ostrich plume. When forty years later David Sherman surveyed a portion of his patrimony into village lots, he named the village after that Indian—Tecumseh. But, there being already a post office of that name in Essex, our village had to find another and was called Thamesville.

The battle of the Thames was fought in the Gore of Zone, and lots 2, 4, 5 and 6 have been entered for the honor of being the site. Lots 5 and 6, the farm until recently owned by Mr. G. J. Watts, who inherited it from his grandfather, whose patent is dated 1849, was long known as the Tecumseh Farm, as it was supposed to be the actual battle ground. But I am assured by Mr. John McDowell, the present owner of the Tecumseh farm, as well as of the adjoining land west, that all the relics known to have been found,—bayonets, muskets and human remains, and skeletons of horses—have been found on the latter—lot 4. Mr. McDowell has a collection of bullets of two sizes, picked up by himself within the past seven years. When the little army was arrayed Tecumseh rode along the lines, shaking the officers by the hand and trying to cheer the weary, hungry and dispirited men about to encounter a foe outnumbering them at least three to one. (The British had 367 of all ranks and their Indian allies were about 800, whereas Harrison's troops numbered at least 3,000 of which almost half were cavalry.) He was dressed in a close fitting suit of buckskin and his favorite white ostrich plume waved above his head. How it recalls another hero—him whose commission Samuel de Champlain carried in 1908:

"The King hath come to marshall us
In all his armor dressed,
And he hath bound a snow white plume
Above *his gallant crest.*"

Proctor with his staff took his stand behind the rear line. He may well have been ashamed to face the men whose confidence he knew he had lost and whom he was flinging to the enemy as the wicked man in the children's story flung the child from his arms to the wolves. I have no technical terms at my command but this is what happened: Harrison's advancing cavalry was met by a fire from the front rank who then retired. The second attempting to fire were borne down by the horsemen and in two minutes or less all was over. The Indians held out the longest; but when Tecumseh fell they also broke and fled. Of the British only about fifty men under Lieutenant Bullock escaped.

Where was Proctor? Two minutes after the first volley was fired he was galloping east to Moraviantown, where his treasures were, and onward through the forest towards Burlington. The enemy pursued him fifteen miles plundered the baggage which he was compelled to abandon—and which included his carriage—and returned, burning Moraviantown en route. Proctor was courtmarshalled at Montreal in December, 1814, and sentenced to a suspension from rank and pay for six months and a public reprimand. In his defense he had the meanness to throw the blame upon his little army. The Prince Regent was dissatisfied with the sentence, complaining that he was treated with inexcusable leniency; and one finds oneself for once agreeing with his Royal Highness.

The morning after the battle Lemuel Sherman and his son, David, were amongst those who went down to bury the dead. The bodies were thrown into a pit from which relic hunters have since carried off many a trophy. Mr. William Sherman assures me that he knows where Tecumseh was buried—that his father (then the boy David) had witnessed the burial and showed *him* the spot when a boy. There is a strong opinion, however, amongst historians "that no man knows that sepulchre, and no man saw it e'er"—no white man at least.

Harrison left the sick and wounded at Sherman's and many of them spent the winter there, using the barn already mentioned as their hospital. The names of some of them cut into the boards are still to be seen. One of the Kentucky troops remained behind altogether. When David Sherman married he took up his abode with him, died in his house in 1857 and is buried in the family plot on the spot where Lemuel Sherman's house stood in 1813.

I have left for the last the few words I wish to say on Tecumseh. That great Shawnee Chief was born in 1768 in the valley of the Mad River within the present State of Ohio. Like his brother the prophet, he was believed to be of supernatural birth, being thus a hero to his own people in the classic sense, as he is a hero to us according to the better meaning of the word—not the one that came in about the time of the

Boer War. From his earliest years he nourished wrath against the Americans from the belief that his people had been unjustly treated concerning their lands. He was of course a warrior. But a warrior of the best type known to our military age—wise in council, fertile in resource, magnanimous and fearless. If we may believe the story that he fled on the occasion of his first battle, it is interesting as indicatory that his courage had a moral rather than a physical origin. When war was declared in 1812 it was natural that he should come forward in aid of the British. Richardson says that he had nothing of the savage about him save the color and the garb. Kipling calls the savage people of to-day "half devil and half child," and the description suits our own red men well enough. They were children for instability and devils for cruelty. Yet from the day Tecumseh took his stand beside Brock at Detroit till that on which Johnston's bullet stilled forever his noble heart he never wavered in his determination and loyalty. And he had learned from civilization her noblest lesson that mercy "which becomes the throned monarch better than his crown," and which shines with even greater lustre from the untutored savage. Richardson, who knew him well, speaks of him with affectionate enthusiasm. Harrison, against whom he fought, respected him while living and lamented his death. In the story of the war he towers above the short-sighted, selfish and unready Proctor. He stands, an equal, besides the heroic Brock.

Such he was; and of his great gifts he gave all in the Canadian cause. "Green leaves of his labor," he gave, "white flower of his thought, and red fruit of his death." Should we not then honor him "as we honor our bravest who fall?"

In five years will come round the one hundredth anniversary of the battle of the Thames. How fittingly on that day would the Canadian people unveil a monument to the memory of the brave, the noble Shawnee who died in battle against the Invaders of Canadian Soil!

III.

THE HIGHLAND PIONEERS OF THE COUNTY OF MIDDLESEX.

It is difficult, if not impossible, for men of the present generation to estimate aright the courage and heroism of their Highland ancestors. Inspired by a noble patriotism, knit to their homes by sacred associations, and the traditions of many centuries, qualified by their mental equipment to admire and enjoy its beautiful scenery, bound to race and clan with the strong ties of friendship and affection so characteristic of the Gael. It is hard to appreciate fully the intensity of the strain, or the severity of the trial of their expatriation. Before them was an ocean voyage in sailing vessels, both tedious and dangerous, and a scarcely less tedious and difficult journey from Quebec or Montreal to their western forest homes. But to counterbalance all this there was a prevailing dissatisfaction with their condition in the Highlands, a noble ambition to better themselves by securing perfect freedom and independence, and a calm, firm reliance on an overruling Providence.

Once arrived at their destination their hardships, so far from ended, were only really beginning. A vast stretch of almost pathless forest, with only here and there a clearing, surrounded and comforted them, and the situation taxed to the utmost their native energy as well as their powers of endurance. It is not necessary here to do more than simply mention the struggle of years in clearing the land and bringing it into cultivation, the many privations, the simple life in the old log cabins, their devoted attachment to their native land, and their loved Gaelic, their steadfast persevering battle with obstacles, and their final success and victory. It is proper to say here that though this paper is confined entirely to the Highland settlers, the pioneers of other origins are no less worthy of honorable mention.

As a people they carried with them from their Highland homes and grandly illustrated the characteristics of their races. Their stalwart physique and capacity for endurance were not only proved and tested, but exercised and strengthened by the inevitable hardships and exertions of their environment. They were gifted with strong intellects and keen powers of observation. No less prominent was their moral stamina and their reverence for religious worship and institutions. With few exceptions their lives were upright, and their economy and thriftiness, a necessity in the early days, were continued in the days of their prosperity. In the midst of the great woods and their howling denizens, so complete a contrast to their Highland abode, even more strikingly were the traits of friendship and hospitality displayed, and their souls knit together in fraternal fellowship. Gaelic was practically the only language spoken, and all their customs, not only from their early training, but from their surroundings, were simple and primitive. The old Highland "Ceilah" kept in the long winter evenings, around great blazing log fires, rested and refreshed them as the pleasant hours were spent in recalling the scenes, incidents, and even superstitions of their native land, and reciting or singing Gaelic songs or hymns. They had their faults but they were like spots in the sun. The Celtic fire was sometimes associated with an irascible temper. Firm as their granite hills at times this degenerated into obstinacy, or the open, honest, straightforwardness passed into abruptness, or their whole-souled hospitality was maimed by prejudice against people of other origins.

The dawn of civilization in Middlesex County first appeared in the township of Delaware, and here we also find a trace, but only a trace, of the pioneer Highlander of the County, Ronald McDonald, who in 1798 obtained a patent of the land on which Delaware village stands, but soon after sold out to Dr. Oliver Tiffany. It is stated that John Sutherland came in 1829, but as far as known there were no others till the close of the pioneer period. In London township there appear to have been two distinct settlements, one near what is now Ilderton, and one near Hyde Park. In the former the first settler was John Carmichael, and in the latter Duncan McKenzie; both came in 1818, and were probably, except Roderick McDonald, the first Highland pioneers in the county. In Mosa the Highland settlers occupied the northern part of the township from the 4th to the 10th concession, and the first settler was Archibald Sinclair, 1827. Many others followed in the next few years, a large number of whom had come to Aldborough, Elgin County, at an earlier date. In Lobo about two dozen families settled in 1820, and from that time till 1835 they continued to come till they had taken possession of the greater part of the township. Among these were the Johnsons, the Grahams, the McKellars and McIntyres. The first Highlanders who come into Ekfrid were Angus Campbell, his two sons, John and Malcolm, and his son-in-law, John McIntosh, in 1821. From that time till 1835 the stream continued to flow till it had filled practically the whole township. The first in Caradoc were Archibald and Malcolm Campbell, 1822. Not many followed till 1829-1835, when possession was taken of the northern part of the township. In 1831 a dozen stalwart Highlanders, prominent among whom was Donald McIntosh, settled in East Williams. The wave of immigration continued during that and the two following years until about 100 families had come in, chiefly from the northern counties of Scotland. There was a second wave of immigration in 1848-49-50, which not only completely filled this township, but overflowed into West Williams, and was chiefly from the western islands of Scotland. In this latter settlement it is said the first pioneer was Donald McGregor, 1846. In Westminster there were comparatively few Highlanders located south of the sixth concession, and John Munro appears to have been the first, 1831. As the early history of London has been so elaborately written by others, I need only say from what I can glean the pioneer Highlander of London was Patrick McGregor, 1826. As far as could be ascertained there were no Highland pioneers in Biddulph, and very few in Nissouri. A few Highlanders, all from Inverness, came into McGillivray in 1849, and about fifty years ago a small colony from the island of Uist settled there, but are now said to be extinct. There were also a few Highlanders in North Dorchester, of whom the first is said to have been Dan. McCallum, 1830. Except as mentioned, nearly all came from Argyleshire. I say nothing of Metcalfe, as it was included in Ekfrid and Adelaide till near the close of the pioneer period.

It is a historical fact that in the matter of public or common school education, Scotland was very considerably in advance of England. All through the Highlands, parish schools had long been established, and the instruction was valuable, even if not very extensive. It was, therefore, only what might be expected that the early Highland settlers, from their past associations and their strong intellectual bias, would lose no time in giving attention to the education of their children. The buildings and equipment in the early years were rude and primitive, but as time passed conditions improved. The first log school house in Mosa was erected in S. S. No. 8, about 1836, followed by another in No. 9, soon after. Patrick McGregor was probably the first teacher in No. 8, and others were Duncan McCallum, Findlay Munroe, and Walter Payne. In Metcalfe the first school was opened in 1839, and the first teacher was Duncan McCallum. The pioneer school in Ekfrid was on lot 6, Longwoods' Road, 1836, and the pioneer teacher was Mr. Smith, followed by William Livingstone, and he by Malcolm Campbell. The first log school house in Canada was erected in the early thirties, on the 9th concession, but it was burned down, and a blacksmith's shop on lot 1, concession 7, Lobo, was utilized for the purpose and attended by children from both townships. Some years after the Caradoc academy, on the Longwoods' Road was opened and conducted by Wm. Livingstone, until it was burned down in 1857. In Lobo a log school house was erected as early as 1826, on lot 7, concession 6, but never roofed or occupied. The first school house to be used was built about 1831 on lot 1, concession 6, and was soon followed by others when the township was divided into sections from 1835 to 1840. Among the pioneer teachers of those years were John Irvine, Donald McRae and Robert Dixon. In East Williams the first school opened in 1837 on the exact spot on which the Nairn hotel afterwards stood, and the first teacher was William Munro, long kindly remembered by his pupils and the people generally. In 1839 or 1840 the next school was opened at Beechwood, and one of the first, if not the very first, teacher was Wm. Wells. In West Williams, which was settled at a much later date, the first log school house in S. S. No. 12 was built in 1857, and the first teacher was Miss Dewar, of Lobo. In Westminster the first school house (a little log one) was in S. S. No. 13, and Mr. McCormick, who had been engaged as teacher in the old land, was the first teacher. The pupils who attended those primitive schools, in most cases knew only Gaelic, but they soon acquired a knowledge of English, and made such rapid progress in their studies that before many years had passed they could compare favorably with those of other origins. An unusually large number entered into intellectual pursuits, and twenty-five years ago Rev. Wm. R. Sutherland, of Ekfrid, in response to an inquiry, stated that he had made a careful estimate and found that up to that time in Western Ontario, 300 of the descendants of the early Highland pioneers had become teachers, or entered into the ministry or learned professions. Faith in a presiding Almighty Ruler of all things was a prominent trait of Highland character. The physical features of their country, the grand scenery, the glens and bens, and locks and islands, the great old ocean, and even the mountain mists and torrents, were all well calculated to imbue an impressible and emotional people with belief in the supernatural. Their acute powers of observation, their vivid imagination, their lofty conception of moral obligation and physical and mental beauty, were abundantly shown in the large volume of Gaelic poetry which had been gathering and increasing for centuries. But in addition it may be said that many of them, even in the early ages, received the gospel as the power of God unto Salvation through the labors of St. Columbus and others, and the mighty impulse which the career of John Knox gave to religion in Scotland was felt, even in the Highlands. Not only were parishes and parish ministers established throughout, but for many decades preceding the coming migration, many able, scholarly, fervent and faithful men by their zealous and extended labors, helped 'to keep alive the flow of true devotion and genuine religion. To this people, in the great woods the change was great, and the contrast in almost every feature sharp and clear, but it did not efface old memories, nor was it less unfavorable to their religious tendencies or convictions. So it comes about that before being visited by pioneer preachers of any kind, the more devout and spiritual met together for prayer, conference and worship. They were also helped and comforted by reading their Gaelic Bibles, reading and singing the Gaelic Psalms and paraphrases, and perusing the "Pilgrim's Progress," and many other good books which had been translated into their native language.

The great majority of the Highland pioneers of Middlesex were Presbyterians. Those who settled in West Williams at a later date were in part Roman Catholic, and there were a few of the same faith in Ekfrid. There were also a few Baptists, and a considerable number in some of the townships became Baptists at a later date. Speaking of Presbyterian Churches, a house for public worship was erected in East Williams in 1835 on a splendid lot of 118 acres, granted by the Canada Company, and was succeeded by a large frame church in 1842. A commodious church was erected in Ekfrid in 1849, and in the area then included there are no less than 10 separate congregations. About 1835 a small log house for religious services was built in Mosa, followed in a few years by a large one, and in 1867 by a brick church. In Westminster services were for a time held in a school house until a church was built in 1854. In 1860 the first log church was erected in Caradoc. The first Baptist churches were erected in Lobo in 1837, followed by a brick structure in 1855, and in Ekfrid in 1840, succeeded by a frame building in 1854.

Among the pioneer ministers of the Church of Scotland who labored in Middlesex in the early days, were Alex. Ross, and Donald McKenzie, 1830; W. McKellar, 1833; Dugald McKellar, Lobo, 1839. Soon after a minister, named Cameron, spent some time among the people of Ekfrid, and among the others may be mentioned Wm. R. Sutherland, Ekfrid, 1848-1898; Donald McKenzie and Donald Allan, as visitors, 1834; in East Williams, Duncan McMillan, 1839; and Lachlan McPherson, 1849, as settled pastors in the same township. Also Wm. McGillivray and Alex. Fraser in the late forties. Robert Stevenson, 1856; Dr. John Scott, D. McKenzie and D. McMillan, Hyde Park, in the forties. John McEwen, 1852, and Duncan McColl (an ordained chatechist), 1841, both in Westminster. Archibald Stewart, Kilmartin, 1862; John Ferguson, Caradoc, 1860. Among the pioneer Baptist ministers who labored with great success among the early settlers in Lobo, Caradoc and Ekfrid from 1827 onwards were Dugald Campbell, Thomas McColl, Duncan Lamont, and Duncan McCallum. Dugald Sinclair, a minister of the Disciples or Christian Church, labored in Lobo from 1831 to his death, in 1870. In the decade ending 1856 Father Kirwan visited the Roman Catholics who had settled in West Williams. A church was built in 1861, and the succeeding priests were Fathers O'Donavan, Kellehan, O'Shea, Lamont, Corcoran and McRae. Fathers O'Danavan, Lamont and McRae, as well as nearly all of the ministers mentioned, could speak and preach in Gaelic. The preaching in the early years was mostly in that language, but I believe there is only one place—Kilmartin—where it is still continued.

From three important documents of the pioneer period, two of which have come into my own possession, I am able to glean some interesting information. The assessment roll of the township of Lobo for 1825, written in a plain legible hand and signed by John Baskin, contains altogether 49 names, 29 of whom were Highlanders. The total value of assessed property was £2,675 8s., Halifax currency at $4 to the £, and the total taxes were £13 9s. 9d. One-fourth of a penny per pound was for payment of members of the Assembly for their services. The tax paid by Joel Westbrook was only four pence, and Captain John Matthews paid the highest tax, £1 12s. 5d.

Much more full and complete than the similar roll for Lobo is the assessment roll for Ekfrid for 1827, probably the first one prepared there. It also bears the signature of John B. Askin, as clerk of the London district. It contains 46 names of whom only about ten were Highlanders. The lot and concession as given shows that all settled along and on both sides of the Longwoods' Road, which had been opened up in 1812. It was the only road then open, and there was not one settler in the rest of the township to the north and south, which was all unbroken forest. As a rule each one of the settlers had 100 acres or a total of 4,312 acres; only 121 acres was arable land in patches of from one to twenty acres. The total population was 107, total valuations £1,198 8s., total taxes £7 13s. 4d., and the wolf hunger, the overshadowing influences of friendship and fraternity and the higher claims of religion so occupied their attention that politics had little or no place in their horizon. Besides, they had no means of obtaining the knowledge on which alone intelligent political opinion could be based. But the upheaval of 1837, the mission of Lord Durham, the granting of responsible government in 1841, the establishment of municipal institutions in 1842, and the publication of newspapers constituted the beginning of a new era. Almost from the first there was a more or less distinct line of cleavage between the two great political parties, which have ever since steadily maintained their organization and identity, and Highlanders and their sons have not been slow to take their places in the political arena, and fill the most exalted positions in the gift of the people.

To Andrew J. Ross, who unearthed what was probably the first assessment roll of Williams for 1833, I am indebted for some of its interesting contents. There were on this roll forty names in all, and with scarcely an exception they were all Highlanders. The wild land is put down at 4,590 acres, cultivated land 141 acres, assessed value £1,254. This last in 1837 had increased to £4,627. At the foot of the list *is the entry,* "in the County of Huron." In the early years there was practically no politics among the Highland pioneers. The franchise was to them a new privilege, which, as a rule, they had never before enjoyed, and it took some time to estimate its value and realize its responsibility.

IV.

CENTENARY OF THE DEATH OF BRANT.

BY HERBERT F. GARDINER, M.A., PRINCIPAL OF THE ONTARIO INSTITUTION FOR THE BLIND, BRANTFORD.

Joseph Brant, or Thayendanegea, the celebrated Mohawk Chief, died in 1807, and the one hundredth anniversary of his death, which fell on Sunday, November 24th, 1907, was fittingly observed by the inhabitants of Brantford and the adjacent Indian Reserve, the newly organized Canadian Club of Brantford taking a special interest in the proceedings.

On the afternoon of Saturday, November 23rd, the Brant monument in Victoria Park, Brantford, was decorated with impressive ceremonies in the presence of a large assemblage. The first speaker was Chief A. G. Smith, who explained the object of the gathering and called upon Chief Jacob General to perform the condolence ceremony, which is an ancient rite observed whenever a death occurs in a chief's family. Chief Jacob General, on behalf of one side of the council, addressed the Mohawks. He repeated all the names of the dead Chief.

The response to the condolence was made by Chief A. G. Smith, who, on behalf of the other side of the council, thanked them for the condolences which had been so kindly extended. Condolence, he said, was a great help, and it was able to clear away the lump in the throat and brighten the dimmed eyes. In closing, he stated that if any death occurred on the other side of the house he could say, on behalf of his side, that they would be willing to offer condolence and wipe away the tears with a clean linen handkerchief.

Mr. Frederick O. Loft, of the Provincial Secretary's Department, Toronto, said that on this occasion they were gathered to commemorate the death of a man who was true to his cause. Brant was a soldier from the top of his head to the soles of his feet, and he proved his fidelity to the British crown. The speaker then reviewed the life of Brant.

Chief A. G. Smith placed a beautiful wreath of roses on the Brant monument. The floral piece was two feet in diameter, and across it was the word "Thayendanegea." Beside the wreath were placed two small Union Jacks as a fitting tribute to the Chief who loved and was true to that flag.

A. D. Hardy, Judge of Brant County, and Superintendent Smith, of the Indian Office, made short addresses in which they referred to the life of one of the noblest of red men.

This closed the proceedings at the monument.

SERVICES AT THE MOHAWK CHURCH.

On Sunday morning, November 24th, a special service at the Mohawk Church was attended by a large number of Indians, and also by many residents of the city. After the regular matins had been said and sung, Rev. R. Ashton, Superintendent of the Mohawk Institute and Rector of the Church, referred in his sermon to the great Chief Joseph Brant, saying that there were many misapprehensions in regard to him. Many thought, for instance, that Joseph Brant built the church they were in. This was not so, as the church was built under the direction of King George III. in 1785. Chief Joseph Brant, the speaker stated, had received a fair education, and even translated the Gospel of St. Mark into the Mohawk tongue. This translation was printed in 1778 by George III's. order, and the books were sent to the Mohawk Church. Joseph Brant, the preacher also stated, had translated the Apostles' Creed, the Ten Commandments and the Lord's Prayer into Mohawk. These translations were placed on three tablets, which were sent out from England in 1786. These are at present in the church and greatly valued. The reverend gentleman paid high tribute to the great Chief, for he was much ahead of his time, and his great idea was to restrain his tribe from being a wandering one and leading an aimless life. Brant also wanted to have the white man teach the Indians agriculture, but the authorities thought that Brant was trying to get the land for himself and this scheme was never taken up during his lifetime.

The pupils of the Mohawk Institute attended the church in a body.

A piece of the famous Queen Anne silver plate, which was sent to the Mohawk Indians in New York in 1712, was used to take up the collection. This valuable silver plate was brought here by Brant's tribe when they came from the other side.

GRAVE DECORATED.

After the service the grave of Chief Joseph Brant was decorated by two wreaths, one being placed on the tomb by the Six Nations and the other by the Canadian Club. The first was of red roses, typifying the red man; the second of white roses, symbolical of the white friends of the dead Chief.

Judge Hardy, Chief Smith and several others delivered short addresses. Those present then inspected the church and graveyard, and a most interesting memorial service was brought to a close. The weather Saturday and Sunday was ideal for this celebration, and the ceremonies at the monument, at the church and at the grave were all most reverently participated in by large numbers of people.

At the Council House.

On Monday, November 25th, the proceedings in connection with the centenary of the death of Brant were continued on the Six Nations Reserve. The chiefs assembled in the Council House at Ohsweken, the Mohawks and Senecas sitting at the right; the Oneidas, Cayugas, Tuscaroras and Delawares at the left; the Onondagas, who as fire-keepers, sit in the centre, were back at the extreme edge of the two sides. A debate is never settled by show of hands. If the Chiefs to right and left cannot agree, the decision remains with the fire-keepers, whose voice is final. If the two sides agree, the fire-keepers have nothing to say.

The Chiefs sit at the far end of the Council House and their portion is railed off, with seats on the outside for the warriors and women. The Superintendent occupies a chair on a small raised platform.

Proceedings opened at 11 o'clock in the forenoon, the Chiefs occupying the positions above described. To the right and left of Superintendent Smith sat Judge Hardy, President, and Mr. F. D. Reville (Editor of the *Brantford Courier*), Vice-President of the Canadian Club of Brantford. Other guests within the Chiefs' enclosure were Mrs. A. D. Hardy, W. G. Raymond (Postmaster of Brantford), Mrs. and the Misses Raymond, Mrs. Smith, Mrs. F. D. Reville and Mr. W. F. Cockshutt, M.P. for South Brant. The council room outside of the dividing barrier was crowded.

Rev. Mr. Carpenter, Dr. and Mrs. Holmes, and many of the teachers on the Reserve were present. The Chiefs, who were grouped according to their nation, were:—

Mohawks—Chiefs D. Doxtater, A. G. Smith, Simon Bomberry, J. W. M. Elliott and Abram Lewis.

Senecas—Chiefs John Gibson, Johnson, Williams and John Hill.

Onondagas—Lawrence Jonathan, Joseph Olsey, Joseph Porter and William Echo.

Oneidas—Simon Douglas, J. S. Johnson, Daniel Sky, William C. Hill, A. H. Lottridge, Robert Isaac.

Cayugas—William Hill, Jacob General, Alexander McNaughton, Joseph Jacobs and Daniel McNaughton.

Tuscaroras—Chiefs Josiah Hill, Joseph Green and Richard Hill.

The addresses throughout the day dealt principally with the education of the Indian, for which Joseph Brant had worked throughout his life. Most of the Chiefs spoke in their own language, some of the speeches being translated into English for the benefit of the white guests.

All the speakers paid tribute to the man who died one hundred years ago. They crowned his head with wreaths of eloquence in referring to his history, and recalled many incidents in his life which showed the excellent character of the man who, born in the woods, was later patronized by leading British soldiers and scions of royalty. Brant was described as loyal to his followers and to the British crown, unselfish and always anxious to find ways to better the condition of his people.

The meeting was declared open by an Onondaga Chief, who laid a string of wampum on the table. Chief Echo, who performed this ceremony, said that the council had seen fit to hold a commemoration in honor of the death of a member of the Six Nations, who had lived over one hundred years ago. He charged the people, no matter of what standing, to be prepared for death at a moment's notice, as the Great Spirit called souls to the great beyond in a minute's time. He welcomed the white visitors with a few appropriate words.

The ceremony of condolence was conducted by Chief John Gibson, who spoke in the Indian language.

Letters were read from Lieut.-Col. and Mrs. Delamere, of Toronto; Principal Gardiner, of the Ontario Institution for the Blind; T. H. Preston, M.P.P. for South Brant; and Hon. William Paterson, Minister of Customs, expressing regret at being unable to be present.

Superintendent Smith said the federation of the Six Nation Indians was the oldest established government on the continent. The constitutions of the present governments were modeled after the Six Nations' constitution. They had shown forethought in framing their system. They believed that at some later day there would be a great confederacy of all the tribes, and they had worked to that end.

Chief A. G. Smith (Mohawk) spoke at some length on the "Life and Times of Joseph Brant." He considered him a thoughtful, unselfish man, who sacrificed many things in order to better the condition of his people. When the Government had given the land grants for the use of the Indians, it was Joseph Brant who advised them to settle and learn to till the ground, rather than to spend their time in laziness. It was he who brought the white man in to teach them the art of agriculture, and it was he who said: "We cannot succeed unless we obtain education."

Judge Hardy spoke at some length on the career of Joseph Brant, touching on many interesting incidents of his life which brought out the true worth of the man. He considered it a fitting thing to hold a celebration in honor of one so great as Joseph Brant, and he had a feeling of intense interest in all the Indian brethren concerned in such an event. The experiences and exploits of these first inhabitants of our great Dominion were interesting, and Joseph Brant figured as greatest of them all. He referred to the natural endowments possessed by Brant. He was the possessor of an educated, cultivated and trained mind, making friends with all men with whom he came in contact. To show the attitude of Captain Brant as regards education, Judge Hardy read a letter written by Brant to Mr. Wheelock, Principal of a Seminary at Lebanon, Conn., in which he gave Mr. Wheelock full charge of his two sons, that they should be thoroughly educated in all lines, and particularly in morals. Brant was solicitous of education, and desired to educate the Six Nations in the same manner as his own sons. He had also assisted in the promotion of religion, thus proving himself an accomplished man, of broad and noble culture. Judge Hardy read a letter from Aaron Burr to his daughter, recommending Brant to her as a man of education, well bred and a suitable person to be introduced to their friends. Judge Hardy described the interview between John Brant and the poet, Campbell, in which John convinced the author of Gertrude of Wyoming that he had done a grave injustice to his father, Joseph Brant. He also referred to Brant's interview with General Herkimer, in which the former announced his fixed intention to adhere to the British side in the war.

W. F. Cockshutt, M.P., made a capital speech, interspersed with humorous stories, which the Indians enjoyed thoroughly. He said his first speech in the House of Commons was on behalf of the Indians, whom he had always been proud to regard as his friends. It was Sir Wilfrid Laurier who had asked him to make that speech on the effect of education on the red man. The Indians had once had the franchise and he believed they should still have it. They were a living, not a dead, race, and they should have legislative privileges. Many of them had demonstrated their capabilities under educational advantages. The late Dr. Oronhyatekha had become the head of a large fraternal order, and at the time of his death he was enjoying a salary as large as that of the Premier of the Dominion. He knew of an Indian girl who had charge of a large hospital in the United States, and examples of similar success could be found in other walks of life. The Indian was capable of the highest education. The Six Nations had proved their ability to occupy the highest positions in peace as well as in war. They formed the largest reserve on the American continent, possessing over 4,000 souls, and they were the most advanced of all the tribes. He had heard the late Senator Plumb, who was an authority, say that no people had made greater advancement within a given time than the Six Nations; that it had taken the whites nearly 2,000 years to reach a position which the Six Nations had largely attained in one century. As a matter of fact, Longboat had recently shown that he was able to go far ahead of all the whites.

He considered Brant a statesman as well as a warrior. Brant's reputation would remain when his detractors were dead and forgotten. The truth was that he had been earnest, loyal and true; he had nobly done his duty in his day and generation, and bequeathed wise measures which had left their impress to the present time. Look at his influence in this vicinity—Brant county and Brantford city perpetuating his name. To the Indians Canada also owed her very name. "Okanada" was an Indian word, meaning a village or settlement, and thus had become transformed into Canada. He knew that some people tried to make out that the Spanish, when they first landed in the country looking for gold, exclaimed "Acanada"—there is nothing here—and that this was the derivation of Canada, but the first explanation given was obviously the true one. The Indians of the Grand River had been the possessors of many valuable relics, too many of which had found their way to Montreal, to England and to the United States. He was sorry that so many of these things had been taken away from this neighborhood, and he would like to have Judge Hardy start a collection of local Indian relics. He knew that some regarded him as a sentimentalist about the Six Nations, but he believed them to be capable of attaining any heights, becoming members of parliament, and perhaps even providing a premier for the land they once owned. He had heard some men say that the Six Nations should be removed to the north or the west, and their lands be opened for white settlement. He protested most strongly against that. In former times it was largely the Indian trade that had made Brantford, and he was old enough to know how much that fact had been appreciated by the business men of the earlier days. They deserved—richly deserved—the lands given them in Brant county for loyalty to the British crown in a time of peril, and to attempt to force them back from the present reserve would be to break faith and pledges. It could never be done.

After luncheon Chief William Hill was the first speaker. His address was in the Indian language and seemed to please those who understood it.

Warrior Jacob Hill, dressed in regular war costume, his face covered with vermilion and his hands filled with bows and arrows, was called on for a speech. He said he had dropped in accidentally and did not know what the multitude of people meant. On being told the cause of the gathering, he said he was prepared for war but not for speech-making, so he would withdraw.

John Gibson, of the Senecas, made an address in his own language.

William G. Raymond, Postmaster of Brantford, said that if Brant could but stand for a moment on the banks of the Grand River, and view the great changes, he would see naught but what he had laid the foundation for. This successful application of methods by Brant and his followers, he considered, was an example to be followed by all men. He thought that the Six Nations Indians had justly earned every privilege that was granted by the Government and sincerely hoped that the removal of the Reserve was not contemplated.

Frederick Loft, of the Six Nations, employed in the Provincial Secretary's office, Toronto, spoke on the constitution of the Six Nations. He thought that the Indian was rapidly gaining a position of equality with the white man. If the Government contemplated any steps in the removal of the Reserve, they should send a delegation to discuss the matter with the Indian Council. He appreciated all the Government had done for the Indians in teaching them the different departments of agriculture, and sincerely hoped that nothing would be done to retard them from their rapid advancement. The old system of rule which had been in force in Brant's time has passed down through these many years, and though it might have many failings, yet it was a most wonderful constitution. It provided for a great many things just as modern Governments have done, and there is a great resemblance between the two constitutions. He knew that the Chiefs would never consent to be put back and hoped there would be nothing done to mar the peace of the people.

Chief J. S. Johnson considered education the means of elevation for the Indian.

Mr. F. D. Reville, seconded by Mr. E. L. Cockshutt, moved a hearty vote of thanks for the cordial reception tendered the white visitors. The proceedings closed with cheers for the King and the Indians, the latter responding with three war whoops, led by Chief J. S. Johnson.

Sketch of Brant's Life.

A very large audience assembled in Victoria Hall, Brantford, on Monday evening, November 25th, to listen to a patriotic lecture on the life and works of Joseph Brant, delivered by Principal H. F. Gardiner of the Ontario Institution for the Blind, a well-selected program and a speech by Chief William Smith of the Six Nations Indians. The affair was held under the auspices of the Canadian Club, which has a primary object in the dissemination of a broader knowledge of Canadian affairs. Needless to say, the lecture of Principal Gardiner was instructive in its every detail, and was of a highly patriotic color from beginning to end. The days of the early revolutionary wars, especially in relation to the settlement of this part of the province by the Six Nations brought about by their removal from the Mohawk valley before the onslaughts of Sullivan and his artillery, were lucidly portrayed by the speaker. He suggested that one good object the Canadian Club could accomplish would be to mark out the place where Joseph Brant lived between the Mohawk Church and the locks at the river, by the erection of a stone monument. He thought it was a subject calling for the patriotic attention of Brantfordites.

Miss Russell, graduate of the Toronto Conservatory of Music, contributed to the program in very fine style. She recited a poem of Miss Pauline Johnson's, and received a meritorious encore. Miss Russell possesses a very pleasing manner, and is an elocutionist of rare ability. Mr. Joyce also contributed solos to the program, and was in very fine voice. Chief William Smith of the Reserve, was the representative of the Six Nations present, and made a patriotic but brief address in which he expressed unswerving loyalty to the British crown and the Canadian Government. The evening was brought to a close with the singing of the National Anthem, and proved a most enjoyable one in every respect.

Mr. Gardiner said he felt complimented by the invitation of the Brantford Canadian Club to speak about Joseph Brant, especially as he was not a native of the city or the county whose names commemorate the great Indian chieftain, who died 100 years ago. He must be a poor Canadian who could not appreciate the labors and the services, the achievements and the character of a man who had devoted the best years of his life to the interests of the British crown and the welfare of his own race. In the time at his disposal he could not attempt to tell anything like the full story of Brant's life, but without regard to style or method he would endeavor to crowd into his remarks as much information as possible about the man in honor of whose memory the meeting had been called.

BRANT'S BIRTH, PARENTAGE AND EDUCATION.

In the eighteenth century the Indian tribe to which Joseph Brant, or Thayendanegea, belonged, dwelt in the valley of the Mohawk, a river 135 miles long, which flows in a southeasterly direction and empties into the Hudson about 10 miles north of Albany, N.Y. But his parents must have strayed many miles from home, for Joseph is said to have been born in the year 1742, "on the banks of the Ohio," a sufficiently indefinite location, since the length of the Ohio River, from Cairo, Ill., to Pittsburg, Pa., is 975 miles. The Ohio at one point comes within little more than 100 miles of Lake Erie, and its chief branch, the Alleghany, approaches within 14 miles of that lake. According to one account, Brant's father died in the Ohio country, and his mother came back to the Mohawk with Joseph and his sister Mary, where she took for her second husband a man named Barnet or Burnet, which was contracted into Brant. Another version makes Joseph Brant the grandson of the Indian Brant, who visited Queen Anne in England in 1710, and the son of Nickus Brant, who lived in the Mohawk country and was mentioned in the papers of Sir William Johnson. Colonel Stone says that Brant was a well-known family name in England. In 1458— nearly 300 years before the birth of Joseph Brant on the banks of the Ohio—Sebastion Brant was born in Strasburg, Germany. He wrote a book containing a poem called the Narrenschiff, or Ship of Fools, which was translated into Latin, French and English (1508), and it was the first book published in the English language which contained any mention of the New World.

It is not recorded that Brant went to school when a child, but after he had seen some service as a warrior he attended Dr. Wheelock's school at Lebanon, Conn., probably from 1759 to 1761. The labors which he performed as a translator of the Scriptures, his letters and speeches, and his intimate friendship with learned men, indicate that Brant attained considerable culture, probably to a great extent by private study. His essay on "American Antiquities and the Relative Advantages of Savage and Civilized Life," quoted by Stone, betokens extensive reading and keen, intelligent observation. An illiterate savage could not have been esteemed by men like Boswell, Sheridan, the Earl of Moira and the Duke of Northumberland, as Brant undoubtedly was.

When a mere child, during the war between the English and the French, he listened to the call to arms.

BRANT THE WARRIOR.

Brant was at the battle of Lake George, under Sir William Johnson, in 1755, being then only about 13 years old. The Mohawks were led by their King Hendrick, who was slain. For his success in that expedition Sir William received a baronetcy and £5,000.

In 1759 Brant accompanied Sir William Johnson against the French at Niagara. General Prideaux being killed, Sir William assumed command and the fort was taken, thus breaking the chain of forts that the French had designed to establish from Canada to Louisiana.

In 1763-64 Brant was engaged in the war against Pontiac, the Ottawa chief, who captured Mackinaw and besieged Detroit, having combined Delawares, Wyandots, Shawnees, Mingoes and Chippewas against the western garrisons and settlers. Pontiac submitted to the British in 1766. Brant returned from the expedition in 1764 and lived a peaceful life until the outbreak of the Revolution.

In May, 1776, Brant led the Indians at the battle of The Cedars, 40 miles above Montreal. Major Sherbourne surrendered to the British.

Brant's first raid on any of the New York settlements was in May, 1777. In June of that year he went south through the Mohawk country as far as Unadilla on the Susquehanna. He there had an interview with General Herkimer, and announced to him that he was engaged to serve the King. Thence he went to a council at Oswego, where the alliance of the Six Nations with the British was cemented.

Later, in 1777, returning from St. Leger's expedition against Fort Stanwix, Brant met with a severe loss in an engagement, which he attributed to the Oneidas, and attacked them. In retaliation they plundered Miss Molly at the Upper Mohawk Town, and she and her family fled to the Onondagas. She got and gave information which enabled Brant to ambuscade General Herkimer at Oriskany, where there was a drawn battle, both sides losing heavily and both claiming the victory.

In the spring of 1778 Brant was again on the Susquehanna below Unadilla. His first movement was on Springfield, ten miles west of Cherry Valley. He was not at Wyoming, where Colonel John Butler was in command. The fact of his absence from that alleged "massacre" was fully established by John Brant and acknowledged by the poet Campbell, who wrote "Gertrude of Wyoming."

In July, 1778, Brant attacked and wiped out of existence Andrustown, and in August of the same year he laid waste German Flats.

In November he served under Walter Butler in the attack on Cherry Valley.

In July, 1779, Brant destroyed Minisink, and devastated other small places in the Mohawk Valley.

In August, 1779, General Sullivan defeated Brant at Newtown on the site of the present Elmira. The Indians could not stand against Sullivan's artillery, and they were not only defeated, but demoralized. Sullivan proceeded through their country, utterly destroying the houses, their corn and their orchards, which he was surprised to find in such abundance. This policy was adopted by order of General Washington and the American Congress. Sullivan went as far west as the Genessee country and he could have taken Fort Niagara, the winter quarters of the British and Indians, if he had pursued his victory.

In the winter of 1779-80 Brant invaded the Oneida Indians.

On April, 1780, he surprised and destroyed Harpersfield, but saved the life of Col. Harper, ancestor of the New York publishers.

In May, 1780, Brant attacked the Saugerties settlements; in August he burned Canajoharie; in October he successfully invaded the Schoharie country.

After the close of the war, Brant was interested in the formation of a confederacy of the Northwest Indians against the United States. He attended councils on the Detroit River, and in the Miami country, helped to defeat General St. Clair in 1791, and kept in close touch with military affairs until the conclusion of Wayne's Treaty in 1795.

How Indians Fought.

Rev. Peter Jones, in his chapter on the mode of Indian warfare, says that "the more scalps they take the more they are revered and consulted by their tribe. Their mode of action is entirely different from that of civilized nations. They have no idea of meeting the enemy upon an open plain face to face, to be shot at like dogs, as they say. Their aim is to surprise the enemy by darting upon them in an unexpected moment, or in the dead of night. They always take care, in the first place, to ascertain the position of the enemy. When they find them unprepared or asleep, they creep up stealthily and slowly, like panthers in pursuit of their prey; when sufficiently near, they simultaneously raise the war whoop, and before the enemy awake or have time to defend themselves, the tomohawk is rattling over their heads. When a village, a wigwam, or a party is thus surprised, there is seldom any mercy shown either to age or sex; all are doomed to feel the weight of the tomahawk and the deep incision of the bloody scalping knife. Such close battles, if they may be so called, seldom last more than a few minutes. If a captive is not adopted by some family who have lost a relative in the war, he is compelled to undergo the most painful death, by being burned alive either at the stake or tree. It is stated that the Indian victims thus burned have never betrayed any weakness in complaining of the severity of their punishment by shedding a tear, or uttering a groan; but, on the contrary, have been known to upbraid their tormentors, telling them that they did not know how to give pain."

With the wisdom that comes after the event, it is now generally conceded that it was a mistake for Britain to employ Indians in the war against the revolting colonies; not that the Americans can afford to throw stones, for they were anxious to get the Indians to fight on their side, and there was not much to choose between the treatment of the whites by the Indians, and the treatment of the Indians by the whites. The Indians practiced the trade of war—always dreadful—in conformity with their own usages and laws. The scalping of a slain foe was not in their opinion barbarous. The scalplock was an emblem of chivalry. The warrior was careful to leave the lock of defiance on his crown, for his enemies to take if they could get it. The stake and the torture were identified with their rude notions of the power of endurance. But whatever degree of hardship and suffering their female captives were compelled to endure their persons were never dishonored by violence; a fact which can be predicated of no other victorious soldiery that ever lived.

The name of Brant has been connected with every species of atrocity from the "massacre" of Wyoming, at which he was not even present, to the deliberate murder of a prisoner. But Colonel Stone has collected evidence to show that on many occasions Brant saved the lives of those who were opposed to him, and while he says that "no matter for the difficulties or the distance, wherever a blow could be struck to any advantage, Joseph Brant was sure to be there." He adds that "there is no good evidence that Brant was himself a participator in secret murders or attacks upon isolated individuals or families." He fought and he fought to win—to kill rather than to be killed. "Whether in the conduct of a campaign or of a scouting party, in the pitched battle or the foray, this crafty and dauntless chieftain was sure to be one of the most efficient, as he was one of the bravest, of those who were engaged. Combining with the native hardihood and sagacity of his race the advantages of education and of civilized life—in acquiring which he had lost nothing of his activity or his power of endurance—he became the most formidable border foe with whom the Provincials had to contend, and his name was a terror to the land."

Brant's Domestic Relations.

Some time previous to 1765 Joseph Brant married Margaret, the daughter of the Oneida chief, and for several years he lived at Canajoharie on the Mohawk. When Rev. Dr. Stewart visited him there in 1771, he found him comfortably settled in a good house, with everything necessary for the use of his family, consisting of his wife, his son, Isaac, and his daughter, Christina. After Margaret's death, he married her half-sister, Susanna, who died shortly after her marriage without issue. In 1780, at Niagara, he was regularly wedded to his third wife, Catharine, with whom he had been living, according to the Indian fashion, for some time previous. She survived him for thirty years, dying in 1837 at the Mohawk village on the Grand River. By his third wife, Brant had seven children, Joseph, jr., who died in 1830, leaving a daughter, Catharine, who married Aaron Hill; Jacob, who died in 1846, leaving six children; John, who died in 1832, unmarried; Margaret, who died in 1848, leaving several children; Catharine, who died in 1867, having had three children; Mary, who married Seth Hill, and Elizabeth, who died in 1844, having married William Johnson Kerr, a grandson of Sir William Johnson. She had four children, one of whom, Chief Simcoe Kerr, was living at Burlington in 1871. Brant's two children, by his first wife, married and left issue. His sister, Mary, or "Miss Molly," as she was called, is described in Sir William Johnson's will as "my faithful housekeeper," and to her children he left money and land. Dr. Canniff says: "We cannot excuse the conduct of Sir William, when he had lost his European wife, in taking the sister of Brant, Miss Molly, without the form of matrimonial alliance; but we must concede every allowance for the times in which he lived. But while grave doubt may rest upon the moral principle displayed by him, we see no just reason to reflect in any way upon the Indian female. Miss Molly took up her abode with Sir William, and lived with him as a faithful spouse until he died. However, this must not be regarded as indicating depravity on the part of the simple-minded native. It must be remembered that the Indian's mode of marrying consists of but little more than the young squaw leaving the father's wigwam, and repairing to that of her future husband, and there is no reason to doubt that Miss Molly was ever other than a virtuous woman. And this belief is corroborated by the fact that four daughters, the issue of this alliance, were most respectably married."

Captain Campbell, who visited Brant's house on the Grand River in 1792, reported that "Captain Brant, who is well acquainted with European manners, received us with much politeness and hospitality. Mrs. Brant appeared, superbly dressed in the Indian fashion. Her blanket was made up of silk and the finest English cloth, bordered with a narrow strip of embroidered lace. They have a fine family of children. Tea was on the table when we came in, served up on the handsomest china plate; our beds, sheets and English blankets were fine and comfortable. Two slaves attended the table."

A few years before his death, Captain Brant built a residence on a fine tract of land at the head of Lake Ontario, given to him by the King, but after his death Mrs. Brant came back to the Grand River to live.

Brant the Business Man.

Brant's record and ability as a man of business cannot be completely understood without reference to the Canadian Archives, in which his name frequently appears. His caution was displayed in going to Montreal in 1775 to negotiate with Carleton and Haldimand about compensation for the lands of the Six Nations in the Mohawk Valley in case the British arms should not be successful. His visit to England to have the King and Government confirm the arrangement and to have his standing in the service confirmed, before committing any overt act against the enemy, was well advised. After the war, he insisted that Haldimand should implement his promise, and made a second visit to England. He had managed to have the women and other non-combatants removed from the Mohawk Valley to Canada early in the struggle, and when peace came he soon got them comfortably settled on the Grand River reserve. How he provided for his own household has been described. He doubtless had many unrecorded difficulties in the distribution and disposal of the land grant, but he seems to have taken a broad view of the future of his people, and his personal honesty is conceded.

The Land Grant on Grand River.

The Neuter nation, on the north shore of Lake Erie, like the Eries or Cats on the south shore of the same lake, had been practically exterminated by the Iroquois about the middle of the seventeenth century, so that there were few human beings in that part of Canada between the Niagara and Detroit Rivers. The Chippewas or Mississaugas laid claim to the country, so the Government bought out their right to a tract bounded on the east by a straight line running from the north end of Burlington Beach to the Falls of the Grand River (Elora), and on the west by a line from the Falls of Elora to the mouth of Catfish Creek, on Lake Erie, about midway from the present Port Stanley to Port Burwell.

Out of this tract, on October 25th, 1784, Sir Frederick Haldimand, by an instrument under his hand and seal declared that the Six Nations "and their posterity should be allowed to possess and enjoy a tract of land six miles in depth on each side of the Grand River," from its mouth to the Elora Falls, a distance of 100 miles. This grant would include, counting land and water, 1,200 square miles, or 768,000 acres, covering the present townships of Sherbrooke, Moulton, Dunn, Canboro', Cayuga, Seneca, Oneida, Tuscarora, Onondaga, Brantford, Dumfries, Waterloo, Woolwich, Pilkington and Nichol. This tract, though much smaller than that which they had been obliged to forsake in the United States, amply satisfied these loyal Indians; indeed, it was not long before they began to dispose of part of their grant. Brant and his people had supposed, it was alleged, that the territory allotted to them had been conveyed in fee by a perfect title. W. H. Smith says: "It is hardly necessary to remark that an estate in fee simple in lands, belonging to the crown, could not be conveyed by Sir Frederick Haldimand's mere license of occupation under his seal. Letters patent, under the Great Seal of England, or of the Province of Quebec, could alone have conferred such a title." It had been expressly declared in 1763, and again in 1788 and 1789, that the Indians were never to alienate their lands without the assent of the crown.

The Indians had not been long in occupancy of the new territory on the Grand River before the white settlers began to plant themselves in their neighborhood. Brant saw that the hunting grounds of his people would be thus circumscribed, and he also saw without regret that the effect would be to drive his people from the hunter to the agricultural state, in which case the territory would be too large, instead of too small. He conceived the idea of selling part of the land for money for the immediate improvement of the people, and part in such a way as to secure a permanent revenue for the Indians. This led to disputes with the Government, especially in Governor Simcoe's time.

The principal chiefs and warriors, in the name of the whole, executed on November 2nd, 1796, a formal power of attorney, authorizing

Captain Brant to surrender into the hands of the Government certain portions of the lands possessed by them, and for which they had found, or intended to find, purchasers, so that His Majesty, thus holding those portions of their lands, relieved from the pledge which had been given for their exclusive possession, might make a clear and free grant, in fee simple, by letters patent, to such persons as the Indians might agree to sell to. This method of proceeding was clearly in accordance with the nature of the tenure under which the Six Nations held, and was, in principle at least, as proper as could be devised for protecting the interests of the Indians and guarding them from hasty and indiscreet sales. The tract which Captain Brant was authorized to surrender was described in the power of attorney referred to, and was stated to contain 310,391 acres. From a report made to the Government in 1830 the disposition of those lands can be ascertained:

94,305 acres, now constituting the township of Dumfries, were sold to P. Steadman for £8,841. This tract passed into the possession of Hon. William Dickson, who paid the price and opened the land for settlement.

94,012 acres, the township of Waterloo, were sold to Richard Beasley, James Wilson and John B. Rousseaux for £8,887.

3,000 acres additional were given to Mr. Beasley to make up a deficiency in Waterloo township.

86,078 acres, the township of Woolwich, were sold to William Wallace for £16,364. Mr. Wallace paid for 7,000 acres, and the Indians reported to the commission that they had given from this tract 10,000 acres to Mrs. Claus, daughter of Sir William Johnson, and 5,000 acres to Captain Brant. Jacob Erb had bargained for 45,185 acres of Woolwich township at half a dollar per acre.

28,152 acres, Nichol township, were sold to Hon. Thomas Clark for £3,564, payable in 1,000 years from the date of the bond, the interest to be paid annually.

30,800 acres, the township of Moulton, were sold to W. Jarvis for £5,775; sold out to Lord Selkirk, who sold to Henry J. Boulton.

The township of Canboro' was granted to John Dockstader, who transferred it to Benjamin Canby for the benefit of Dockstader's Indian children. It was reported that Canby had paid neither principal nor interest.

The township of Sherbrooke appears to have been given to Mr. Dickson, on his agreement to transact all necessary business of a professional character for the Indians.

15,000 acres, comprised in the township of Pilkington, were sold to Captain Pilkington.

The commissioners reported: "Whether Captain Joseph Brant did or did not on all occasions execute the trust reposed in him faithfully towards the Indians the trustees are unable to judge, no evidence having been laid before them upon that subject; and it is indeed only right to observe that no improper conduct whatever has been imputed to him before the trustees; and they are, therefore, bound to assume that he discharged his duty with due fidelity."

Until long after Brant's death, that is to say, until 1830, the entire area of what is now Brantford township remained in possession of the Six Nations Indians, but at that date the town plot of Brantford and the north part of the township were deeded away and further surrenders were made from time to time until the whole township was ceded and settled.

Brant the Patriot.

Brant was to the day of his death an Indian chief, owing his first duty to his kindred and his nation. He was ready to contest Indian rights with Governor Simcoe, Agent Claus or any other disputant. Nor were his sympathies confined to the Six Nations. For years he was active on behalf of the Indians west of the Detroit River, and only gave up the struggle when he became convinced that the cause could expect no assistance from Great Britain. It was Brant's proud boast that he had never taken pay for work done on behalf of the Indians. He also claimed that his loyal devotion to the British cause during the War of the Revolution was in fulfilment of the pledges given by his forefathers.

One of his biographers says that the interests of his people, which were ever uppermost in his mind while in the fulness of health and strength, seemed to be foremost in his thoughts to the end. His last words were: "Have pity upon the poor Indians; if you can get any influence with the great, endeavor to do them all the good you can." With these sentiments paramount in his thoughts, Joseph Thayendanegea died. His remains were brought to the burying grounds which surround the old Mohawk Church, and there interred among those of many of his kindred.

Forty-three years passed away. The flight of time and the corroding hand of neglect were fast obliterating the little mounds of earth which marked the last resting place of Joseph Brant and his son and successors, John Brant. In the year 1850 the remains of the two chiefs were re-interred in one common vault. The Brantford *Herald* of November 27th, 1850, said:

"On Monday last the remains of Thayendanegea, which had been previously exhumed, were placed in the tomb at the Mohawk that had been recently prepared for their reception. This was done with no small degree of pageantry. The vast multitude of people who had assembled from different quarters went in procession from the town of Brantford to the Mohawk village. Addresses were delivered by Rev. A. Nelles, Rev. P. Jones, Sir Allan McNab, D. Thorburn, Esq., and others, among whom was an American gentleman whose father had many years ago been most generously treated by Brant. After the speaking was concluded the interment took place, when three volleys were fired over the grave of the brave and faithful Indian soldier, Captain Joseph Brant."

In his address on that occasion Rev. Peter Jones said that Brant's adherence to Great Britain was strong and sincere; and in consequence of that attachment the Six Nations lost their extensive fertile country, now the garden of the state of New York. No one can dispute his gravery. In Indian language it may be said of him: 'His eye was like the eagle's—his motions like arrows from the bow—his enemies fell before him as the trees before the blast of the Great Spirit.' Brant was the principal means of the erection of this church, now the oldest in Canada, and procured the bell which has so often summoned the people of God together to worship in his holy courts; and has tolled for hundreds of those whose bones now lie in that sacred yard. I am informed that it tolled, when Brant died, 24 hours. I am happy to learn that our white friends have it in their hearts to erect a monument to the memory of the Indian brave, that succeeding generations may see and know the hero after whom the town of Brantford is named."

BRANT, THE GENTLEMEN.

Mr. Stewart denies that the family of Brant occupied a pre-eminent position in their village on the Mohawk River, and contends that Joseph's influence was acquired by his uncommon talents and address as a councillor and politician. "Distinguished alike for his address, his activity and his courage—possessing in point of stature and symmetry of person that advantage of most men even among his own well formed race—tall, erect and majestic, with the air and mien or one born to command —having, as it were, been a man of war since his boyhood—his name was a tower of strength among the warriors of the wilderness." Regarding his first visit to England in 1776, it has always been said that he was not only well received, but that his society was courted by men of rank and station—statesmen, scholars and divines. He had little of the savage ferocity of his people in his countenance; and when, as he ordinarily did, he wore the English dress, there was nothing besides his color mark to mark wherein he differed from other men. He was provided with a splendid costume after the manner of his own nation, in which he appeared at court.

On his second visit to England in 1785-86, he was received with even greater favor, for he had made the acquaintance of many officers of the army and other persons of prominence who vied with one another to do honor to Brant. Lord Dorchester, Earl Moira, General Stuart, the Duke of Northumberland, the Earl of Warwick, Charles Fox, the Bishop of London and the Prince of Wales were among his intimates. With King George II. and the royal family he was a great favorite. Speaking of the people he met at the table of the Prince of Wales— Fox, Burke and Sheridan, and others of that splendid galaxy of eloquence and intelligence—Col. Stone says that, "though deficient in his literary acquisitions, Brant, with great strength of mind and shrewdness of observation, had moreover sufficient taste and cultivation to appreciate society, even of this elevated and intellectual character. The natural reserve of the Indian he could assume or throw off at pleasure and with a keen sense of the ludicrous he could himself use the weapons of humor and sarcasm with a good share of skill and dexterity." Brant's method of impressing the Turkish diplomat who had allowed his curiosity to get the better of his caution is too well known to require repetition.

BRANT'S RELIGION.

About the time of Brant's second marriage (1772-3) he became the subject of serious religious impressions. He attached himself to the church, was a chastened and regular communicant at the celebration of the Eucharist; and from his serious deportment, and the anxiety he had ever manifested to civilize and Christianize his people, great hopes were entertained from his future exertions in that cause. No doubt has ever been entertained of his sincerity at that time; and it has been attributed to the counteracting influences of the dreadful trade of war, in which it was his fortune afterward again so actively to become engaged, that those manifestations of Christian utility were effaced; entirely eradicated they were not, as was shown at a subsequent stage of the career of this remarkable man. As far back as 1762 Rev. Charles

J. Smith, a missionary to the Mohawks, took Brant as an interpreter. Rev. Dr. Wheelock receiving a report from Rev. Mr. Kirkland that, on account of the outbreak of the war, Mr. Smith was obliged to return, but Joseph tarried and went out with a company against the Indians and was useful in the war; in which he behaved so much like the Christian and the soldier that he gained great esteem; adding "he now lives in a decent manner, and endeavors to teach his poor brethern the things of God, in which his own heart seems much engaged. His house is an asylum for the missionaries in that wilderness."

Brant assisted in translating the prayer book and portions of the Scriptures into the Mohawk language, and after he came to reside in Canada, his efforts for the moral and religious improvement of his people were indefatigable. One of his first stipulations with the commander-in-chief, on the acquisition of his new territory, was for the building of a church, a school house and a flouring mill and he soon made application for a resident clergyman. It is no less interesting than true that the first Episcopal Church erected in Upper Canada was built by Brant, from funds collected by him while in England in 1786. The communion service is of beaten silver, each piece bearing an inscription stating it to have been given to the Mohawks for the use of their chapel by Queen Anne. The church bell was made by John Warner, Fleet Street, London, 1786. Brant died at Wellington Square (now Burlington), on November 24, 1807, at the age of 64, and his remains were interred by the side of the Mohawk Church on the Grand River. Not far away is the institute for the education of Indian children, maintained by the New England Company, which was originally constituted a corporation under the name of "The President and Society for the Propagation of the Gospel in New England," by an ordinance issued in 1649. It was this Company which supported various missionary undertakings in New England during the seventeenth and eighteenth centuries, until interrupted by the war between Britain and her colonies. The operations of the Company have since been carried on in what is now the Dominion of Canada.

THE MAN BRANT.

As a warrior, Brant was cautious, sagacious and brave; watching with sleepless vigilance for opportunities of action, and allowing neither dangers nor difficulties to divert him from his well settled purposes. His constitution was hardy, his capacity of endurance great; his energy untiring, and his firmness indomitable. He was at once affable and dignified, avoiding frivolity on the one hand and stiffness on the other. His temperament was decidedly amiable; he had a keen perception of the ludicrous, and was both humorous and witty himself. In his dealings and business relations he was prompt, honorable and expert, and a pattern of integrity. The purity of his private morals has never been questioned, and his house was the abode of kindness and hospitality.

F. W. Halsey, in his book on "The Old New York Frontier," says that in the town named after him an imposing monument perpetuates the memory of Brant. In that soil, therefore, sleeps in his last sleep the most interesting Indian, who, in that eventful eighteenth century, forever linked his name with the history of central New York. Stone is not alone among Brant's eulogists. William C. Bryant, of Buffalo, had remarked that the evidence is incontestable that he was a great man—in many respects the most extraordinary his race has produced since the advent of the white man on this continent; and John Fiske, in one of his later books, declares that he was the most remarkable Indian known to history. Schoolcraft calls him the Jephtha of his tribe, and lauds his firmness and energy of purpose as qualities, which few among the American aborigines have ever equalled. But the best evidence of the man's personal worth lies in the high respect and friendship which he inspired among educated and titled Englishmen, as shown in many ways and notably in his correspondence. Brant, says Halsey in conclusion, has deserved no large part of that load of obloquy which on this frontier for many years rested upon his name. He was better than the Tories under whose guidance he served, and far better than most Indian chiefs of his time. There was much in the man that was kindly and humane. If he loved war, this was because he loved his friends and his home still more. He fought in battle with the vigor and skill of a savage, but we are to remember that he fought where honor called him. To the story of his life peculiar fascination must long be attached, a large part of which springs from the potent charm of an open personality. In Brant's character were joined strength and humanity, genius for war and that unfamiliar quality in the Mohawk savage, bonhomie.

Mr. Gardiner said he had not attempted to depict Brant as a man free from imperfections. He had his faults, as which of us has not? Doubtless, he made mistakes. His judgments were not infallible. Could he have foreseen that, within one hundred years from the time when he sold hundreds of thousands of acres for 50 cents an acre, payable either in spot cash or at the end of 1,000 years, Woolwich, Waterloo, Dumfries and the other townships bordering the Grand River would be filled with smiling farms, while the hum of manufacturing industry would be heard from such busy centres of population as Berlin, Preston, Galt, Paris and Brantford, he would probably have advised the leasing of the lands at a ground rent adjustable every 40 or 50 years, and would thus have secured for his people an ample income for all time to come. Doubtless, in the lust of battle, he committed acts for which he was afterwards sorry. But Brant has now been dead long enough for an unprejudiced public to estimate him fairly, and the verdict will surely be that the good in him far outweighed the evil, and that his name is entitled to rank with the Robinsons and Ryersons, the Merritts and McNabs, the Tisdales and Sherwoods, the Cartwrights and Hamiltons whom by common consent Canadians delight to honor. Joseph Brant was a man, take him for all in all, we shall not look upon his like again.

V.

THE PIONEERS OF MIDDLESEX.

Mr. President, Ladies and Gentlemen:—

You will see by the addenda that the paper I have promised to read is entitled "The Pioneers of Middlesex," though that scarcely correctly describes my attempt. What I intend to speak to you about is certainly men who were pioneers in the county of Middlesex, though I intend to deal principally with them in their character as pioneers and founders of the city of London.

London, often spoken of as the Forest City, from the fact that when and for many years after it was first laid out, indeed, until a period well within living memory, there remained a wide expanse of unbroken forest within a very short distance of the site upon which this beautiful city of the west now stands.

In the year 1826 Thomas Talbot, Mahlon Burwell, James Hamilton, Charles Ingersoll and John Matthews were appointed by government Commissioners to erect county buildings in the town of London, in the Province of Upper Canada, which had been named as the county town of the county of Middlesex in the same province in the place of Victoria previously named.

Before going any further a few words may be said about some of these commissioners. Thomas Talbot was the famous Colonel Talbot, who came to Canada with Governor Simcoe in 1792, and eleven years later, in the year 1803, founded the town of St. Thomas. It would occupy more time than the Ontario Historical Society has at its disposal for the whole of its meeting, to attempt to give any history of the famous Thomas Talbot.

His whole life is bound up with the city of St. Thomas, with the early settlers on Lake Erie, with the Talbot Settlement and the county of Elgin. He is one of the most notable characters of the early days of Upper Canada, now Ontario, and one could only deal efficiently with the circumstances of his advent in Canada and his subsequent sojourn here in a long series of papers.

Mahlon Burwell, another of the commissioners, was a Colonel of Militia. He was one of the very earliest settlers on the shores of Lake Erie, the town of Port Burwell receiving its name from him.

James Hamilton was a member of the famous Niagara family of that name. They were, 80 years ago, greatly interested in the lake trade; built several steamers themselves and exercised a wide influence in the province.

Charles Ingersoll was the founder of the town of Ingersoll in the county of Oxford, where he was a very large land owner. Of John Matthews I do not possess any very accurate information, beyond the fact that he was a prominent figure of Lobo.

Every student of Canadian History is aware that Governor Simcoe, when he first visited Upper Canada, had it in his mind to plant his capital on the River La Tranche, on the site now occupied by London. This idea, though, was speedily abandoned, and it was quite thirty years after Governor Simcoe's time before the present city of London was founded.

In 1826 the first survey was made for the proposed town. The work was carried out by Colonel Mahlon Burwell, assisted by Freeman Talbot and Benjamin Springer as chain bearers.

Everything must have a beginning and the first beginning of the present city of London was very modest, indeed, some two or three log cabins being the first houses erected.

Colonel Talbot had a very great deal to do with settling the place. He was apparently land commissioner, the patents all being in his hands; but it must also be admitted that the conditions entitling a proposed settler to a tract of land were not very rigid. They were the payment of a fee of £8 currency or $32 upon the patent, with the additional condition that they built a house, the quality not being specified, though the size was to be 24 feet by 18. There were no stipulations as to it being a one or a two-storey building, and it goes without saying that no sanitary regulations were enforced; all the settler had to do was to pay the patent fee and build any kind of a shack that he fancied so long as it was at least 24 feet in length.

The boundaries of the first town were Wellington Street on the east, North Street, now know as Carling Street, on the north, and the River Thames on the south and west.

Among the very early settlers were Robert Carfrae, who was related to a well known resident of York, Hugh Carfrae; John Yerex, Dennis O'Brien, Patrick McMannis and Thomas Fisher. John Yerex was father of the first native born Londoner, Nathaniel Yerex, who first saw the light of day in 1826, very shortly after the survey was made for the new town. Information is very vague as to the first year or two of London's history, though it is known that in the year 1827 the total population of the place numbered 133, there being in all thirty-three families. The first marriage, which took place in the town, was that of Thomas Carling, father of the late Senator Carling, to Miss Anne Routledge, and it was performed not by a clergyman but by a magistrate, Colonel Mahlon Burwell.

Reference has been made previously to the county buildings. These were duly erected and completed in 1827, the builders being Ewart & Clarke, who were contractors in the town of York, now Toronto, the former of whom, two years later, erected the buildings on the north side of King Street West in that city, between Simcoe and John Streets, which for more than sixty years was the home of Upper Canada College.

Among the very early merchants in London was an American citizen, George Goodhue, who soon became a naturalized British subject and for many years occupied a prominent and responsible position, both as business man and a politician in the Province of Upper Canada. Mr. Goodhue commenced business in London in 1829, and very shortly afterwards was joined by Lawrence Lawrason, who was the first postmaster in the place.

There are many of Mr. Goodhue's relatives and descendants still living in the province, while there are still not a few residents in the city who have a vivid recollection of the gentleman himself.

Lawrence Lawrason, his partner, was a Canadian by birth, having been born in the Province of Upper Canada early in the last century. His father had emigrated to this country at a period the date of which I am uncertain.

Lawrence Lawrason married Miss Abigail Lee, a daughter of Dr. Hooker Lee and a sister of Dr. Hiram D. Lee, one of the pioneer medical practitioners in the London district. By this marriage there were two daughters and one son born to Mr. and Mrs. Lawrason. The latter married a Miss Bettridge, of Woodstock, and died in Muskoka from the effects of an accident about twenty years ago. One of Mr. Lawrason's daughters, Mrs. Reed, of British Columbia, survives, while the remaining one, the late Mrs. Lionel Ridout, died about fourteen years since. Mr. Lawrason was a Conservative among Conservatives in his political views and sat in the Provincial Parliament as member for London in the year 1844. He continued in business in partnership with Mr. Goodhue for many years. When that partnership was dissolved he was joined by his wife's nephew, Hiram Chisholm, and then a few years later, having retired from active business, he was appointed the first police magistrate for London. He died in 1881. His wife survived him for about sixteen years.

Another of the early settlers whom I have mentioned was Thomas Fisher. He only lived in London for two or three years, but he was one of those who assisted in making the first clearing. After leaving the newly-founded town, which he did somewhere about 1829, Thomas Fisher removed to the township of Etobicoke in the county of York, and there on the River Humber established a grist mill which continued in operation under various owners from early in the thirties until about 1860. Mr. Fisher died about 1878 at a very great age, but to the very last he was pleased to relate that he had taken part in the foundation of London.

The first two-story frame house and store erected in London was the work of G. J. Goodhue, and the first post office was opened by Lawrence Lawrason, who afterwards joined the former in business, as I have previously stated. One of the very first, if not the very first, doctor in London, to whom belongs the honor of establishing what is now the present city hospital, was Archibald Chisholm. Dr. Chisholm married Selina, the eldest daughter of Dr. Hooker Lee and sister of Lawrence Lawrason's wife. Dr. Chisholm died in 1832 or 1833. The date is somewhat uncertain but the former is the more probable one. His widow, on January 29th, 1834, married Colonel Edward William Thompson of Toronto township, who died in 1865, and Mrs. Thompson, formerly Mrs. Chisholm, died in Toronto in 1884.

Dr. William Hooker Lee, who has previously been mentioned, died in London, Ontario, March 30th, 1829, aged 67 years. One of Dr. Lee's sons, Hiram Davis Lee, who had studied medicine and taken his degree, played a very prominent part, not only in the history of the province but in that of the town of London. Having in his earlier days seen service in the War of 1812 and thus brought himself under the notice of the authorities, he was, on October 14th, 1833, appointed Government Medical Officer for London District. Dr. Lee married in 1819 Anne Terry, daughter of Parshall Terry, one of the most notorious of the U. E. Loyalists, who settled in Canada, he having been a Lieutenant in the famous corps of Butler's Rangers who fought with such intrepidity and vigor during the Revolutionary War. When the revolted colonists attained their independence Parshall Terry and the whole of the other officers of the rangers found it highly desirable to leave the new United States of America and become settlers in Canada. Parshall Terry was one of the best known of the U. E. Loyalists. He first settled in Kingston, then removed to York, being one of the most prominent of the early citizens of that place, where he also possessed a considerable amount of land, granted to him for his services. Terry was also a land owner in the county of Middlesex. He was a member of the second provincial parliament, and died in Toronto in 1807.

Dr. Lee who was Terry's son-in-law had a very large family, one of whom is still alive, though in extreme old age, was Grace Simcoe Lee, the well-known actor of fifty years since. Dr. Lee died a victim to his own sense of public duty and heroic self-forgetfulness, whilst doing his duty among the fever-stricken emigrants suffering from the dreaded ship-fever in the emigration sheds of London in 1847.

My paper has already taken up a considerable amount of time, and yet it seems to me as if I had scarcely touched the fringe of my subject, namely, the Pioneers of London. Let me, though, go on a little further. The first Anglican clergyman in London was the Rev. E. J. Boswell, who came here in the year 1829 and established St. Paul's parish. For some reason or other Mr. Boswell does not seem to have had a very happy sojourn in London, for he only remained for about three years, being succeeded in 1832 by Benjamin Cronin, for more than thirty years rector of St. Pauls, and for nearly fourteen years Bishop of Huron.

The Anglicans in 1830 had no place of worship in London. This is shown by the fact that on January 16th, 1830, in reply to an application from Mr. Boswell that his congregation might use the court room for divine service, Colonel Mahlon Burwell writes:—

"The magistrates cannot grant the congregation the use of the court room, as it was erected for the only purpose of accommodating his Majesty's courts of law in the administration of justice. They do not conceive that they possess the right of granting you your request."

In the year 1835 there was a small frame church built near where the present custom house stands. This was destroyed by fire in the early part of 1844, but to the credit of the congregation, almost immediately rebuilt.

The first Presbyterian minister was the Rev. William Proudfoot. His name is mentioned in many places as early as 1831. Among the Baptists the earliest name of any accredited minister belonging to that denomination is that of the Rev. Thomas Hutchins, who officiated at the solemnization of a marriage on February 4th, 1833.

The Methodist Church appears to have been fairly established in the London District about the year 1833, the name of the Rev. John Beatty frequently recurring in documents relating to that denomination.

In the Congregationalist body there was a church formed so far back as 1835, the minister of which was the Rev. William Lyall.

The Roman Catholic Church first established a congregation in the London District about 1830. It was not a remarkably strong one, as there were in the early days not a very large number of adherents of that faith in this part of Canada.

Turning to municipal matters. The first president of the village council was George J. Goodhue, who has often been mentioned already. The second in 1841 was James Givins, better known as Judge Givins.

Judge Givins was a son of Colonel James Givins, an officer in the Queen's Rangers, commanded by Governor Simcoe. He occupied a very conspicuous position in military and political circles in the early part of last century. He had great influence with the government of the day and was appointed Indian Commissioner. He was one of the very first householders in the town of York and built what was for the time a very handsome residence in the western portion of the city, which was only pulled down about 1888.

The first town warden of London was John Jennings, a well known distiller, who was appointed in 1838. The village was created a town in 1848, the first mayor being Simeon Morrell. It was created a city on January 8th, 1855, Murray Anderson being the first mayor.

The members of the Provincial Parliament were as follows:—

Hamilton Killaly, 1841.
Lawrence Lawrason, 1844.
John Wilson, 1847.
T. C. Dixon, 1851.
John Wilson, 1854.
John Carling, 1858, until Confederation.

I cannot conclude this paper without referring to two notable events in the history of London. The first was the great fire which occurred in 1845 when more than 150 buildings were destroyed and damage done to the extent of $100,000, an enormous sum for such a poor and small place as London was then.

The next event happening in London that I wish to refer to was happily one which was for the benefit and not the injury of the town. It was the fact that in 1854 the Provincial Agricultural Association held their first exhibition there during the month of October, that exhibition being the precursor of the Western Fair which will open here next week.

VI.

THE BEGINNING OF LONDON.

By Cl. T. Campbell, M.D.

When Canada passed under the control of the British Government, the problems arising in the effort to govern an alien race, were rendered more serious by the influx of the loyal English, who left the United States after the establishment of the Republic. To relieve the burden of Government it was decided to divide the territory into two sections—Lower Canada, where the French element would predominate, and Upper Canada, which would be essentially English. The proclamation of Lord Dorchester, the Governor-General, announcing the new order of things, was issued on May 26th, 1791. The Governor-General, having his headquarters in Lower Canada, his authority in Upper Canada was, to some extent, delegated to a Lieutenant-Governor—Colonel John Graves Simcoe being the first appointed to that office. At the time of its constitution the population of the new province would be about 20,000. There were villages at Kingston and Newark, and a number of small settlements generally located near the St. Lawrence River and Lakes Ontario and Erie.

Col. Simcoe had served in the British army during the American Revolution. He had personal knowledge of the intense anti-British feeling in the States; and was certain that many years would not elapse before the war would be renewed. This thought dominated his policy during his administration. To settle Upper Canada with loyal Britons—soldiers, especially, and to place it in a state of defence, that would protect it from hostile raids from over the border, was to be his mission.

As he looked over the map, he saw the western part of his province especially liable to attack; for at two points—the Niagara River and the Detroit River, the enemies' forces could be easily concentrated and an invasion easily affected. To establish a strong military centre from which his forces could be promptly despatched either east or west, seemed to him a necessity.

His map at the Home Office indicated the River La Tranche to be a large stream extending from the lake well up to the northeast, with only a short portage necessary to connect it with the Ouse or Grand

River. Here was a military highway which he thought could be utilized to good advantage. Of course the maps of those days were not the most accurate. Gallinee's map (1670) the first drawn, only outlined the coast; Farquharson's (1684) indicated a river where the Thames might be, and so did that of Jeffery in 1762. A report accompanying Billini's map (1744) refers to it as the Askenessippi or Antlered River; and it appears to have been about this time that the trappers had dubbed it La Tranche (the cut or trench). Later geographies give it a fuller outline, and hinted at greater magnitude. But Cartography in the past never hesitated to draw on its imagination; and Col. Simcoe might be excused if his expectations were tempered by his desires.

Coming to Canada in the latter part of 1791, the Governor pursued his enquiries at Montreal with apparent success. In a letter to the Hon. Henry Dundas, Colonial Secretary, written from Montreal, on the 7th December, 1791, he says:—

"I am happy to have found in the surveyor's office an accurate survey of the River La Tranche. It answers my most sanguine expectations; and I have but little doubt that its communications with the Ontario and Erie will be found to be very practicable, the whole forming a route which in, all respects, may annihilate the political consequence of Niagara and Lake Erie. . . . My ideas, at present are to assemble the new corps, artificers, etc., at Cataraqui (Kingston), and to take its present garrison and visit Toronto and the heads of La Tranche, to pass down that river to Detroit, and early in the spring to occupy such a central position as shall be previously chosen for the capital."

The Governor had doubtless a busy winter in Newark, his temporary capital, during the first year; but he was laying his plans for the future. In a letter to the Colonial Office of April 28th, 1792, he writes:

"Toronto appears to be the natural arsenal of Lake Ontario, and to afford easy access overland to Lake Huron. The River La Tranche, near the navigable head of which I propose to establish the capital, by what I can gather from the few people who have visited it, will afford a safe, more certain, and I am inclined to think by taking advantage of the season, a less expensive route to Detroit than that of Niagara."

Again, on the 30th of August, he announces his intention of establishing himself at the forks of La Tranche in the spring following. It was in a proclamation issued this year that he christened the river the Thames.

The spring of 1793 came; and as a first step towards locating himself midway between the Niagara and Detroit Rivers, he made a trip across the peninsula. It required two months for the journey; and that without any unnecessary delay at any point. His Secretary, Major Littlehale, kept a diary which was published in a pamphlet by Dr. Scadding some years ago. A portion of the original manuscript is in possession of the family of the late Mr. Shanly of this city.

It is not possible to map out with precision the route of this first British journey of exploration across the southwestern peninsula of Ontario. There were no cities to be seen; few settlements to be visited. The major does not seem to have taken any observations of latitude or longitude; and his references to points which were considered of interest are not always sufficiently clear for us to identify them; nor are the descriptions we get of the physical aspect of the country as exact as a scientific observer would make.

Speaking in general terms, and using the well-known names of places not then existant, we may say that, leaving Newark on the 4th of February, 1793, the governor and his party went by way of St. Catharines, Hamilton, Brantford and Woodstock, following a line from there south of the south branch of the Thames through Westminister Township to Delaware. Here they took to the ice on the river for a short distance; returning to *terra firma* they passed through the newly-established Moravian Missions to Dolson's, near Chatham, and from there to Detroit by canoe. Returning from Detroit the Governor retraced his steps to Delaware, and on Saturday, the 2nd of March, came to the forks of the Thames. Here I give the record in full:—

"March 2nd. We struck the Thames at one end of a low, flat island, enveloped with shrubs and trees. The rapidity and strength of the current were such as to have forced a channel through the mainland, being a peninsula, and to have formed the island. The Governor wished to examine the situation and its environs, and therefore remained here all day. He judged it to be a situation eminently calculated for the metropolis of all Canada. Among many other essentials it possesses the following advantages: command of territory, internal situation, central position, facility of water communication up and down the Thames into Lakes St. Clair, Erie, Huron and Superior, and for small craft to probably near the Moravian settlement; to the northward by a small portage to the waters flowing into Lake Huron; to the southeast by a carrying place into Lake Ontario and the River St. Lawrence; the soil luxuriantly fertile; the land rich and capable of being easily cleared and soon put into a state of agriculture; a pinery upon the adjacent high knoll, and other timber on the heights, well calculated for the erection of public buildings; a climate not inferior to any part of Canada. To these natural advantages, an object of great consideration is to be added; that the enormous expense of the Indian department would be greatly diminished, if not abolished. The Indians would, in all probability be induced to become the carriers of their own peltries; and they would find a ready, continuous, commodious and equitable mart, honorably advantageous to the Government, and the community generally, without their becoming a prey to the monopolizing and unprincipled trader.

"March 3rd. We were glad to leave our wigwam early this morning, it having rained incessantly the whole night; besides, the hemlock branches upon which we slept were wet before they were gathered for our use. We first ascended the height at least 120 feet, into a continuation of the pinery already mentioned; quitting that we came to a beautiful plain, with detached clumps of white oak and open woods, then crossing a thick swampy wood, we were at a loss to discover any track; but in a few moments we were released from this dilemma by the Indians, who, making a cast, soon discovered our old path to Detroit."

Analyzing the record in the diary, we should infer that the Governor coming from Detroit, south of the Thames, struck the river at what is now called "The Cove." The stream had here made a sharp curve to the south, then west, then north, near where the curve began, thus forming a peninsula. During a heavy flood its waters had cut across the neck of the peninsula, and formed an island. How long that was before the Governor's visit we cannot tell. Spending the night at the Forks, probably where the bowling club grounds are situated, he turned southward, climbing the high bank at the Ridgeway near Becher Street, which seems to have been covered with pines. Going south, in order to strike the trail by which he had passed to Detroit the previous month, he found a plain with clumps of white oak, then a swampy wood, and finally came to the site of his former encampment on the 14th of February, which, as we learn from an earlier part of the diary, was at an Indian village, some four miles distant from two little lakes, presumably the ponds well known, between the second and third concession of Westminster.

During the summer the Governor sent Mr. McNiff to make a survey of the Forks, and in forwarding this to Mr. Dundas on the 30th of September, he wrote:

"The tract of country which lies between the river (or rather, navigable canal, as its Indian name and French translation import), and Lake Erie, is one of the finest for all agricultural purposes in North America, and far exceeds the soil or climate of the Atlantic States.

There are few or no interjacent swamps, and a variety of useful streams empty themselves into the lake or the river... They lead to the propriety of establishing a capital of Upper Canada, which may be somewhat distant from the centre of the colony... The capital I propose to be established at new London."

The settlement of the peninsula, at first confined to the lake shore and the river bank, now began moving to the interior. A treaty with the Indians, dated May 22nd, 1784, had secured for the new settlers a legitimate title to their lands. The earliest pioneers in our own neighborhood appear to have located at Delaware. James R. Brown, of Edinburgh, who published his "Views of Canada and the Colonists," in 1844, and who claimed to have his information direct from some of the original settlers, tells us that: Shortly after the landing of the U. E. Loyalists in the Niagara District, a party of them left Ancaster for the West, with tobacco, whisky, calico, knives and trinkets for the Indian trade. Striking La Tranche, about the present site of Woodstock, they took canoes and followed the river down past the forks, and camped near the present village of Delaware, making it the headquarters of their traffic with the Indians. The location pleased them, and they sent word back to their friends in Ancaster, some of whom speedily joined them, and the foundation of the first settlement was made. More precise knowledge of Delaware refers to a later period, when Governor Simcoe, following his regular policy of encouraging settlement, made a number of grants of land—including one of two thousand acres to B. Allen, on condition that he would erect a grist mill. This was commenced in 1797, on Dingman's Creek; but before he finished it Allen had to go to jail for counterfeiting. He seems to have been an energetic person, but not an exemplary citizen. A post office was established at Delaware, with Dan Springer for Postmaster. This was, at the time, the only post office between Niagara and Detroit.

The name London was connected with this locality at an early period in its history. At first it was applied only to the Governor's town site, but later to a distinct section of country. In 1787 Lord Dorchester divided Upper Canada into four districts, named from west to east, Hesse, Nassau, Mecklenberg, and Lunenberg. A few years later (1792) this intensely German momenclature was dropped by Gov. Simcoe, and they were called Western, Home, Midland and Eastern. Subsequently there was a rearrangement: 38 George III., chap. 5, passed in 1789, divided up the province into nine districts—Western, London, Gore, Niagara, Home, Midland, Newcastle, Johnston and Eastern. These districts were subdivided into counties or "circles," though the latter title appears to have been used only in some official documents. Section 36 of the Act gives the county of Middlesex as made up of the townships of London, Westminster, Dorchester, Yarmouth, Southwold, Dunwich, Aldboro and Delaware. In 1821, Lobo, Mosa, Ekfrid and Caradoc were added to Middlesex, and McGillivray and Biddulph in in 1865. The southern townships were formed into the county of Elgin in 1852.

Townships at first were numbered, but names soon took the place of numbers; and the one laid out at the forks of the Thames and north of its south branch was called London.

The most extensive grants of land in the peninsula were made to Col. Talbot, who located not far from Port Stanley in 1803—Lord Durham's celebrated report credits him with having received 48,500 acres. North of London township the Canada Company controlled the land; at the western extremity of the peninsula Col. Baby had a large section; while east of London, Reynolds, Ingersoll and Nelles had extensive grants. And throughout the peninsula the hardy pioneer entered and took possession.

But the site of the Governor's capital remained vacant. That, however, was not his fault. Reading Canadian history casually, one might get the idea that he changed his mind and selected Toronto. As a matter of fact he never changed. His correspondence with the home office shows this clearly.

I have given an extract from his letter to Mr. Dundas in 1793, inclosing McNiff's survey, October 23rd, of the same year, he urges upon the imperial authorities the advisability of at once occupying London in the public interests; and in December he advises that the troops should be removed from Detroit—one-half to be located at Chatham, which he had selected for his future navy yard, and the rest sent to London.

A letter which he received from Dundas, dated March 16th, 1794, showed that the Government approved of his ideas as to the future capital, and he was told that the Governor-General, Lord Dorchester, had been instructed to raise two batallions of 700 men each, and from these he would receive a sufficient detachment to garrison his proposed post on the Thames and his capital city.

In all his correspondence up to the date of his removal from Canada, Simcoe persistently clung to the idea of founding his capital on the Thames. Even after buildings had been erected at York, or Toronto, for Government purposes, he would only consider them as temporary works, and in one letter we find him suggesting that, "should the seat of Government be transferred to the Thames, the proper place, the buildings and grounds at York can be sold to lessen or liquidate the cost of their construction." (Letter to Portland, February 27th, 1796). He left the country this year, and his successor in the administration—Peter Russell—inherited his views, speaking in his reports to England of York as "The temporary seat of Government;" until Portland in September, 1797, gave him to distinctly understand that the matter was finally settled and that "the selection of York had been made on mature reflection."

The trouble was that Simcoe was only Lieut.-Governor of Upper Canada, while Lord Dorchester was Governor-General of the entire colony, though Simcoe had great difficulty in realizing his subordinate position. He was in the west, and thought he knew the requirements of his own province; but Dorchester, who lived in Lower Canada, could not see the wisdom of placing the capital of Upper Canada so far away, and preferred to have it in a place more accessible by water from Montreal and Quebec. So he decided on York, and the home Government very naturally accepted the view of their chief officer in the colony. But Londoners may well bear in grateful recollection the first governor of our province, who could see no place to equal "Georgina-upon-the-Thames," as he was once inclined to name it, or London as it has ever since been known.

And so, while all around, farms were being located, and the lands being cleared, London remained in primeval beauty. George Heriot, Deputy Postmaster General of British North America, who saw it about 1807, writes of it in his "Travels through Canada." Coming eastward from Detroit up the valley of the Thames he pictures the country for us:

"In proceeding upward, the sinuosities of the river are frequent, and the summits of the banks rather elevated, but not broken. On either sides are villages of the Delawares and Chippewas. Somewhat higher up at the confluence of the two forks of the river, is the site of which Governor Simcoe made choice for a town to be named London. Its position with relation to Lakes Huron, Erie and Ontario is central, and around it is a fertile and inviting tract of country. It communicates with Lake Huron by a northern or main branch of the same river and a small portage or carrying place.

"Along the banks of the Thames are several rich settlements, and new establishments are every week added to this as well as to other parts of the neighboring country by the immigration of wealthy farmers from the United States.

"On the east side of the forks, between the two main branches, on a regular eminence, about forty feet above the water, there is a natural plain denuded of wood except where small groves are interspersed, affording in its present state the appearance of a beautiful park on whose formation and culture taste and expense have been bestowed."

The war of 1812-15, though it moved over the western peninsula, found London still the natural park that Heriot described, and left it unstained by blood of friend or foe. A sharp skirmish occurred a few miles west. Lieut.-Governor Sir Gordon Drummond had established a military post at Delaware, and from it a sortie of 240 men under Captain Basden was made against a United States post at Longwoods, on March 3rd, 1814. Our troops did not succeed in capturing the post attacked, but the United States Commandant evidently found the neighborhood too warm for comfort and retreated to Detroit. The Delaware post was strengthened during the summer by the addition of some light infantry and a party of dragoons, but there was no more fighting.

At the close of the war the surrounding townships began to fill up more rapidly with settlers. What is now Middlesex, had been generally surveyed and lands granted. The earliest settlers in Middlesex and Elgin were doubtless those who came through the instrumentality of Col. Talbot. Here are a few of the names: Daniel Springer, R. B. Bingham, Timothy Kilbourn, Joseph Odell, Andrew Banghart, Seth Putnam, Mahlon Burwell, Jas. Nevills, Jacabus Schenck, Leslie Patterson, Sylvanus Reynolds, William Orr, Henry Cook, Samuel Hunt, Richard Williams, Peter Teeple, John Aikens, Maurice Sovereign, Henry Daniels, James Smiley and Abraham Hoover.

Westminster had been surveyed by Watson in 1809-10, and we find the Odells there in 1810, Norton in 1810 and Griffith and Patrick in 1812. George Ward purchased land from the Indians in 1810; his name is familiar to us in connection with Wardsville. About the same time A. McMillan settled in Byron. Nissouri was surveyed in 1818, and its settlement began with the McGuffins, Vinings, Hardys and Scatcherds.

Prior to 1818 London township had very few families, but in that year a large addition was made. Richard Talbot, an Irish gentleman, received a large grant from the Imperial Government—a condition being that he should bring out at least sixty adults. To insure the stability of the new settlement each man was required to advance 50 pounds, which was to be returned to him as soon as he had built a log house. On the way out some dropped from the ranks at Kingston, but about forty families came on to London. Among them were: Richard

THE BEGINNING OF LONDON.

Talbot, John and Edward Talbot, William Gerrie, Thomas Brooks, Peter Rogers, Thomas Guest, Frank Lewis, Benjamin Lewis, William Haskett, William Mooney, William Evans, William O'Neil, Edmund Stoney, Joseph O'Brien, Geo. Foster, Thos. and James Howay, John Phalen, Jos. Hardy, John Grey, Jos. Keays, Robt. Ralph, John Sifton and Thos. Howard.

Probably the nearest settler to the site of London was John Applegarth, who about 1816 commenced cultivating hemp, an industry which was at that time encouraged by money grants from the English Government. He located on a ridge east of Mount Pleasant Cemetery and built a log cabin. He was not very successful, however, and shortly after moved south to the neighborhood now occupied by Mr. A. C. Johnstone; and his deserted cabin fell into the occupation of some squatters. There was no bridge over the river at this time, but a canoe ferry, a short distance below the forks, served the purpose of communication.

During this period the official centre of the London District was off to one side, at Vittoria, about six miles south of the present town of Simcoe, and fifty miles in a straight line from the forks. A court house had been erected in that village, and the district school was also located there. It had been started at Charlotteville in 1807; John Mitchell, who had come from Scotland to act as tutor for Col. Hamilton's children, secured two lots, and in a small building opened the school. It was removed to Vittoria shortly after. Mitchell was made a judge in 1819, and remained on the bench until 1844.

Great inconvenience was experienced by the residents of the district in their enforced attendance at Vittoria. They had now reached a very respectable number. Gourlay's statistics, in 1817, places them at 8,907, while Fothergill's record in 1825 showed an increase to 12,351. The roads were not of the best. By an act passed in 1793, every settler was required to clear a road across his own lot; but as crown lands and clergy reserves came between lots, the road often began on one side of a man's farm and ended on the other. Of course there was the Government road, running westward from York, which had been originated by Governor Simcoe. Col. Talbot was also engaged in constructing Talbot Street through his own settlement. But the facilities for travel were primitive at the best. And when the court house in Vittoria was burned in 1825, the people of Middlesex made a vigorous effort to remove the headquarters of the district to a more convenient locality. Especially persistent in their labours to this end were Charles Ingersoll and Peter Teeple, of Oxford; M. Homer, of Blenheim; Dan Springer, of Delaware, and Ira Schofield, of London township—leading merchants and magistrates of this section. They were determined, if possible, to have the seat of Government transferred from Vittoria to London; and though they met with considerable opposition, especially from the southern townships, they were finally successful.

On the 30th of January, 1826, an act was passed by the Provincial Parliament (George IV., chapter XIII) "to establish the district town of London in a more central position." After reciting the burning of the court house in Vittoria, and noting the inconvenient location of that place for the business of the district, it declares that "it is expedient to establish the district town at the reservation heretofore made for a town near the forks of the River Thames, in the townships of London and Westminster;" and orders that "the court of quarter sessions for the peace, and the district courts in and for said district, shall be holden and assembled within some part of the reservation . . . so soon as a jail and court house shall be erected thereon;" and in the meantime at such place as the sheriff may appoint.

The original reservation made by Simcoe appears to have extended to the 3rd concession, London, north of London West, and south to the present southern limit of the city in Westminster, all the lots in this space having been laid out in park lots. The grants to settlers in the vicinity had, however, encroached somewhat on the limits of the reservation.

Another act, passed at the same session (Chap. XIV.), makes provision for the survey of the town and the building of the court house. The first section provides that "a town shall be layed out and surveyed under the direction of the Surveyor-General within the reservation heretofore made for a town near the forks of the Thames in the townships of London and Westminster, in the county of Middlesex in the said district of London, and a plan thereof shall be furnished by the said Surveyor-General to the commissioners hereinafter named; and in the said plan or survey a tract of space of not less than four acres shall be designated as reserved for the purposes of a court house and jail."

Section 2 appoints Hon. Thomas Talbot, Mahlon Burwell, James Hamilton, Charles Ingersoll and John Matthews, of Lobo, as commissioners, for erecting the court house and jail.

Section 3 authorizes the justices of the peace to levy by assessment on every inhabitant householder in the district, an additional rate of one-third of a penny in the pound to defray the cost of building. Section 4 gives the commission power in the meantime to borrow not more than 4,000 pounds, at interest not exceeding 6 per cent.

Section 5 requires the commissioners to meet at St. Thomas, on the first Monday in March, 1826, and organize by the election of a president and secretary.

The first step taken under the acts above cited was the appointment of Mr. Mahlon Burwell to make the survey of the proposed town. The plan in the Crown Lands Department, Toronto, a copy of which I have here, shows that it contained about 240 acres. The river formed the southern and western boundaries of the town; to the east it extended as far as Wellington Street; on the north it was bounded by North Street or Queen's Avenue, as it is now called. North Street, however, did not run in a straight line; a short distance west of Richmond the line of survey turned southwest, striking what is now Carling Street, about where the police court stands, and running from thence direct to the river. This was owing to the fact that the land to the northwest of this jog was part of the Kent farm, which extended westward over the river. The land along the river bank was not surveyed into lots, but was left as a strip of meadow surrounding the town plot on two sides, and varying from one to six chains in width. It is evident, from an inspection of the map, that there were a number of small streams in the locality, all signs of which have long since disappeared. The most important commenced on York Street, probably beyond the town boundary, and running south and west, entered into the river near the foot of Bathurst Street. It was subsequently converted into a covered drain, which the older property holders of that section can well remember.

In selecting names for the streets, the surveyor chose some well-known to the people of the colony at that time. North and South Streets appropriately marked the boundaries of the town in those two directions, while Thames Street was but a proper compliment to the river which ran near by. Loyalty was satisfied by naming one street King and giving two others to members of the royal family—the Dukes of York and Clarence, Dundas, Bathurst, Horton and Grey were called after British ministers, whose departmental duties had brought them into frequent contact with Canadian affairs. The Duke of Wellington was complimented by having one street named after him, and another, Hill, for his mother. Simcoe Street kept in memory the name of the first Lieutenant-Governor of Upper Canada, while the name of the popular Governor-General, the Duke of Richmond, whose sad death from hydrophobia in 1819, created a melancholy interest throughout the country, was given to what is now one of our leading thoroughfares. Two streets were named after local celebrities—Col. Talbot, the uncrowned king of the country, and Thomas Ridout, Surveyor-General of Upper Canada, or possibly his son, equally well-known in London.

The first man to move into the new town was a Scotch tailor, Peter MacGregor, who came in from the neighborhood of Byron, and took up a lot (21 S. King), on which he erected a little shanty to serve the purpose of a hotel. He wanted to be on hand to provide for the comforts of the London pioneers; though the first provision seems to have been little more than a jug of whiskey on the stump of a tree at the front door. His wife, formerly a Miss Poole, of Westminster, was an energetic, bustling woman, and developed the hotel business as rapidly as she could—though for some time the accommodation was limited; and when there was an influx of visitors at the first courts holden in town, most of them, we are told, had to go some three miles to Flanagan's to find shelter. This first house built in London was situated on the south side of King Street, a short distance west of Ridout. MacGregor did not obtain a patent from the crown for some years—the record in the registry office giving the date as July 25th, 1831. It was the lot on which now stands the Grand Central Hotel. The first lot patented was by J. G. Goodhue, the pioneer merchant, who received his deed for lot 20, N. Dundas Street, being half an acre on the corner of Dundas and Ridout Streets, on September 11th, 1830. He had, however, commenced business before that date, in fact, he seems to have opened his store in 1826—the same year in which MacGregor arrived. Other lots were rapidly taken up and a number of settlers made the new town their home.

The commission appointed to attend to the erection of the court house met in St. Thomas, in March, 1826, and commenced their work as speedily as possible. The plan of the building is said to have been in imitation of one of the baronial homes of Great Britain, and was adopted more as a compliment to Col. Talbot than with any view to public convenience. At first, a temporary building was constructed on the northeast corner of Dundas and Ridout Streets, and in this the first Court of Quarter Sessions was held January 9th, 1827, Col. Ryerse being chairman of the bench of magistrates. It was scarcely completed before it was required. Thomas Pomeroy, a sheriff's officer, was murdered, and his murderer tried, found guilty, and hanged in three days after sentence was pronounced. It was not convenient to keep a prisoner any length of time in these primitive jails.

In the *Gore Gazette* of July 31, 1827, a paper published by Geo. Gurnett, Ancaster, appears a letter from a traveller who had visited London during the holding of a court, and who tells a very amusing story of a trial for assault made by a little Irish pensioner on a big Yankee from Delaware, who had offended the loyalty of the Irishman by some insulting remarks, and received a blow on the mouth, which knocked out some of his teeth. The fiery pensioner was defended by Mr. TenBrock in an eloquent speech, and was sentenced to a fine of one shilling. The writer says:

"I was much pleased with the delightful situation of the town, commanding as it does a most extensive view of the richest, most fertile, and most thickly settled part of the province; as well as a delightful prospect of both branches of the picturesque river Thames. The new court house, which is to be a fine building in the gothic style, 100 feet long, 50 feet wide and 50 feet high, having an octagon tower fourteen feet in diameter at each of its angles, is now building by Mr. Edward, an architect of first-rate ability. The house in which the law courts are now held is a building erected by subscription, and eventually intended for the district school-house."

The new court house was built by Mr. John Ewart of Toronto. Thomas Park, father of the late Police Magistrate, was his foreman, or partner, and had charge of the wark. He became a citizen of the new town. One of the employees was Robert Carfrae, whose widow died on Carfrae Street a few years ago. The brick for the building, as I am informed by Hon. Freeman Talbot, was manufactured by a Toronto man, William Hale, who also became a resident of London. There were two brickyards, one at the rear of the present Robinson Hall, and the other in London West, on land subsequently belonging to Walter Nixon.

As soon as preparations were commenced for the building of the court house and goal, a post office was opened, with Major Ira Schofield as Postmaster. The office was kept in a little log house on Dundas Street. As near as I can discover, its site would be about the Queen's Avenue entrance to the Sacred Heart Academy, between Colborne and Maitland Streets.

Thus the beginning of London centred in a tavern, a goal and a post office. Churches came later; for the pioneer clergymen held services in private houses. And three or four years elapsed before any building was erected for religious worship.

When the court house was completed, the temporary building was converted into a school-house, according to the original intention; and Peter Van Every, jr., who had been acting as jailer, became the first schoolmaster. The early teachers in Upper Canada, it is said, were largely recruited from the ranks of retired soldiers, and were mostly Irish. I am not sure whether Van Every was an Irishman or not; his name is not good Irish, at all events.

The construction of the court house definitely marked the foundation of London; though, at first, it was not a distinct municipality, and its officials exercised their authority over a larger tract of country than the few acres of which the new town was composed. Of the first settlers, some like Parke, and Carfrae, and Hale, came in connection with the building of the court house; some, like John TenBrock, a lawyer, who came from Long Point to practice in the courts. Others came to London as a suitable place from which to supply the wants of the people of the surrounding country, at that time the most important element in population of this section.

Peter McGregor's little pioneer hotel soon took second place, for in 1828 Abraham Carroll built the Mansion House on the north side of Dundas Street, east of Ridout, a more pretentious establishment, and one which provided ample accommodation for the travelling public for many years. Mr. Goodhue's store was the general emporium, which supplied the material needs of the community as well as any of our modern departmental stores. Rev. E. J. Boswell came as a Church of England Clergyman in 1829; though Rev. Mr. McIntosh, of Kettle Creek, held occasional services before that date. Mr. TenBrock was the pioneer lawyer; and Dr. Arch Chisholm the first physician.

The first officials, as near as I can find, were the following: Sheriff, Daniel Rappalge; judge, James Mitchell; clerk of the peace, John B. Askin; deputy clerk, William King Cornish; high constable, John O'Neil; jailer, Samuel Park; court crier, Gideon Bostwick; registrar, Mahlon Burwell; treasurer, John Harris.

For the first few years London did not seem to grow very rapidly, though all circumstances were radiant with hope for its future. Andrew Picken's book "The Canadas," published in England in 1832, has this to say of it as it appeared in 1829:

"London is yet but inconsiderable; but from its position in the heart of a fertile country, is likely to become of some importance hereafter, when the extreme wild becomes more settled. The town is quite new, not containing above 40 or 50 houses, all of bright boards and shingles. The streets and gardens are full of black stumps, etc. They were building a church, and had finished a handsome gothic court house."

Such was the beginning of London. This is not the place to trace its development to its present condition; or to forecast its future. The population represented at the beginning, by Peter McGregor and his wife, has increased to 50,000. The area of 240 acres in the first survey, has broadened to 4,500. The nominal value of the original site has advanced to $30,000,000. The beginning of London was humble; its growth has been steady; its condition is prosperous; its future is bright; and the most sanguine hopes of its loyal citizens will doubtless, in due time, be realized.

VII.

AN EPISODE OF THE WAR OF 1812. THE STORY OF THE SCHOONER "NANCY."

By Lieut.-Col. E. Cruikshank.

In the summer of 1789, the firm of Forsyth, Richardson & Co., fur merchants of Montreal, undertook the construction of a schooner for the navigation of the upper lakes. As I have related in a former paper, John Richardson, one of the partners, went to Detroit to superintend the work, in which he was deeply interested.

"The schooner," he wrote on the 23rd September, 1789, "will be a perfect masterpiece of workmanship and beauty. The expense to us will be great, but there will be the satisfaction of her being strong and very durable. Her floor timbers, keel, keelson, stem, and lower uttock are oak. The transom, stern-post, upper uttocks, top timbers, beams and knees are all red cedar. She will carry 350 barrels."

He ordered a suitable figure-head of "a lady dressed in the present fashion with a hat and feather" from the carver Skelling of New York. The schooner was launched on the 24th September, 1789, "a most beautiful and substantial vessel," and in the spring following made her first voyage from Detroit to Fort Erie, whence she sailed upwards in June with a full cargo, bound for the Grand Portage at Sault Ste. Marie, with the intention of visiting Mackinac on her way back.

"She is spoken of here," Richardson wrote from Niagara, "in such a high strain of encomium as to beauty, stowage, and sailing, that she almost exceeds my expectations."

By 1793, the Nancy had become the property of George Leith Co., and is described as being of sixty-seven tons burden. Sometime before the end of the century, she passed into the possession of the Northwest Fur Company, by whom she was employed in the transportation of furs and merchandise on Lakes Erie, Huron and Michigan. In 1805 she was navigated by Capt. Wm. Mills, who had some years before owned her in connection with Forsyth, Richardson and Sir Alexander Mackenzie of Montreal.

In a list of merchant vessels prepared early in 1812 by Colonel Matthew Elliott for the information of Major-General Brock, the Nancy is described as a schooner of about one hundred tons, lying at McIntosh's wharf, at Moy, opposite Detroit.

On July 1st, 1812, when the declaration of war by the United States became known to Lieutenant-Colonel St. George, the commandant of the British Garrison at Amherstburg, she was still lying at Moy waiting for a favorable wind to carry her into Lake Huron, and he at once ordered her to be brought down under the guns of that post to secure her from capture. Some light brass guns with which she had been armed were mounted in row-boats to patrol the river, and the schooner was impressed into the government service as a transport. On July 30 she sailed for Fort Erie under convoy of the Provincial schooner, Lady Prevost. Five days later she left Fort Erie on her return voyage, in company with the armed brig General Hunter, having on board sixty soldiers of the 41st Regiment and a quantity of military stores. The timely arrival of this small reinforcement had considerable weight among the reasons which induced General Hull to evacuate Canada.

During the summer and autumn of that year the Nancy was constantly employed in the important service of transporting troops, stores, and provisions between Detroit and Fort Erie.

On April 23rd, 1813, she was included in the small squadron assembled to transport General Procter's division from Amherstburg to Miami Bay, to undertake the siege of Fort Meigs.

The next recorded incident in her history is narrated in a letter from her commander, Captain Alexander McIntosh, to Captain Richard Bullock of the 41st Regiment, commanding the garrison at Mackinac, dated "5 miles from St. Joseph's," on the 16th of October, 1813. On the 4th of that month he had sailed from St. Joseph's for Amherstburg to obtain a much needed supply of provisions, and arrived at the mouth of the St. Clair river on the following afternoon when he sent two men ashore to ascertain whether it would be safe for him to enter the river. As they were prevented from returning by rough water, he decided to venture as far as the foot of the rapids. There he learned that the whole of the British squadron on Lake Erie had been taken and that the Americans were in possession of Detroit and Amherstburg. It was also reported that two of their armed schooners and two gun-boats were awaiting his appearance in the river below.

"Next day about noon," Captain McIntosh wrote, "a white flag was seen coming towards us in a canoe. About half an hour afterwards I was hailed from the shore by a Canadian, ordering me to give up the vessel and that my property, as also that of the crew, should be respected. I went ashore to see who this man was. It was Lieutenant-Colonel Beaubien, of the militia, who wished me to surrender the vessel to him, repeating what he had already said. I told him I would give an answer in an hour's time. I immediately went back and got all ready to defend the vessel. After the time had elapsed I went to him, gave him my answer, which was that I would defend the vessel until necessity compelled me to give her up, and that if the wind proved strong enough, I would attempt going back to the lake. He then replied, 'We shall fire on you.' I asked what number of men he had. 'Fifty,' was his answer. I returned to the vessel, made sail and was fishing the anchor when they commenced firing. I returned the fire as quickly as I received it, which continued for a quarter of an hour or more. They then ceased, whether from want of ammunition or that we had killed any, I know not. During the action I was placed at the helm and exposed to the whole of their fire, but luckily escaped. Several shots struck the main boom and railing. No person was injured from their fire, but the blowing up of a couple of cartridges burnt one of the men severely on the face and hands. Whether it was from a piece of the cartridge or their fire, our main sail was blazing which was no sooner seen than extinguished. During the engagement my men behaved with the greatest coolness, and I cannot say too much for them. We were all this time sailing with a very light breeze but not sufficiently strong to ascend the rapids. That night I received a letter from the same Lieutenant-Colonel, repeating what he had already said. I returned no reply. This was brought by Reaume, who is now with Mr. D. Mitchell, prisoners of war, they having gone ashore the morning of the action. Next morning at daylight we got under weigh. At 8 a.m. (we) entered the lake on which we have been fighting the elements these nine days, twice narrowly escaping going ashore."

As early as the 3rd of October, Captain Bullock had received information of the disastrous result of the battle on Lake Erie from Major-General Proctor, who informed him that he had already recommended that supplies for his garrison should be forwarded from York to Machedash Bay. His stock of provisions was then nearly exhausted, but by purchasing everything that could be obtained in the small settlements on the mainland he succeeded in laying in enough to keep his men until February. The Nancy arrived on the 18th with her sails and cables so badly damaged as to render her unfit to navigate the lake during the storm of autumn, and Captain McIntosh determined to take her to the Northwest Company's post, at Sault Ste. Marie, in the hope of procuring the necessary materials to refit her during the winter. Before he sailed, Robert Dickson, Agent for the Western Indians, arrived from Machedash on his way to Prairie du Chien. After consulting with him, Bullock proposed that six gun-boats should be built at Machedash to keep open the communication and protect supplies on their way to Mackinac, and requested that the garrison should be reinforced early in the spring by twenty artillerymen and two hundred infantry with four field guns. An officer and twenty-seven men of the Michigan Fencibles were at once detached with Mr. Dickson to establish a post at Green Bay and the remainder of the garrison was put on short rations.

Continued stormy weather made it impossible to send forward any supplies from Machedash before navigation closed, but it also prevented the American squadron from entering Lake Huron to undertake the reduction of Mackinac as had been at first intended.

The Governor-General was, however, fully impressed with the great importance of maintaining possession of that place, and lost no time in preparing a small force for its relief as soon as the lake again became navigable.

"Its geographical position is admirable," he wrote to Lord Bathurst. "Its influence extends and is felt amongst the Indian tribes at New Orleans and the Pacific Ocean; vast tracts of country look to it for protection and supplies, and it gives security to the great establishments of the Northwest and Hudson's Bay Companies by supporting the Indians on the Mississippi; the only barrier which interposes between them and the enemy, and which if once forced (an event which lately seemed probable), their progress into the heart of these Companies' settlements by the Red River is practicable and would enable them to execute their long-formed project of monopolizing the whole fur trade into their own hands. From these observations, your Lordship will be enabled to judge how necessary the possession of this valuable post on the outskirts of these extensive provinces is becoming to their future security and protection."

The failure to forward supplies caused him considerable uneasiness, but having been informed that there were some cattle and a quantity of potatoes on the island he anticipated that the garrison would be able to subsist until spring. Their stock of provisions might be increased considerably by fishing.

Lieutenant-Colonel Robert McDouall, of the Glengarry Light Infantry, an officer of tried courage and discretion, was selected for the command of this expedition. About the end of February, 1814, McDouall crossed Lake Simcoe on the ice, following the Nine Mile Portage from Kempenfeldt Bay to the head waters of the Nottawasaga River, where he was directed to select a suitable place for building the necessary boats for the conveyance of troops and stores across Lake Huron. He was accompanied by a party of shipwrights, twenty-one seamen, eleven artillerymen in charge of four field guns, and two companies of the Royal Newfoundland Regiment, many of whom were expert boatmen. Although this route had the merit of being shorter than that by way of Machedash, yet it was less known and much obstructed by rocks and shoals which in many places rendered the channel so narrow that nothing larger than batteaux could pass. Favored by the unusual mildness of the season, McDouall began the descent of the river on the nineteenth of April, with thirty batteaux of the largest class, heavily loaded with provision and military stores. Six days later, he sailed from its mouth, and after an extremely hazardous and stormy voyage, arrived at Mackinac, on May 18th, with the loss of but a single boat, the crew and cargo of which were saved.

"The difficulties which were experienced in conducting open and deeply-laden batteaux across so great an extent of water as Lake Huron, covered with immense fields of ice and agitated by violent gales of wind," Prevost wrote to Lord Bathurst, "could only have been surmounted by the zeal, perseverance, and ability of the officer commanding the expedition. For nineteen days it was nearly one continued struggle with the elements, during which the dangers, hardships, and privations to which the men were exposed were sufficient to discourage the boldest amongst them, and at times threatened the destruction of the flotilla."

Dickson arrived at Mackinac a few days later, bringing with him two hundred picked warriors, and every effort was made to strengthen the defences of the island. It was proposed that the Nancy should be cut down to the dimensions of a gunboat and armed with the guns brought from the Nottawasaga, but as it was evident that she could not keep the lake in the face of the overwhelming force which the enemy could bring up from Lake Erie, McDouall became satisfied that he could make better use of these guns on shore and she was accordingly retained in service as a transport and sent away for a cargo of supplies.

On June 21st information was received that the trading post of Prairie du Chien, where Dickson had established his headquarters during the winter, had been taken by a large force under the command of General William Clark, Governor of the Missouri Territory, which had ascended the Mississippi in boats from St. Louis, and next day a Winnebagoe chief came in to demand assistance, relating that besides several Indians of his own tribe, the wife of Wabash, a leading Sioux chief, who was then at Mackinac on his way home from Quebec, had been murdered in cold blood. This news caused an irresistible outcry for vengeance from the Indians who demanded to be led against the enemy without delay.

"I saw at once the imperious necessity which existed of endeavoring by every means to dislodge the American general from his new conquest and make him relinquish the immense tract of country he had seized upon in consequence and which brought him into the very heart of that occupied by our friendly Indians," McDouall wrote. "There was no alternative, it must either be done or there was an end to our connection with the Indians, for if allowed to settle themselves in place by dint of threats, bribes, and sowing divisions among them, tribe after tribe would be gained over or subdued and thus would be destroyed the only barrier which protects the great trading establishments of the Northwest and the Hudson's Bay Company."

He, therefore, promptly decided to attempt the recovery of Prairie du Chien at the manifest risk of imperilling his own position by greatly weakening his garrison. A company of sixty-three volunteers was enrolled in forty-eight hours. Sergeant Keating of the Royal Artillery, with a sergeant and thirteen men of the Michigan Fencibles, was put in charge of a field gun and the whole of the Sioux and Winnebagoe warriors on the island, 155 in number, were detailed to accompany them. The expedition set off on its voyage of more than six hundred miles on the seventh day after the news had been received under command of Major William McKay, a veteran fur trader. At Green Bay, McKay was joined by a second company of volunteers, which increased his white force to one hundred and twenty men, and during his advance by way of the Fox and Wisconsin Rivers, the number of his Indians was gradually argumented to 450. The journey was accomplished in nineteen days, and on the 17th of July, McKay unexpectedly invested the American Fort at Prairie du Chien, which was surrendered forty-eight hours afterwards by its garrison of three officers and seventy-one men of the regular army.

Meanwhile, a formidable expedition for the recovery of Mackinac had been organized at Detroit. The land force consisted of a detachment of United States Artillery, with several field guns and howitzers, a battalion of regular infantry, composed of picked companies from the 17th, 19th and 24th regiments, and a battalion of Ohio Volunteers, numbering in all nearly a thousand men. Lieutenant-Colonel George Groghan, who had gained much reputation among his countrymen by his successful defence of Fort Stephenson, was selected for the command of these troops, and Major A. H. Holmes, who had lately conducted a vigorous raid from Detroit up the Thames as far as Delaware, was given the second place as commandant of the regulars. Six of the largest vessels of the Lake Erie squadron, mounting sixty guns and manned by more than five hundred seamen and marines under Commodore Sinclair, provided with launches for landing artillery, were detailed to convey these troops to their destination. Sinclair sailed from Detroit on the 3rd of July but did not succeed in entering Lake Huron until the 12th, when he shaped his course for Machedash Bay where he had been informed that the British had established a depot of supplies and were building gunboats, but having no pilot familiar with those waters and being enveloped for several days in a dense fog in a perfect maze of islets and sunken rocks, the attempt was abandoned and he steered for the Island of St. Joseph. Arriving there on the 20th July, he learned that the military post had been abandoned a few weeks before and the garrison withdrawn to Mackinac. While his squadron lay windbound near this place, the Northwest Company's schooner Mink, on her way from Mackinac to Sault Ste. Marie, was intercepted and taken by its boats, which were then despatched to destroy the trading station at the latter place. This was accomplished without opposition, but much of the property deposited there had been removed before their arrival.

On July 26th the American squadron came in sight of Mackinac. Its presence in the lake had been known to the garrison for some time, and every possible precaution had been taken in anticipation of an attack. A strong redoubt had been completed on the summit of the cliff overlooking the former works which so greatly increased their strength that McDouall considered his position one of the strongest in Canada. "We are in a very fine state of defence here," he wrote "the garrison and Indians are in the highest spirits and all ready for the attack of the enemy. We apprehend nothing for the island but from want of provisions."

The Nancy had already made two successful trips to the Nottawasaga and sailed again for that place a few days before. A message to her commander, warning him of the appearance of the American squadron off Mackinac and advising him to take his vessel as far up the river as possible and remain there until the blockade of the island was at an end, was entrusted to Lieutenant Robert Livingston, a daring and adventurous officer of the Indian Department, who volunteered to deliver it. After serving for several years as a midshipman in the Royal Navy, Livingston obtained a commission in the Royal Canadian Volunteers, which he retained until the disbandment of that corps at the peace of Amiens. He then became a fur trader and was living at St. Joseph's when the war began. Having raised a company of volunteers, he was appointed adjutant of the battalion organized for the capture of Mackinac, in July, 1812. Being despatched to Detroit in charge of the prisoners, he was detained by the enemy but soon effected his escape. Two days later, he was wounded and taken prisoner in a skirmish, again recovering his liberty at the surrender of Detroit. After receiving his commission in the Indian Department, he was frequently employed in conveying important despatches owing to his intimate knowledge of the country, and in this service travelled a distance of 8,890 miles, mainly by canoe or on snow shoes. In the summer of 1813, Livingston assembled a body of Indians on the north shore of Lake Huron, whom he conducted to Niagara to assist in the investment of Fort George. In a skirmish near the Four Mile Creek, on the 17th of August, he received four severe wounds and was again taken prisoner, but on the night of the 19th October, he escaped from Fort Niagara and secreted himself in the woods until he found means to cross the river, subsisting for seven days on acorns only. He had acted as pilot for McDouall's force during its voyage to Mackinac and conducted the Nancy to the Nottawasaga on her first trip. Although two of his wounds were still unhealed, his zeal and energy seemed unimpaired and he eagerly undertook this difficult and important mission.

Foul weather prevented the American vessels from approaching the shore for several days, but on August 1st a party of soldiers was landed on Round Island where they had a skirmish with some Indians. After carefully reconnoitering the harbour and the vicinity of the forts, Croghan decided to adopt the advice of former residents of the island who accompanied him as guides and attempt a landing on its western coast where there was a break in the cliffs and his largest ships could anchor within three hundred yards of the shore. From this place, however, he would be compelled to advance for nearly two miles through dense woods before reaching an open space where a favorable position existed for assailing the works "by gradual and slow approaches" under cover of his artillery which he knew to be superior in range and weight of metal. Nearly a thousand men, including a body of marines, were accordingly landed on the morning of August 4th and began their march across the island.

McDouall promptly advanced to meet them with one hundred and forty men of the Royal Newfoundland Regiment and Michigan Fencibles and about one hundred and fifty Indians, mostly of the Folles Avoines or Menomonee tribe from the Wisconsin River, whom he considered the bravest and best fighting men of any at his disposal. With this force he occupied an excellent position in which his men were hidden among thickets and underwood on the edge of a small clearing across which the enemy must pass in their advance, yet it could easily be turned as there were paths leading around either flank which he had not force enough to guard. When the enemy came in sight, he opened fire upon them from two field guns, without effect except to check their advance and cause them to attempt a movement around the clearing in the direction of his left flank. But the battalion of regular troops which undertook this flank march was suddenly assailed by a party of Menomonees from an ambush among the thickets. Their first fire killed Major Holmes and severely wounded Captain Desha, next in command. Two other officers, Captain Van Horne of the 19th and Lieutenant Jackson of the 24th Infantry, were mortally wounded and their men instantly fell into great confusion. A field piece was brought up, but the fire of their unseen foes was so effective and the disorder became so great that Croghan soon decided to retire to his shipping to avoid a worse disaster, leaving behind him two wounded men and the bodies of Major Holmes and others of the dead.

Captain Sinclair stated that "it was soon found that the further the troops advanced, the stronger the enemy became and the weaker and more bewildered our force were; several of the commanding officers were picked out and killed or wounded without seeing any of the enemy. The men were getting lost and falling into confusion natural under such circumstances, which demanded an immediate retreat or total defeat and a general massacre must have ensued."

In all three officers and fifteen men were killed and one officer and fifty-eight men wounded, while McDouall's force was so well concealed that he had not a single man hurt.

Sinclair had learned from a prisoner taken in the Mink that reinforcements and supplies had arrived at Mackinac from the Nottawasaga River and that the Nancy had lately been despatched thither for more. By destroying her and blockading the river he hoped to retrieve his defeat and ultimately compel the garrison to surrender for want of provisions, and also prevent the Northwest Company from receiving any further supplies.

About the middle of July, Lieutenant Miller Worsley, of the Royal Navy, with a small detachment of seamen, had arrived at the mouth of the Nottawasaga, where he awaited the appearance of the Nancy for more than a week, suffering much discomfort from bad weather and swarms of mosquitoes. On her arrival, the schooner was loaded with three hundred barrels of provisions and a quantity of much-needed military stores, and on August 1st, she again set sail for Mackinac. Before she entered the lake, Livingston met her with McDouall's instructions, and Worsley at once turned back. The Nancy was towed up the river about two miles to a place where she was hidden from view from the bay by intervening sandhills and the construction of a log blockhouse for her protection on a commanding position on the right bank was begun. Information of her perilous situation was sent to Lieutenant-General Drummond, who was then besieging Fort Erie, and he promptly gave orders for the assembly of a body of militia and Indians for her defence. But on the 13th of August, before these instructions could be fully carried into effect, part of the American squadron, consisting of the brig Niagara and the schooners Scorpion and Tigress, made their appearance in Nottawasaga Bay, having on board a detachment of artillery with several field guns and three companies of regular infantry under the command of Lieutenant-Colonel Croghan.

Lieutenant Livingston, who had returned that morning from York with despatches, was at once employed in assembling the neighboring Indians, but only succeeded in mustering twenty-three. Worsley had under his command Midshipman Dobson and twenty-one seamen of the Royal Navy and nine French Canadian boatmen. Three guns had been mounted in the blockhouse, two of which were twenty-four pounder carronades, taken from boats lying in the river, and the other was a six pounder field piece. With such inadequate means Worsley gallantly undertook to offer the stoutest resistance possible. Late in the afternoon, Croghan landed his troops on the narrow peninsula separating the lower reach of the river from the bay, and while exploring it for the purpose of selecting a suitable place for encamping, he discovered the Nancy lying on the opposite side of the stream close under the guns of the blockhouse. Next morning Sinclair anchored all his vessels near the shore within easy range and opened fire with little effect, as both vessels and blockhouse were screened from view by the sandhills, surmounted by a thin belt of trees and bushes. About noon, however, two howitzers were landed and placed in a favorable position within a few hundred yards. Their fire speedily became so damaging that Worsley determined to destroy the schooner and retire into the woods. The guns had accordingly been spiked and a train of powder laid to the Nancy when a well directed shell burst inside the blockhouse, setting fire to a quantity of combustible material near the magazine which soon blew up, communicating the flames to the schooner which was entirely destroyed with her valuable cargo still on board. Worsley had defended himself "very handsomely," as Sinclair said, but lost only one man killed and another severely wounded. The Indians continued to fire for some time from the edge of the woods and no pursuit was attempted. Eventually Sinclair sent a party of men across the Nottawasaga in boats who brought off the guns from the smoulding ruins of the blockhouse and took away a batteaux which had escaped destruction, after which they endeavored to obstruct the river by felling trees across it. On the following day Sinclair sailed for Lake Erie in the Niagara, leaving Lieutenant Turner in command of the Scorpion and Tigress, with instructions to maintain a rigid blockade until "driven from the lake by the inclemency of the season, suffering not a boat or canoe to pass in or out of this river," but authorizing him at the same time to detach the Tigress to cruise for a week or two at a time in the vicinity of St. Joseph's to intercept fur canoes passing between Sault Ste. Marie and French River. Twenty-five picked men from the 17th United States Infantry were detailed to serve on these vessels as marines, and the Scorpion was provided with a boarding netting as a protection against a night attack by small boats.

"Against attacks of this kind, which he might be driven to by his desperate situation, as this blockade must starve him into a surrender, I must particularly caution you," Sinclair said in his instructions. "If we can keep their boats from passing until October, I think the bad weather will effectually cut off all communication by anything they have on float, and in the spring an early blockade will possess us of Mackinac."

A brigade of boats from Montreal, by way of French River, under Captain J. M. Lamotte, laden with supplies for Mackinac, received timely warning of their presence before entering Lake Huron and turned back to a place of safety.

Upwards of a hundred barrels of provisions still remained in a store-house several miles up the Nottawasaga which the enemy had not discovered, and two batteaux and Livingston's large canoe had escaped destruction. In these circumstances Worsley determined to elude the blockading vessels. The obstructions were quietly removed from the river, seventy barrels of provisions were taken on board, and on the night of the 18th, he entered the bay without being observed. Six days later, when within a few miles of St. Joseph's, after rowing three hundred and sixty miles along the north shore of the lake, he was greatly surprised to discover both the schooners which he had seen in Nottawasaga Bay a week before, cruising among the islands ahead. As it would be scarcely possible to pass them unobserved, with his heavily-loaded boats in the narrow channel known as the Detour which they were evidently watching, he turned back and concealed them in a secluded bay. His whole party of twenty-five persons then embarked in Livingston's canoe on the night of August 29th, and after passing one of these vessels within a hundred yards in the darkness, arrived at Mackinac at sunset on September 1st.

Worsley lost no time after reaching the island in soliciting permission to lead an attack on the two schooners which were lying about fifteen miles apart when last seen by him. Next day four large rowboats were equipped for this enterprise. One of these, armed with a six pounder, was manned by Midshipman Dobson, a gunner's mate and seventeen seamen of the Royal Navy, under Worsley himself. The other three were manned by a picked detachment of two sergeants, six corporals and fifty privates of the Royal Newfoundland Regiment, commanded by Lieutenants Bulger, Armstrong, and Radenhurst. Bulger's boat was armed with a three-pounder in charge of a bombardier and a gunner of the Royal Artillery. As it was reported that the blockading vessels were accompanied by a body of Indians, whom they had induced to co-operate with them, about two hundred warriors were also embarked in nineteen canoes, under the orders of Dickson and four officers of his department. The expedition left Mackinac that evening, and at sunset on the 2nd of September, arrived at the Detour, thirty-six miles distant, where they expected to find one of the schooners. The men were landed on the island and the boats concealed in a secluded bay. Early next morning Worsley and Livingston went out in a canoe to reconnoitre and soon discovered one of the schooners at anchor about six miles away. It was thought prudent to defer the attack until night when they could approach her unseen. At six o'clock the whole force was re-embarked and rowed as quietly as possible towards the enemy. When about three miles from the schooner the Indians were directed to remain behind and await further orders, but Dickson and three of their principal chiefs were taken on board the boats, making a total of ninety-two of all ranks. The night was very dark and still. About nine o'clock the outline of the schooner was described close ahead. It was then arranged that Worsley's and Armstrong's boats should board her upon the starboard side and Bulger's and Radenhurst's on the larboard. Their approach was so noiseless that Worsley's boat was within ten yards of her and Bulger's not far behind when they were discovered and hailed. No answer being returned, a gun was fired without doing any injury and a hasty and ill-directed fire of musketry was opened upon them. In the face of this the boarders quickly gained the deck on both sides nearly at the same instant and within five minutes the commander of the schooner, Sailing Master Champlain, and all his officers were cut down with several of his men and the remainder driven below. From between decks they kept up a desultory fire which killed one of Worsley's seamen. After all resistance had ceased it was ascertained that the prize was the Tigress, having a crew of thirty-one persons, of whom four were killed and four wounded. Worsley lost two seamen killed and one seaman wounded, but Lieutenant Bulger, Gunner McLaughlin and six privates of the Royal Newfoundland Regiment were also wounded. The prisoners were sent away in boats under guard, and Livingston was despatched in a canoe to ascertain the position of the other schooner. In two hours he returned with information that she was apparently beating down toward the Tigress under sail. As it seemed highly improbable that the firing could have been heard by her crew, Worsley determined not to alter the position of his prize and to keep the American colors flying. During the night of the 5th, the Scorpion anchored within two miles of the Tigress without making any effort to exchange signals or communicate with her in any way. At break of day next morning, Worsley slipped his cable and ran silently down towards her under the jib and foresail only with a dozen sailors in sight besides a few soldiers who were lying down covered with overcoats. Four or five of the Scorpion's crew in charge of the gunner were scrubbing her deck, and although the approach of the Tigress was observed and duly reported it excited no suspicion in the minds of her officers. At the distance of a dozen yards the twenty-four-pounder on the Tigress was fired into the Scorpion's hull as a signal for the remainder of the soldiers to rush on deck. Worsley then ran alongside and grappled with her. The boarders fired a single volley and sprang on her deck, meeting with scarcely any resistance from her bewildered crew, of whom two were killed and two wounded before they surrendered. Like the Tigress the Scorpion mounted a single twenty-four-pounder but also had a twelve pounder in her hold, the carriage of which had become unfit for use. She was commanded by Lieutenant Daniel Turner and had a crew of five officers and thirty-one soldiers, seamen and soldiers. It appeared that these vessels had been forced out of Nottawasaga Bay by a fierce gale which had nearly driven the Niagara on shore after parting from them and even compelled Sinclair to cut loose his launch and the captured boat which he was towing astern. For the last five days the Scorpion had been cruising between St. Joseph's and the French River in the hope of intercepting Lamotte's Brigade of boats from Montreal, of whose approach they had received some information. In her capture Worsley had but a single seaman wounded. He had regained entire control of Lake Huron and effectually relieved Mackinac from all danger of being forced to surrender from want of provisions. This expedition was admirably planned and executed and certainly richly deserved the success with which it was crowned. The prizes were fine vessels for lake service and were at once placed in commission under the names of the Surprise and the Confiance. They sailed at once for the Nottawasaga whence they returned in the beginning of October with a supply of provisions sufficient to maintain the garrison of Mackinac for six months.

ILLUSTRATIVE DOCUMENTS.

Major-General Brock to the Earl of Liverpool.

YORK, 23rd November, 1811.

(Extract.)

I have directed a survey of a tract of land on Lake Simcoe belonging to the Indians to meet your views. The merchants are particularly anxious to obtain a route for their goods unconnected with American territory.

"It is proposed to purchase 428 acres of land and erect grist mills for the convenience of a populous neighborhood."

From a memorial enclosed in the foregoing letter from General Brock to the Earl of Liverpool, signed by William McGillivray, William Hallowell, Roderick McKenzie, Angus Shaw, Archibald McLeod, James Hallowell, jr., and others composing the Northwest Fur Company.

NOTE. For two round trips of the Nancy from Detroit River to Fort Erie, in 1812, the Northwest Company claimed and received £500. For her services in 1813-14, her owners were allowed £1,243 5s. 0d. and the further sum of £2,200 as compensation for the loss of the vessel.

(Extract.)

"We have been continually subjected to the vexatious interference of the United States customs' officials since 1796, and have had boats and property seized. We suggest the establishment of a road from Kempenfeldt Bay to Penetanguishene and will change our route in that direction as soon as practicable. We apply for a grant of land at each end of the road and at the landing at Gwillimbury.—2,000 acres on Kempenfeldt Bay, 2,000 acres at Penetanguishene, 200 at Gwillimbury—consideration, £4,000 in goods to be paid the Indians."

Extract from a letter unaddressed and unsigned in the Canadian Archives. Series C, Volume 257, page 144.

"It appears to be a matter of essential expediency, if not of indispensable necessity, that Mr. Dickson should be sent on forthwith to Michilimackinac by Machedash or if he finds it more convenient to go only to the mouth of the French River in Lake Huron, and in either case to wait for the canoes with the Indian presents which will in all probability reach Lake Huron in the month of September."

From Robert Dickson to Noah Freer, Military Secretary to the Governor-General.

YORK, 29th September, 1813.

With the assistance of Mr. Cameron, I have got the provisions in the way of being transported to Lake Huron and shall set out for Michilimackinac to-morrow. I shall attend particularly to the route and shall transmit my remarks on the return of the canoe by the Grand River. . . .

Should our fleet be totally destroyed on Lake Erie, as we have reason to believe, the bay at Machedash or Penetanguishene are both good harbors and there is plenty of excellent wood in the vicinity for constructing a vessel of any dimensions.

From an unsigned memorandum addressed to Major-General Procter, dated 6th October, 1813. (Canadian Archives, Series C, Volume 680, page 146.)

(Extract.)

"Penetanguishene Bay is an excellent harbor, and easy of access from Lake Huron; the entrance into it is not half a gun-shot across, and the ground very commanding. Near to the water's edge is the finest oak and pine timber that can be imagined. Here (if there are ships' stores in the country for the purpose), vessels might be built in the winter to command Lake Huron and secure the Indians notwithstanding our being driven from Lake Erie.''

From Robert Dickson to Noah Freer.

MICHILIMACKINAC, 23rd October, 1813.

(Extract.)

"I send you a map of Lake Simcoe on a large scale. I think that if a road is to be cut the best route is from Kempenfeldt Bay to Penetanguishene."

From Captain Richard Bullock, 41st Regiment, to Noah Freer.

MICHILIMACKINAC, 23rd October, 1813.

(Extract.)

"Mr. Dickson and I have consulted together as to the best means of defence for the security of Michilimackinac, and we are of the opinion that should the enemy not attack us here this fall, the first and most essential thing to be recommended is the building this winter of six large gunboats at Machedash Bay to protect supplies of any description from falling into their hands; that a re-inforcement of at least two hundred men with an officer of engineers and twenty artillerymen would be required and ordnance as per the enclosed return. . . . .

"The pork and flour which you mentioned in your letter that Mr. Dickson was to take in charge and which we are so much in want of, I am sorry to say, he has not brought. I understand from him that it was to be forwarded from York to Machedash on Lake Huron, to which place, he informs me he must send for it, and I shall lose no time in sending what canoes I can for that purpose."

From Earl Bathurst, Secretary of State for War and the Colonies, to Sir George Prevost, Governor-General of Canada.

DOWNING STREET, 3rd December, 1813.

(Extract.)

"From every information which I have been able to collect, the port of Machedash at the mouth of the Severn is peculiarly well calculated for a naval depot. It has been long used as a post by the persons trading with the Indian nations; it has a good land and water communications with Kingston and is less distant than the former dockyard at Amherstburg. It has moreover this advantage that nothing short of the most serious disaster could render it necessary to abandon it or its communication with Kingston.

"Upon a consideration of all these advantages, His Majesty's Government have determined to convey to you the necessary authority for erecting such block-houses and other defences as may be required to secure this post from attack or insult. As soon as these shall be completed you will make every exertion to build and fit out vessels calculated to meet those which the enemy may transfer to the lake. As the success of this measure depends much upon the rapidity of execution, I would recommend to your serious attention the advantage of laying down vessels at Quebec or Montreal which might afterwards be transported in frame to Machedash and set up there in a much shorter time than would have been required to build them there."

From Captain Richard Bullock to Noah Freer.

MICHILIMACKINAC, 30th December, 1813.

(Extract.)

"In my letter to you of the 23rd October, I mentioned that I should lose no time in sending what canoes I could to Machedash for the flour and pork Mr. Dickson had directed to be sent to that place from York. . . . . .

"Having no alternative, on the 28th October I despatched two large canoes and a bateau manned with Indians and some of the Michigan Fencibles with an interpreter and a sergeant of the veterans for that place. Previous to this party leaving the island I was told by the oldest residents the impracticability of the undertaking, but our situation warranted me to make the trial. On the 2nd of November the bateau with the sergeant and one of the canoes returned, the Indians having refused to proceed, owing to the weather setting in very severe with frost and snow, and they had to cut their way through the ice to get back. It was now too late to send off another party, nor indeed could I get any person on the island to undertake it notwithstanding a large sum was offered by the commissary for that purpose. The other canoe with Indians, having presents for a few of the inhabitants on the north shore of Lake Huron, were prevailed on by the interpreter to go on for the purpose of delivering them. The interpreter on his return informed me that when the presents were delivered the weather becoming more moderate, he further prevailed on the Indians to go to Machedash for what provisions they could bring in the canoe, where they arrived on the 15th November, but to their great disappointment the provisions had not been brought to that place. In consequence lest they should be frozen up, they lost no time in returning here, and after suffering very severely, arrived on the 2nd instant.''

From Lieutenant-General Sir Gordon Drummond to Sir George Prevost.

KINGSTON, 19th January, 1814.

(Extract.)

In reply to Your Excellency's letter of the 2nd instant, marked private, I beg to assure you that I have lost no time in giving ample instructions relating to the supply of troops and provisions to be forwarded to Michilimackinac by Lakes Simcoe and Huron, as also with regard to the building of gunboats and bateaux at Panatanguishene for their conveyance thither.

"In fact I had, prior to the receipt of Your Excellency's letter, already ordered two of the latter description of boats to be constructed at that place for the transport of the provisions and stores for some time since deposited at Machedash, and also for 100 barrels of flour and 50 of pork which I had ordered in addition before I left York."

From Lieutenant-Colonel R. H. Bruyeres, R.E., to Sir George Prevost.

YORK, 23rd January, 1814.

(Extract.)

"I have made every enquiry since I have been here respecting the practicability of building four gunboats in Penetanguishene harbor on Lake Huron for the purpose of communicating from thence to the island of Michilimackinac as early as the opening of navigation will permit. I have seen the only person here that could be competent for this service (Mr. Dennis, late master builder at Kingston). He is at present unemployed, but from the conversation I have had with him he is unwilling to engage in this business, owing to the impossibility of obtaining workmen here for that purpose. Captain Barclay, whom I have seen on this subject, very strongly recommends a Mr. Bell, who was master builder at Amherstburg. He is now at Kingston and I have written to General Drummond to endeavor to engage him for this service and to procure twelve shipwrights to accompany him. I have stated fully all that will be necessary, and I still hope that this business will be accomplished. . . . .

"Mr. Crookshank, the Commissary, is at present at Lake Simcoe where I understand he is gone to make arrangements for the building of five bateaux to convey provisions that were left on the communication to be sent to Michilimackinac."

From Lieutenant-General Drummond to Sir George Prevost.

KINGSTON, 28th January, 1814.

(Extract.)

"I have the honor to acquaint Your Excellency that I have received a communication from Deputy Assistant Commissary-General Crookshank, at York, on his return from Lake Simcoe where he had been to make arrangements for forwarding supplies to Michilimackinac.

"He informs me that from the authority of several credible persons and likewise from Mr. Wilmot, the surveyor, who had been employed in running the line from Lake Simcoe to Penetanguishene Bay that it is impracticable to transport anything by that route previous to a road being cut upwards of thirty miles in length, and that it was calculated to take 200 men for at least three weeks before it could be made passable, and in case of deep snow it could not be done at all.

"In consequence of the delay and difficulty attending such a measure Mr. Crookshank has made arrangements for forwarding the supplies to Nottawasaga Bay on Lake Huron, a distance of only 20 miles from Penetanguishene.

"The opening of the road to the river leading to Nottawasaga Bay will take but 12 men for about 10 days, and in the course of a few days, as soon as a shed can be erected on the other side of Lake Simcoe, he will commence sending the stores across it, should a thaw not prevent.

"As Mr. Crookshank found it almost impossible to procure hands to build boats and altogether no person to contract for the whole or even a part, I have had a communication with the Commissioner of the Navy here who says he could furnish 30 workmen with an able foreman that would ensure the measure being completed in a given time and contract at once the building of as many as should be required, and they could set out from hence at a day's notice well furnished with tools and oakum, and every other requisite for the occasion.

"This mode of proceeding would undoubtedly prove somewhat expensive, but I see no alternative.

P.S. Since writing the above I have received a letter from Lieutenant-Colonel Bruyeres from York corroborating that part of Mr. Crookshank's letter relative to the inability of procuring persons there to build at Penetanguishene Bay, and asserting the only way this object can be accomplished is by sending up builders with the necessary materials of pitch, ironwork, etc., from Kingston."

From Captain Richard Bullock to Noah Freer.

FORT MICHILIMACKINAC, 26th February, 1814.

(Extract.)

"The number of boats I can send to Nottawasaga and Penetanguishene Bay in the ensuing spring to assist in bringing in the supplies, etc., will be two bateaux, two large birch canoes and a keel boat."

From Lieutenant-General Drummond to Sir George Prevost.

KINGSTON, 21st May, 1814.

(Extract.)

I have the honor to enclose herewith the copy of a report I have just now received from Colonel Claus, Deputy Superintendent-General of Indian Affairs, from which I am concerned to learn that the enemy have passed up the River St. Clair with two vessels and six gunboats containing about 300 men, about the 22nd or 23rd of last month for Lake Huron.

"Lieutenant-Colonel McDouall's last brigade of boats for Michilimackinac left Nottawasaga on the 20th of the same month, which I most anxiously hope has arrived at its destination in safety."

(Extract from Colonel Claus's Report Enclosed.)

Thirteen Indians from Naywash's band arrived at Burlington, on the 9th instant, from Flint River, and say that they were informed that two vessels and six gunboats with about 300 men had passed the River St. Clair about the 22nd or 23rd April for Michilimackinac and that no more than about 250 men remained at Detroit.

From Lieutenant-Colonel McDouall to Lieutenant-General Drummond.

MICHILIMACKINAC, 26th May, 1814.

(Extract.)

"The Nancy being just under way, I refer to my letter to Colonel Harvey for particulars of our voyage. I avail myself of the few minutes left me before she sails to urge in the strongest terms the necessity of Mr. Crookshank being immediately directed to deposit for us at the mouth of the Nottawasaga River another supply of provisions consisting of from three to four hundred barrels of flour and pork, otherwise this place will be in great danger from the want of that article, owing to the great issues to the Indians which I have curtailed as much as possible, even at the risk of offending them."

From Lieutenant-Colonel Robert Nichol.

KINGSTON, 30th May, 1814.

(Extract.)

"In addition to the establishment at Long Point, I should strongly recommend the formation of one at Penetanguishene on Lake Huron. The road, however, to the north of Lake Simcoe which is, I understand, about twenty-four miles, should be previously opened. A flotilla on Lake Huron will be found of great service, both as it respects offensive and defensive operations. The remoteness of the situation will keep the enemy ignorant of our movements."

From Lieutenant-General Drummond to Sir George Prevost.

KINGSTON, 2nd July, 1814.

(Extract.)

"I have the honor to transmit herewith a copy of an interesting letter I received from Lieutenant-Colonel McDouall from Michilimackinac. I am apprehensive his Indian allies, unless he can find some method of employing them so as they may in a greater degree supply themselves with food, will cause him some uneasiness and difficulties with regard to provisions. To enable him to meet all their demands, however, as much as possible, I have given directions to Deputy Commissary Couche to take measures for securing a constant supply to his post, and I understand Deputy Assistant Commissary General Crookshank is at

Nottawasaga at present on this business as well as for the purpose of improving the road to that place from Lake Simcoe."

From Lieutenant-Colonel McDouall to Lieutenant-General Drummond.

MACHILIMACKINAC, 17th July, 1814.

(Extract.)

I was greatly disappointed at the Nancy bringing us last trip only eleven barrels for Government. I at least expected three hundred. I also received but little comfort on Mr. Crookshank telling me that by the 20th instant, he was in hopes to have 200 barrels at the Nottawasaga River. However, as it is of great consequence, even the securing of that quantity, I am now despatching the Nancy for it. I, however, beg to represent the great necessity which exist that the supplies should be more liberal for this place. It is now the last point of connection with the Indians and I believe the great importance of their alliance and the policy of conciliating them as much as possible is generally admitted, particularly as the enemy is making such efforts to seduce them from us; and yet what means are placed in my hands to counteract the influence of the Americans? A continual interchange of Indians is going on at this place and some have come a great distance for its defence, and yet I have been compelled to refuse rations to their wives and children, and to many others in a half-famished state; even my own garrison I am compelled to reduce the rations of, and as soldiers have but little foresight and think only of the present, it adds to the general discontent on the subject of provisions. In what a predicament does this leave me, and in what a situation should I be left if great efforts are not made for my relief? Every day adds to my perplexity on this subject. I now only issue 250 rations daily to Indians which make the whole about 550. It is absolutely essential and cannot with prudence be otherwise, that in calculating the supplies for this garrison, at least *three hundred Indians* should be included, and I am fully convinced that they could never be expended to a better purpose. . . . .

(Canadian Archives, C, 685, page 67.)

From Captain A. Slinclair to the Secretary of the Navy.

UNITED STATES SLOOP NIAGARA,
OFF ST. JOSEPH'S, 22nd July, 1814.

SIR,—The wind became favorable on the evening of the 3rd instant, the troops were embarked and I sailed from Detroit that night, but such were the difficulties I had to encounter on the flats of Lake St. Clair, where, instead of ten feet, as I had been led to believe there was, I found only eight, and the rapid current of that river, that I did not reach Lake Huron until the 12th. From thence I shaped my course as directed for Machedash Bay and used every possible effort to gain it, but not being able to procure a pilot for that unfrequented part of the lake, and finding it filled with islands and sunken rocks which must inevitably prove the destruction of the fleet as it was impossible to avoid them on account of the impenetrable fog with which this lake is almost continually covered, and finding the army were growing short of provisions from the time already elapsed, it was agreed between Colonel Croghan and myself to push for this place where we should procure such information as would govern our future operations. We were favored in winds and arrived here on the 20th. The enemy had abandoned his work, consisting of a fort and a large block-house, etc.; those we destroyed but left untouched the town and Northwest Company's storehouses.

From Lieutenant-Colonel McDouall to Lieutenant-General Drummond.

MICHILIMACKINAC, 28th July, 1814.

(Extract.)

"We are here in a very fine state of defence, the garrison and Indians in the highest spirits and all ready for the attack of the enemy. I apprehend nothing for the island but from the want of provisions. I have, therefore, to beg to supplicate, to entreat, my dear General, that every effort may be made, every step be immediately taken which can facilitate our being supplied. There are now three bateaux in the Nottawasaga River, a fourth can be carried over from Lake Simcoe. These should be manned by the crew of the Nancy, mounting one of her carronades in one of them and could bring 140 barrels of flour which should be taken to the depot at the River Sauganock, and being there secured, the party would have sufficient time to return to the River Tessalon which we consider (the secret being well kept) as out of the reach of the enemy, and which (should the blockade not be raised in time) can easily be brought here over the snow in the winter. The River Sauganock is fifteen miles *on our side* of the Cloche and is the place where the Montreal canoes are directed to deposit the cargoes they brought from that place and likewise the first cargo of flour they bring from the River Nottawasaga. The River Tessalon is thirty miles from St. Joseph's and is the place where the second cargoes of both the

canoes and the bateaux must be landed, as by that time the enemy's
squadron may have been obliged to leave us, but be that as it may, we
consider it a safe place. Should the Nancy's crew come with the bateaux
as proposed she must be hauled as high as possible up the river. A
subaltern and 20 men and some Indians stationed for her defence and
that of the depot which, I think, will perfectly secure both."

From Lieutenant Daniel Turner to Captain A. Sinclair.

UNITED STATES SCHOONER SCORPION,
OFF MICHILIMACKINAC, July 28th, 1814.

SIR,—I have the honor to inform you that, agreeable to your orders
of the 22nd instant, I proceed on the expedition to Lake Superior with
launches. I rowed night and day, but having a distance of sixty miles
against a strong current, information had reached the enemy at St.
Mary's about two hours before I arrived at that place, carried by
Indians in their light canoes, several of whom I chased, and by firing
on them and killing some, prevented their purpose, some I captured and
kept prisoners until my arrival, others escaped. The force under Major
Holmes prevented anything like resistance at the Fort; the enemy carrying with them all their light valuable articles, peltry, clothes, etc. I
proceeded across the strait of Lake Superior without a moment's delay,
and on my appearance the enemy, finding they could not get off with the
vessel I was in quest of, set fire to her in several places, scuttled and
left her. I succeeded in boarding her, and by considerable exertions,
extinguished the flames and secured her from sinking. I then stripped
and prepared for getting her down the falls. Adverse winds prevented
my attempting the falls until the 26th, when every possible effort was
used, but I am sorry to say without success to get her over in safety.
The fall in three-quarters of a mile is forty-five feet and the channel
very rocky, the current runs from twenty to thirty knots, and in one
place there is a perpendicular leap of ten feet between three rocks.
Here she bilged but was brought down so rapidly that we succeeded in
running her on shore below the rapids before she filled and burned
her. She was a fine new schooner, upwards of one hundred tons, called
the Perseverance, and will be a severe loss to the Northwest Company.
Had I succeeded in getting her down safe, I could have loaded her with
advantage from the enemy's store-houses. I have, however, brought
down four captured boats loaded with Indian goods to a considerable
amount, the balance, contained in four large and two small store-houses,

were destroyed, amounting to from fifty to one hundred thousand dollars. All private property was, according to your orders, respected. The officers and men under my command behaved with great activity and zeal, particularly Midshipman Swartwout.

From Captain A. Sinclair to the Secretary of the Navy.

UNITED STATES SLOOP NIAGARA,
OFF MICHILIMACKINAC, July 29th, 1814.

SIR,—Whilst windbound at St. Joseph's I captured the Northwest Company's schooner, Mink, from Michilimackinac to St. Mary's with a cargo of flour. Receiving intelligence through this source that the schooner Perseverence was laying above the falls at the lower end of Lake Superior in waiting to transport the Mink's cargo to Fort William, I despatched the ships' launches under Lieutenant Turner of the Scorpion, an active and enterprising officer, to capture, and, if possible, get her down the falls. Colonel Croghan attached Major Holmes with a party of regulars to co-operate in the expedition in which the capture of St. Mary's was included. The official report of the result made by Lieutenant Turner I herewith enclose you. The capture of the Perseverence gave us the complete command of Lake Superior, and had it not been for the strong force at Michilimackinac forbidding a separation of our means of attacking that place and feeling myself bound by my instructions to do so before I was at liberty to enter into any extensive enterprise of my own planning, I should have availed myself of this unlooked for advantage and have broken up all their establishments on Lake Superior. The capture of Fort William alone would have nearly destroyed the enemy's fur trade, as that is his grand depot and general rendezvous from which his extensive trade branched out in all directions, and at which place there is never less than a million in property, and at this season of the year it is said there is twice that amount. I fear such another opportunity may never recur. The capture of those two vessels and the provisions will, however, prove of very serious inconvenience to the enemy in that quarter where the loss cannot possibly be retrieved. Flour was before this loss worth sixty dollars per barrel with them, and salt provisions fifty cents per pound, etc.

From Major A. H. Holmes to Lieutenant-Colonel Croghan.

UNITED STATES SCHOONER SCORPION, 27th July, 1814.

SIR,—Pursuant to your orders of the 22nd instant, I left the squadron with Lieutenant Turner of the Navy, and arrived at the Sault Ste.

Marie the day after. Two hours before the Northwest Agent had received notice of our approach and succeeded in escaping with a considerable amount of goods after setting fire to the vessel above the falls. The design of this latter measure was frustrated only by the intrepid exertions of Mr. Turner with his own men and a few of Captain Saunder's company.

The vessel was brought down the falls on the 25th, but having bilged, Mr. Turner destroyed her. Most of the goods we have taken were found in the woods on the American side and were claimed by the agent, John Johnson, an Indian trader.

I secured this property because it was good prize by the maritime law of nations as recognized by the English courts (witness the case of Admiral Rodney, adjudged by Lord Mansfield), further, because Johnson has acted the part of a traitor, having been a citizen and magistrate of Michigan Territory, and at its commencement and now discharging the functions of a magistrate under the British Government; because his agent armed the Indians from his stores at our approach, and, lastly, because those goods, or a considerable part, were designed to be taken to Michilimackinac. Pork, salt, and groceries compose the chief part. Johnson himself passed to Michilimackinac since the squadron arrived at St. Joseph's.

From Lieutenant-Colonel McDouall to Lieutenant Worsley.

MICHILIMACKINAC, 28th July, 1814.

SIR,—The American expedition destined for the attack of this island having at length made its appearance under the command of Commodore Elliott and Lieutenant-Colonel Croghan, consisting of the Niagara, 20 guns, Lawrence, 20 Hunter, brig 8, and a large schooner of   guns, the Mary of   guns, five gunboats and the Mink, their prize, I hasten to apprise you of the circumstance, lest the Nancy and her valuable cargo fall into their hands, and that you may be enabled to take such steps for her preservation as will appear to you most expedient under the circumstances. I have taken such precautions as were in my power to make you acquainted with this event in case you may be on your passage. If so, I would recommend you to return to the Nottawasaga River and to take up the Nancy as high as possible, place her in a judicious position and hastily run up a log house (such as were made when the boats were built, but larger) with loopholes and embrasures for your two six pounders which will enable you to defend her should you be attacked, which is not unlikely.

The mode of obtaining her cargo which is of such value to us will depend upon the result of the attack which we daily expect, and of the duration of the blockade. I see no other way of obtaining the provisions, but by bringing them protected by carronades in the bows of two of them. You will probably receive instructions from Kingston as to your conduct.

(From Niles' Register, Volume VII, page 132. Captured by Captain Sinclair, at Nottawasaga.)

From Captain Sinclair to the Secretary of the Navy.

UNITED STATES SLOOP NIAGARA,
OFF THUNDER BAY, August 9, 1814.

SIR,—I arrived off Michilimackinac, on the 26th July, but owing to a tedious spell of bad weather, which prevented our reconnoitering or being able to take a prisoner who could give us information of the enemy's Indian force which from several little skirmishes we had on an adjacent island, appeared to be very great, we did not attempt a landing until the 4th instant, and it was then made more with a view to ascertain the enemy's strength than with any possible hope of success. Knowing at the same time that I could effectually cover their landing and retreat to the ships from the position I had taken within 300 yards of the beach. Colonel Croghan would never have landed, even with this protection being positive that the Indian force alone on the island with the advantages they had, were superior to him, could he have justified himself to his government without having stronger proof than appearances that he could not effect the object in view.

Mackinac is by nature a perfect Gibralter, being a high, inaccessible rock on every side except from the west, from which to the heights you have near two miles to pass through a wood so thick that our men were shot in every direction, and within a few yards of them, without being able to see the Indians who did it, and a height was scarcely gained before there was another within fifty or one hundred yards, commanding it where breastworks were erected and cannon opened on them. Several of these were charged and the enemy driven from them, but it was soon found the further our troops advanced the stronger the enemy became, and the weaker and more bewildered our force were; several of the commanding officers were picked out and killed or wounded without seeing any of them. The men were getting lost and falling into confusion, natural under such circumstances, which demanded an immediate retreat or a total defeat, and massacre must have ensued. This was conducted in a masterly manner by Colonel Croghan who had lost the aid of that valuable and ever to be lamented officer, Major Holmes, who with Captain Van Horne, was killed by the Indians. The enemy were driven from many of their strongholds, but such was the impenetrable thickness of the woods that no advantage gained could be profited by. Our attack would have been made immediately under the lower fort so that the enemy might not have been able to use his Indian allies to such advantage as in the woods, having discovered by drawing a fire from him in several instances that I had greatly the superiority of metal of him, but its site being about 130 feet above the water, I could not, when near enough to do him an injury, elevate sufficiently to batter it. Above this, nearly as high again, he has another stronghold commanding every point on the island and almost perpendicular on all sides. Colonel Croghan not deeming it prudent to make a second attempt upon this place and having ascertained to a certainty that the only naval force the enemy have upon the lake consists of a schooner of four guns, I have determined to despatch the Lawrence and Caledonia to Lake Erie immediately, believing that their service in transporting our armies there will be wanting, and it being important that the sick and wounded amounting to about one hundred, and that part of the detachment not necessary to further our future operations here should reach Detroit without delay. By an intelligent prisoner captured in the Mink, I ascertained this and that the mechanics and others sent across from York during the winter were for the purpose of building a flotilla to transport reinforcements and supplies to Mackinac. An attempt was made to transport them by way of Machedash, but it was found impracticable from all the portages being a morass; that they then resorted to a small river called Nottawasaga, situated to the south of Machedash, from which there is a portage of three leagues over a good road to Lake Simcoe. This place was never known until pointed out to them by an Indian. This river is very narrow and has six or eight feet of water in it, and is then a muddy rapid shallow for forty-five miles to the portage where their armada was built and their storehouses are now situated. The navigation is dangerous and difficult, and so obscured by rocks and bushes that no stranger could ever find it. I have, however, availed myself of this means of discovering it. I shall also blockade the mouth of French River until the fall, and those two being the only two channels of communication by which Mackinac can possibly be supplied, and their provisions at this time being extremely short, I think they will be starved into a surrender. This will also cut off all supplies to the Northwest Company who are now nearly starving, and their furs on hand can only find transportation by way of Hudson's Bay. At this place, I calculate on falling in with their schooner which it is said is gone there for a load of provisions and a message sent to her not to venture up while we are on the lake.

From Lieutenant-Colonel Croghan to the Secretary of War.

UNITED STATES SLOOP NIAGARA,
OFF THUNDER BAY, August 9th, 1814.

SIR,—We left Fort Gratiot (head of the straits of St. Clair) on the 12th ultimo, and imagined we should arrive in a few days at Machedash Bay. At the end of a week, however, the Commodore from want of pilots acquainted with the unfrequented part of the lake, despaired of being able to find a passage through the islands into the bay, and made for St. Joseph's where he anchored on the 20th day of July. After setting fire to the Fort of St. Joseph's, which seemed not to have been recently occupied, a detachment of infantry and artillery, under Major Holmes, was ordered to Sault St. Mary's for the purpose of breaking up the enemy's establishment at that place. For particulars relative to the execution of this order, I beg leave to refer you to Major Holmes' report herewith enclosed. Finding on my arrival at Michilimackinac, on the 26th ultimo, the enemy had strongly fortified the height overlooking the old fort of Mackinac, I at once despaired of being able with my small force to carry the place by storm and determined (as the only course remaining) on landing and establishing myself in some favorable position whence I should be enabled by gradual and slo wapproaches under cover of my artillery in which I should have the superiority in point of metal. I was urged to adopt this step by another reason not a little cogent; could a position be taken and fortified on the island, I was well aware it would either induce the enemy to attack me in my stronghold or force his Indians and Canadians (his most efficient and only disposable force) off the island, as they would be very unwilling to remain in my neighborhood after a permanent footing had been taken. On inquiry I learned from individuals who had lived on the island, that a position as desirable as I might wish, could be found on the west end and therefore immediately made arrangements for disembarking. A landing was effected on the 4th instant under cover of the guns of the shipping, and the line being quickly formed, had advanced to the edge of the field spoken of, when intelligence was conveyed to me that the enemy was ahead, and a few seconds more brought us a fire from his battery of four pieces firing shot and shell. After reconnoitering his position which was well selected, his line reached along the edge of the woods at the further extremity of the field and was covered by a temporary breastwork. I determined on changing my position (which was now two lines, the militia forming the front) by advancing Major Holmes' battalion of regulars on the right of the militia, thus to outflank him, and by a vigorous effort to gain his rear. The movement was immediately ordered, but before it could be executed, a fire was opened by some Indians posted in a thick wood near our right which proved fatal to Major Holmes and severely wounded Captain Desha (the next officer in rank). This unlucky fire by depriving us of the services of our most valuable officers, threw that part of the line into confusion, which the best exertions of the officers were not able to recover. Finding it impossible to gain the enemy's left owing to the impenetrable thickness of the woods, a charge was ordered to be made by the regulars immediately in front. This charge, although made in some confusion, seemed to drive the enemy back into the woods from whence an annoying fire was kept up by the Indians.

Lieutenant Morgan was ordered up with a light piece to assist the left now particularly galled; the excellent practice of this brought the enemy to fire at a longer distance. Discovering that this position from whence the enemy had just been driven (and which had been represented to me as so high and commanding), was by no means tenable from being interspersed with thickets and intersected in every way by ravines. I determined no longer to expose my force to the fire of an enemy, deriving every advantage from numbers and a knowledge of the position, and therefore ordered an immediate retreat towards the shipping.

This affair which cost us many valuable lives, leaves us to lament the fall of that gallant officer, Major Holmes, whose character is so well known to War Department. Captain Van Horne of the 19th Infantry and Lieutenant Jackson of the 24th Infantry, both brave and intrepid young men, fell mortally wounded at the head of their respective commands. Captain Desha of the 24th Infantry, although severely wounded, continued with his command until forced to retire from faintness through loss of blood. Captains Saunders, Hawkins, and Sturgis, with every subaltern of that battalion, acted in the most exemplary manner. Ensign Bryan, 2nd Rifle Regiment, acting adjutant of the battalion, actively forwarded the wishes of the commanding officer. Lieutenants Hickman, 28th Infantry, and Hyde, of the United States

Marines, who commanded the reserve, claim my particular thanks for keeping that command in readiness to meet any exigency. I have before mentioned Lieutenant Morgan's activity; his two assistants, Lieutenant Pickett and Mr. Peters, conductor of artillery, also merit the name of good officers.

The militia were wanting in no part of their duty; Colonel Cotgreave, his officers and soldiers deserve the warmest approbation. My acting adjutant-general, Captain N. H. Moore, 28th Infantry, with Volunteer Adjutant McComb, were prompt in delivering my orders. Captain Gratiot, of the Engineers, who volunteered his services as adjutant on the occasion, gave me valuable assistance.

On the morning of the 5th, I sent a flag to inquire into the state of the wounded (two in number), who were left on the field, and to request permission to bring away the body of Major Holmes which was also left, owing to the unpardonable neglect of the soldiers in whose hands he was placed. I am happy in assuring you that the body of Major Holmes is secured and will be buried at Detroit with becoming honors.

I shall discharge the militia to-morrow and will send them down with two regular companies to Detroit. With the remaining three companies I shall attempt to destroy the enemy's establishment in the head of Naw-taw-wa-sa-ga River, and if it is thought best erect a post at the mouth of that river.

Return of the killed, wounded, and missing of a detachment commanded by Lieutenant-Colonel Croghan, in the affair of the 4th August.

11th August, 1814.

Artillery—Wounded—Three privates.

Infantry—17 Regiment. Killed—Five privates; wounded—two sergeants, two corporals, fifteen privates, two privates since dead; two privates missing.

19th Regiment. Wounded—One captain, nineteen privates. Captain J. Van Horne, and one private since dead.

24th Regiment. Killed—Five privates; wounded, one captain, one lieutenant, three sergeants, one musician, five privates. Captain Desha, severely. Lieutenant H. Jackson, and one sergeant since dead.

32nd Regiment. Killed—Major A. H. Holmes.

United States Marines. Wounded—One sergeant.

Ohio Militia. Killed—Two privates; wounded, five privates. One private since dead.

Extract from a letter to W. D. Thomas, M.D., surgeon of the 104th Regiment at York or Kingston.

NOTTAWASAGA, 6th August, 1814.

It is now nearly a month since I left York in company with Lieutenant Worsley of the Navy on my way to the land of promise, but things have turned out rather unfortunately, for you still behold me a sojourner in the wilderness. We had waited about a week on the banks of this river before the Nancy arrived during which time we suffered every misery you can imagine from bad weather and mosquitoes, etc., etc. The land here is the most barren I have seen. It seems to have been formed from time to time by the washing of Lake Huron, it being for upwards of two miles composed entirely of banks of sand on which nothing grows but small brushwood. We found a number of Indians encamped on the lake shore who were extremely troublesome until the vessel arrived. It was not possible to keep them out of our wigwams. You may then imagine what a pleasant sight the Nancy was for us. We found her a very fine schooner with an admirable cabin. Her cargo was not completed before Sunday last and she got under way on Monday with every prospect of reaching Mackinac in a short time, which is only 220 miles from hence. We had been out but a few hours when we met an express from Lieutenant-Colonel McDouall to say that the American squadron from Lake Erie of large force was blockading the island and we could not possibly reach it. We, therefore, had the mortification to put back into this wretched place where we are busily employed in erecting a block-house to contain and defend the stores and schooner in case of an attack which is an event I have no doubt of, but I hope from the strength of the ground Worsley has chosen and the goodness of his crew that we shall be able to beat off a very strong force. The river is too narrow to sail up, we shall, therefore, only have gunboats to contend with. I hope Mackinac has provisions for three months, and the enemy, it is said, cannot keep out so long on account of the climate, so that the Nancy can make a run late in the season with the stores, if we succeed in defending them. I expect the man who brought the express the other day, who has gone on to York, and intends going back to Mackinac in a canoe. I shall trust my person with him as he thinks he can again give Jonathan the slip.

(From Niles' Register, Volume VII, page 132-3. Taken by Sinclair at Nottawasaga.)

AN EPISODE OF THE WAR OF 1812.

From Lieutenant-General Drummond to Sir George Prevost.

CAMP NEAR FORT ERIE, August 11, 1814.

(Extract.)

Instantly on the receipt of these letters, I directed a communication to be made to the officer commanding at York, covering extracts of the most important parts of them, with instructions that the commissariat should be called upon to carry into effect the request of Lieutenant-Colonel McDouall as far as relates to that department in the transport of provisions, etc., and that a detachment of militia and Indians should be sent to Nottawasaga for the protection of the Nancy schooner.

(Canadian Archives, Series C, Volume 685, page 73.)

From Lieutenant-Colonel McDouall to Sir George Prevost.

MICHILIMACKINAC, 14th August, 1814.

SIR,—I have reported to Lieutenant-General Drummond the particulars of the attack made by the enemy on this post on the 4th instant. My situation was embarrassing. I knew that they could land upwards of a thousand men, and after manning the guns at the forts, I had only a disposable force of one hundred and forty to meet them, which I determined to do in order as much as possible to encourage the Indians, and having the fullest confidence in the little detachment of the Royal Newfoundland Regiment. The position I took up was excellent, but at an unavoidable and too great a distance from the forts, in each of which I was only able to leave twenty-five militia-men. There were likewise roads upon my flanks, every inch of which were known to the enemy by means of people formerly residents of this island, which were with them. I could not afford to detach a man to guard them, and it is one of the misfortunes of having to do with Indians and depending upon them, that they will do as they like, and in action it is impossible to form any previous judgment whether they will behave well or ill or are disposed to fight or not.

My position was rather too extensive for such a handful of men. The ground was commanding, and in front clear as I could wish it, on both flanks and rear a thick wood. My utmost wish was that the Indians would only prevent the enemy from gaining the woods upon our flanks which would have forced them upon the open ground in my front. A natural breastwork protected my men from every shot, and I told them that on the close approach of the enemy they were to pour in a volley and immediately charge. Numerous as they were, all were fully confident of the result.

On the advance of the enemy my six-pounder and three-pounder opened a heavy fire upon them, but not with the effect they would have had, not being well manned, and for want of an artillery officer which would have been invaluable to us as they moved slowly and cautiously, declining to meet me on the open ground, but gradaully gaining my left flank, which the Indians permitted even in the woods without firing a shot. I was even obliged to weaken my small front by detaching the Michigan Fencibles to oppose a party of the enemy which were advancing to the woods on my right. I now received accounts from Major Crawford of the militia that the enemy's two large ships had anchored in the rear of my left and that troops were moving by a road in that direction towards the forts. I therefore moved to place myself between them and the enemy, and took up a position effectually covering them from whence collecting the greater part of the Indians who had retired and taking with me Major Crawford and about 50 militia. I again advanced to support a party of the Fallsovine Indians who, with their gallant chief, Thomas, had commenced a spirited attack upon the enemy who, in a short time lost their second in command and several other officers, seventeen of which we counted dead upon the field besides what they carried off and a considerable number wounded. The enemy retired in the utmost haste and confusion, followed by the troops, till they found shelter under the very broadside of their ships within a few yards of the shore. They re-embarked that evening and the vessels immediately hauled off.

Though the enemy, formidable as they were in numbers, have made so poor a business of their attack, yet I must still ever regret their being not more effectually punished which would not assuredly have been the case had not the Indians gradually disappeared, leaving both flanks uncovered. The gallant Fallsovines with a few Winnebagoes, Chippewas, and Ottawas certainly retrieved their character.

I am now fully convinced of the great danger of depending upon these people for the defence of this island, they are as fickle as the wind, and though the American Commodore avowed to Major Crawford his intention of renewing his attack, the instant he received some re-inforcements (by the end of this month), yet all my endeavors have not been able to prevent a great many from going away, according to their custom after an action. Should they be as good as their word (and they say the island must be retaken, cost what it will), I shall have to encounter them with a force considerably diminished while theirs will have been proportionately increased.

I have, therefore to assure Your Excellency that the present garrison is entirely inadequate to the defence of the island which has now assumed a degree of importance which it never had before, and which would be productive of most serious consequences were its safety and due security to be neglected. Indeed, it is of such consequence that this frontier should be kept in a respectable state of defence that when all the re-inforcements have arrived it would be worth while to employ a regiment between this place and the Mississippi. We here require at least one hundred picked men and an officer and twenty artillery and a company (and a small detachment of artillery) are absolutely necessary to defend Colonel McKay's new conquest. The fort is represented to me as being strongly situated and being capable of making an excellent defence.

The enemy's designs upon that fine country have been long formed and they had not a doubt of the whole of it as well as this island being by this time in their possession by which means our connection with all the Indians of the Mississippi would have been completely cut off. Nothing could have opposed them on that river, and they could with impunity have carried their schemes of conquest even to Hudson's Bay.

It will give me uncommon satisfaction should Your Excellency be convinced of the importance of securing the Mississippi and the beneficial consequences which must result therefrom, for I should then consider it practicable that a company under an active intelligent officer might still garrison Fort McKay previous to the winter. They might embark at Nottawasaga in the Nancy and have ample time to reach that place, whereas if omitted till next next year it will be the middle of June before they can reach it, which I much fear will enable the enemy previously to attack it.

Mr. Rolette tells me there are ample supplies to maintain the garrison. The Indians cannot be relied on for its defence, but a company of regular troops would rally round them and firmly retain in our interest all the tribes on the Mississippi. A number of them, particularly those in the neighborhood of St. Louis, being without support from us, and in the power of the enemy, have accordingly temporized and kept back. A similar instance of this lately occurred. Governor Clark on his return route made peace with the Sauks and Renards, but the instant they heard of the capture of the fort and the arrival of the British then they immediately obeyed Colonel McKay's summons, was supplied by him with ammunition and attacking Major Campbell's flotilla, effected the destruction of his whole detachment. This signal and justly deserved punishment together with the capture of Fort McKay and the general union of the Indians will cause great terror in St. Louis, and fully deter them from making any attempts on the reconquered country till the ensuing spring.

(Canadian Archives, Series Q, Volume 128-1, page 229.)

From Captain A. Sinclair to Lieutenant Daniel Turner.

NOTTAWASAGA RIVER, August 15, 1814.

SIR,—Having accomplished the object for which the squadron came into this quarter in the destruction of the enemy's whole naval force on this lake. I am on the eve of returning to Lake Erie, but as it is all important to cut the enemy's line of communication from Michilimackinac to York which is through the Nottawasaga River, Lake Simcoe, etc., and on which his very existence depends, you will remain here and keep up a blockade until you shall be driven from the lake by the inclemency of the season, suffering not a boat or canoe to pass in or out of this river. I shall leave the Tigress with you. In case accident should happen to either one of the vessels, the other may afford her necessary assistance. Should you deem it proper to send the Tigress up to cruise a week or two about St. Joseph's in order to intercept the enemy's fur canoes between Ste. Marie's and French River, you can do so, as one vessel is sufficient to blockade this river.

I should recommend your immediately finding out an anchorage to cover you from the northwest gales, as that is the only wind which can affect you in this bay. I see from the Nancy's log book that the small island on the southwest of this bay is such a place as you could wish, directions for which, I herewith give you. The island north of us may also give you good anchorage, but always be sure of some good bottom before anchoring, as the loss of an anchor might prove of serious consequence to you. Should you find anchorage on both sides, I should recommend your changing frequently, and in a way not to be observed by the enemy who might not only avail himself of your position to move out his boats on the opposite side, but he might attempt surprising you by throwing a number of men on board. Against attacks of this kind which he might be driven to by his desperate situation as this blockade must starve him into a surrender by spring, I must particularly caution you. When the Tigress is here it would be well to be on the opposite shore and sometimes to run out of sight, taking care to scour both shores as you return. I shall endeavor to annoy the navigation of the river by felling trees at its mouth in order that a portage must be performed there which must be seen by you.

I wish you to take an accurate survey of this bay and its islands, and if possible, of the one on the north of it called Machedash, observing all its islands, bays, shoals, anchorages, courses, distances, and soundings, particularly attending to the kind of bottom.

Should anything occur to make it necessary, you can send the Tigress express to me. If we can keep their boats from passing until October, I think the weather will effectually cut off all communication by anything they have on float, and in the spring an early blockade will possess us of Mackinac.

You will be particularly careful in having communication with the shore, and when you send a party for wood, let it be on an island and under protection of your guns and a guard from both vessels. Wishing you a pleasant cruise, I am your, etc.

From George Crookshank to Peter Turquand, Deputy Commissary General.

YORK, 21st August, 1814.

SIR,—I have the honor to report that I have just returned from Nottawasaga. On my arrival there I learned from Lieutenant Worsley, Royal Navy, that the enemy's fleet had appeared off the mouth of the Nottawasaga on the 13th, and on the 14th that they landed a large party of men, in consequence of which I regret to say he had to destroy the Nancy with all the cargo to prevent the same from falling into the enemy's hands, a copy of the invoice and receipts for the same, I herewith enclose. There was also 50 bags of flour, private property, on board which I had directed Mr. Livingston to load a canoe with and proceed and I would replace the same, but the enemy had appeared before Mr. Livingston had reached that place. One of the largest size gunboats which had been brought down from Mackinac for the purpose of loading the vessel fell into the hands of the enemy. I have also enclosed a return of the quantity of provisions remaining in the storehouse at Nottawasaga, part of which Lieutenant Worsley takes on with him in two boats and a large canoe with Mr. Livingston. As Mr. Worsley had hands for manning another boat, I directed one to be sent across from Lake Simcoe to him, and think it probable they have left Nottawasaga to-day in case the boat sent across the carrying place should not have got injured in the transport. In that case Lieutenant

Worsley would proceed with the two boats and the canoe, as it is doubtful whether Mr. La Mothe, who has charge of the government canoes, will return for provisions. I will immediately send out three bateaux and endeavor to get hands for manning the same they they may make two trips with flour to the place pointed out by Colonel McDouall, and shall send out sufficient to make up the 600 barrels required for that post.

All the public letters that were forwarded in charge of Lieutenant Worsley for Lieutenant-Colonel McDouall, I learn were burnt in the vessel, of which I have to request you will inform Colonel Foster as some of the packets that were delivered to Lieutenant Worsley were from General Drummond.

P.S. The enemy's fleet left Nottawasaga River on the 15th instant and stood up the lake.

(Canadian Archives, Series C, Volume 685, page 145.)

From Lieutenant-Colonel George Croghan to Brigadier-General Duncan McArthur.

DETROIT, August 23rd, 1814.

DEAR SIR,—I communicated in my report of the 11th instant my intention of continuing on Lake Huron with three companies for the purpose of breaking up any depots the enemy might have on the east side of the lake.

We were fortunate in learning that the only line of communication from York to Mackinac, etc., was by way of Lake Simcoe and Nottawasaga River which runs into Lake Huron about 100 miles southeast of Cabot's Head. To that river, therefore, our course was directed in the hope of finding the enemy's schooner, Nancy, which was thought to be in that quarter. On the 13th instant the fleet anchored off the mouth of the river and my troops disembarked on the peninsula formed between the river and lake for the purpose of fixing a camp.

On reconnoitering the position thus taken, it was discovered that the schooner, Nancy, was drawn up in the river a few hundred yards above us under cover of a block-house erected on a commanding situation on the opposite shore.

Having landed with nothing larger than four pounders, and it being now too late in the evening to establish a battery of heavy guns, I determined on remaining silent until I could open with effect.

On the following morning a fire for a few minutes was kept up by the shipping upon the block-house, but with little effect as the direction to it only could be given, a thin wood intervening to obscure the view. About 12 o'clock, two howitzers (an eight and a half and a five and a half inch) being placed within a few hundred yards of the block-house, commenced a fire which lasted but a few minutes when the house blew up and at the same time communicated the fire to the Nancy which was quickly so enveloped in flames as to render any attempt which might have been made to save her unavailing. My first impression on seeing the explosion was that the enemy after having spiked his guns had set fire to the magazine himself, but on examination it was found to have been occasioned by the bursting of one of our shells which firing some combustible matter near the magazine gave the enemy but barely time to escape before the explosion took place. The Commodore secured and brought off the guns which were mounted within the block-house (two twenty-four pounder carronades and one long six pounder) together with some round shot, grape, and canister. The enemy will feel severely the loss of the Nancy, her cargo consisting (at the time of her being set on fire) of several hundred barrels of provisions intended as a six months' supply for the garrison at Mackinac.

Having executed (so far as my force could effect) the orders of the 2nd of June, from the Secretary of War. I left Nottawasaga on the 15th and arrived on the 21st at the mouth of the River St. Clair with my whole force, except a few soldiers of the 17th Infantry, who were left as marines on board the two small vessels which still continue to cruise on that lake.

From Captain Sinclair to the Secretary of the Navy.

ON BOARD THE UNITED STATES SLOOP NIAGARA,

ERIE, September 3, 1814.

SIR,—Immediately after the attack on Michilimackinac I despatched the Lawrence and Caledonia with orders to Lieutenant-Commandant Dexter to make all possible despatch to Lake Erie and there co-operate with our army, etc., while I shaped my course in pursuit of the enemy's force supposed to be about Nottawasaga, and I cannot but express my surprise at having passed those vessels and arrived at Erie before them. By that opportunity I informed you of my movements up to the 9th ultimo, since which time I have been fortunate enough to find His Britannic Majesty's schooner laden with provisions, clothing, etc., for the troops at Mackinac.

She was two miles up the Nottawasaga River under a block-house strongly situated on the southeast side of the river, which running nearly parallel with the bay for that distance, forms a narrow peninsula. This and the wind being off shore afforded me a good opportunity of anchoring opposite to her within good battering distance, but finding the sand hills and trees frequently interrupting my shot, I borrowed one of the howitzers from Colonel Croghan, mounted it on one of my carriages and sent it on the peninsula under command of Lieutenant Holdup. A situation was chosen by Captain Gratiot, of the Engineers, from which it did great execution. The enemy defended himself very handsomely until one of our shells burst in his block-house and in a few minutes blew up his magazine. This set fire to a train which had been laid for the destruction of the vessel and in an instant she was in flames. I had made the necessary preparation with boats for getting on board of her, but frequent and heavy explosions below made the risk of life too great to attempt saving her. She was, therefore, with her valuable cargo, entirely consumed. I cannot say whether those who defended her were blown up in the block-house or whether they retreated in rear of their work which they might have done unseen by us as it afforded a descent into a thick wood. I hope the latter. A number of articles were picked up at a considerable distance off. Among them was the commander's desk containing copies of letters, etc., several of which I enclose herein for your information. They seem to show the vessel to have been commanded by Lieutenant Worsley of the Royal Navy; of what infinite importance her cargo was to the garrison at Mackinac, and that they have nothing now afloat on this lake. The Nancy appeared to be a very fine vessel between the size of the Queen Charlotte and Lady Prevost. There were three guns on the block-house, two twenty-four pounders and one six pounder. I cannot say what was on the vessel as all her ports were closed. I also got a new boat called a gun-boat, but unworthy the name, being calculated only to mount a 24 pound carronade.

The Nottawasaga is too narrow and overhung with trees for a vessel to get up except by warping which prevented my sending boats in or Colonel Croghan from attempting to turn his rear as we saw a number of Indians skulking and occasionally firing across from the banks. It was in this way the only man we had touched was wounded.

You will see by the enclosed letters the short state they are in for provisions at Michilimackinac, and I am assured from the best authority that this is the only line of communication by which they can be supplied, that of the Grand River being rendered impassable for anything heavier than a man can carry on his back by sixty portages. I have therefore left the Scorpion and Tigress to blockade it closely until the season becomes too boisterous for boat transportation. Colonel Croghan thought it not advisable to fortify and garrison Nottawasaga as the enemy's communication from York is so short and convenient that any force he could leave there would be cut off in the winter.

I was unfortunate in getting embayed in a gale of wind on a rocky iron bound shore which occasioned the loss of all the boats I had in tow which was the captured gunboat and my launch. I felt fortunate in saving my vessel, lumbered as she was, with 450 souls on board and shipping such immense quantities of water as to give me very serious alarm for some hours. I was compelled to strike some of my guns below, and nothing saved her at last but a sudden shift of wind, as there is nothing like an anchorage in Lake Huron except in the mouths of the rivers, the whole coast being a steep perpendicular rock. I have several times been in great danger of total loss in the extremely dangerous navigation entirely unknown to our pilots except directly to Mackinac, by falling suddenly from no soundings to three fathoms and twice in a quarter less twain all a craggy rock. These dangers might be avoided from the transparency of the water, but for the continued fogs which prevail almost as constantly as on the Grand Bank.

By the arrival of the mail a few hours after I anchored at Detroit I learned the critical state of our army on the peninsula and that the Somers and Ohio had been captured. The craft from the flats with part of my guns had not yet arrived, but being certain that my presence would be necessary at the earliest possible moment, I availed myself of a fair wind and sailed for this place when I am happy to learn that our army feel secure where they are. I have, however, sent the Lawrence, Lady Prevost, and Porcupine to Buffalo, there to render any assistance which may be required and shall follow myself in the course of twenty-four hours. There is such an imminent risk of the loss of the fleet at this season of the year lying to an anchor near Buffalo where the bottom is composed entirely of sharp rock, a strong current setting down and exposed to the open lake from which the heaviest gales are experienced, that I shall not, unless positively ordered to do so from the Department, continue there a moment longer than I can ascertain the commanding general's views, and in what way I can co-operate with him. Daily and dearly bought experience teaches us that we ought not to risk our fleet in a situation where they are so liable to be lost. Lieutenant Kennedy has no doubt informed you of the total loss of the Ariel after being on float and ready to remove from there.

N.B. A company of riflemen from Sandusky has just arrived here and been forwarded on to Fort Erie without delay.

Lieutenant-General Drummond to Noah Freer.

CAMP BEFORE FORT ERIE, August 24th, 1814.

SIR,—Herewith I have the honor to transmit for the information of the Commander of the Forces, a distressing account of the only remaining vessel of any burden in our possession on Lake Huron having been destroyed with her cargo of provisions and stores for Michilimackinac at Nottawasaga.

It would appear that Lieutenant Worsley, of the Royal Navy, who was on his way to relieve Lieutenant Poyntz, and who took charge of the Nancy schooner, was under the necessity of so doing to prevent her falling into the enemy's hands, they having shown themselves with a force at the mouth of that river; Lieutenant Worsley had one seaman killed and one severely wounded, but further particulars I have not been as yet made acquainted with.

P.S. Since writing the foregoing, a letter of which the enclosed is a copy, has been handed to me by Department Commissary General Turquand, from Department Assistant Commissary General Crookshank to him under date of the 21st instant. I presume the senior officer of the Commissariat Department in this Province has duly appreciated the conduct of Mr. Crookshank, and has not failed to report the same in the most favorable point of view to the Commander of the Forces, particularly for his indefatigable and unremitting exertions in procuring and forwarding to the post of Michilimackinac every article of the various stores and provisions required of him, and through a communication, which by his personal observation and perseverance, was completed when scarcely imagined to have been commenced upon.

I feel much pleasure, therefore, in drawing to the notice of His Excellency, the name of an officer so highly deserving of commendation.

(Canadian Archives, Series C, Volume 685, page 138.)

From Lieutenant-General Drummond to Sir George Prevost.

CAMP BEFORE FORT ERIE, September 5th, 1814.

(Extract.)

I take this opportunity of acquainting you that Deputy Assistant Commissary General Crookshank still continues unremitting in his exertions to forward supplies to Michilimackinac. Three only of eleven canoes from Montreal have proceeded to the post, and the crews of the three (the others having altogether refused to proceed) he found it necessary to bribe largely for that purpose. Mr. La Mothe has returned to Montreal to procure fresh canoes. But I have directed Colonel Claus to send steady Indians without delay in charge of the remaining canoes to Michilimackinac, and as the loss of the Nancy schooner has been a very serious one indeed, I have directed as many bateaux as are necessary to be taken from York to Nottawasaga for the purpose of transport across Lake Huron.

(Canadian Archives, Series C, Volume 685, page 168.)

From Lieutenant A. H. Bulger to Lieutenant-Colonel McDouall.

MICHILIMACKINAC, 7th September, 1814.

SIR,—I have the honor to report to you the particulars of the capture of the United States schooners Scorpion and Tigress by a detachment from this garrison under the command of Lieutenant Worsley of the Royal Navy and myself.

In obedience to your orders we left Michilimackinac on the evening of the 1st instant in four boats, one of which was manned by seamen under Lieutenant Worsley, the others by a detachment of the Royal Newfoundland Regiment under myself, Lieutenants Armstrong and Radenhurst. We arrived near the Detour about sunset on the following day, but nothing was attempted that night as the enemy's position had not been correctly ascertained. The troops remained the whole day concealed among the rocks, and about six o'clock in the evening embarked and began to move towards the enemy. We had to row about six miles during which the most perfect under and silence reigned. The Indians which accompanied us from Mackinac remained about three miles in our rear. About 9 o'clock at night we discovered the enemy and had approached to within one hundred yards of them before they hailed us. On receiving no answer they opened a smart fire upon us, both of musketry and from the 24-pounder. All opposition, however, was in vain for in the course of five minutes the enemy's vessel was boarded and carried by Lieutenant Worsley and Lieutenant Armstrong on the starboardside, and my boat and Lieutenant Radenhurst on the larboard. She proved to be the Tigress commanded by Sailing Master Champlin, mounting one long 24 pounder with a complement of 30 men. The defence of this vessel did credit to her officers who were all severely wounded. She had three men wounded and three missing, supposed to have been killed and thrown immediately overboard. Our loss is two seamen killed and seven soldiers and seamen slightly wounded.

On the morning of the 4th instant the prisoners were sent in a boat to Mackinac under guard, and we prepared to attack the other schooner which we understood was anchored 15 miles further down. The position of the Tigress was not altered, and the better to carry on the deception the American pendant was kept flying. On the 5th instant we discovered the enemy's schooner beating up to us. The soldiers I directed to keep below or to lie down on the deck to avoid being seen. Everything succeeded to our wish, the enemy came to anchor about two miles from us in the night, and as the day dawned on the 6th instant we slipped our cable, ran down under our jib and foresail. Everything was so well managed by Lieutenant Worsley that we were within 10 yards of the enemy before they discovered us. It was then too late, for in the course of five minutes her deck was covered with our men and the British colors hoisted over the American. She proved to be the Scorpion, commanded by Lieutenant Turner of the United States Navy, carrying one long 24-pounder and one long 12-pounder in her hold with a complement of 32 men. She had two men killed and two wounded.

I enclose a return of our killed and wounded and am happy to say that the latter are but slight.

To the admirable good conduct and management of Lieutenant Worsley, of the Royal Navy, the success is in a great measure to be attributed, but I must assure you that every officer and man did his duty.

(Canadian Archives, Series C, Volume 685, page 172.)

Return of the killed and wounded of the troops employed in the capture of the United States schooners, the Scporion and Tigress, on the 3rd and 6th September, 1814.

Royal Artillery. One rank and file wounded.

Royal Newfoundland Regiment. One lieutenant and six rank and file wounded.

Officer wounded. Lieutenant Bulger, Royal Newfoundland Regiment, slightly.

          A. H. BULGER,
      Lieutenant Royal Newfoundland Regiment.

N.B.—Three seamen killed.

(Canadian Archives, Series C, Volume 685, page 175.)

AN EPISODE OF THE WAR OF 1812.

From Lieutenant-Colonel McDouall to Lieutenant-General Drummond.

MICHILIMACKINAC, 9th September, 1814.

SIR,—I have the honor to inform you that some Indians on their way to the falls of St. Mary's returned to me with the intelligence that part of the enemy's squadron had, on the 25th ultimo, again made their appearance in the neighborhood of St. Joseph's, likewise occupying the passage of the Detour, their intention evidently being to cut off supplies and prevent all communication with this garrison.

On the 31st I was joined by Lieutenant Worsley, of the Royal Navy, with seventeen seamen, who had passed in a canoe sufficiently near the enemy to ascertain them to be two schooner-rigged gunboats of the larger class. On stating to me his opinion that they might be attacked with every prospect of success, particularly as they were at anchor nearly five leagues asunder, I immediately determined to furnish him with the requisite assistance.

In the course of the next day, four boats were accordingly equipped, two of them with field pieces in their bows. One of them was manned by the seamen of the navy, the remaining three by a detachment of the Royal Newfoundland Regiment under Lieutenants Bulger, Armstrong, and Radenhurst, consisting of fifty men. The whole sailed the same evening under the command of Lieutenant Worsley.

I have now the satisfaction of reporting to you the complete success of the expedition, Lieutenant Worsley having returned to this place on the 7th instant with his two prizes, consisting of the United States schooners, Scorpion and Tigress, the former carrying a long 24 and a long 12-pounder, and the latter a long 24. They were commanded by Lieutenant Turner, of the American Navy, and are very fine vessels. For the particulars of their capture I beg to refer you to the enclosed statement of Lieutenant Bulger, whose conduct in aiding the execution of this enterprise (in which he was slightly wounded) reflects upon him great credit, and I beg leave to recommend him as a meritorious officer of long standing, who has been in many of the actions of this war. Lieutenants Armstrong and Radenhurst possess similar claims, and with the detachment of the brave Newfoundland Regiment, who were familiar with this kind of service, merit my entire approbation. Neither should I omit noticing the zeal displayed by Mr. Dickson and Lieutenant Livingston, of the Indian Department, who volunteered their services on this occasion.

In calling your attention to the conspicuous merit of the officer who so judiciously planned and carried into effect this well concerted enterprise, I am conscious that I only do Lieutenant Worsley a strict justice in acknowledging the eminent services which he has rendered this garrison. You are already acquainted with the unequal conflict which he sustained at the mouth of the River Nottawasaga, and the almost unprecedented defence he made of the Nancy schooner with only twenty-one seamen and a few Indians against the American squadron, and upwards of three hundred troops. Since that period he, with his gallant little band of seamen, has traversed this extensive lake in two boats laden with provisions for this garrison, and having at this extremity of it, discovered two of his former opponents his active and indefatigable mind never rested till he had relieved us from such troublesome neighbors and conducted the blockading force in triumph into our port.

Such, Sir, have been the services of Lieutenant Worsley, during the short time that he has been stationed on Lake Huron. I have to beg that you will strongly recommend him to the protection of Commodore Sir Jas. Yeo, and also to the patronage of His Excellency the Governor-General in order that my Lords Commissioners of the Admiralty may be enabled to appreciate them as they merit.

(Canadian Archives, Series C, Volume 685, page 176.)

From Lieutenant Worsley to Sir James L. Yeo.

MICHILIMACKINAC, September 15th, 1814.

SIR,—In my last despatch from the Nottawasaga River, I informed of my intention to proceed in boats to Michilimackinac. I have now the honor to report to you that I left that place, on the 18th of August, with two bateaux laden with flour for the garrison of Michilimackinac and had the good fortune to arrive on the sixth day, within 8 miles of the island of St. Joseph's, without any accident. On the 24th of August I discovered two of the enemy's schooners under sail between the islands opposite St. Joseph's, and seeing no probability of my being able to pass them in my bateaux, owing to the narrowness of the channel, I determined on concealing them in a secure place, in the choice of which I was greatly assisted by Lieutenant Livingstone, of the Indian Department, who had accompanied me in his canoe from the Nottawasaga River, and whose zeal and activity for the service I beg to acknowledge. As soon as the bateaux were hauled up and concealed, I embarked with my men in a canoe and proceeded in the night for the island of Michilimackinac with the intention of applying to Lieutenant-Colonel

McDouall for assistance in men to attempt cutting out the enemy's vessels. I had the good fortune to pass them unobserved on the night of the 29th of August, and of satisfactorily observing their position and force. I reached the island of Michilimackinac at sunset on the following day, and made known my intentions and wishes to Lieutenant-Colonel McDouall, who immediately granted all the assistance I asked for. A detachment of the Royal Newfoundland Regiment, under Lieutenant Bulger, was nominated to accompany me on that service with which, and my own seamen, I manned four bateaux. In one of which I placed a six-pounder, and in the second a three-pounder, which boat I gave the command of to Lieutenant Bulger. On the 1st of September, I left Michilimackinac and arrived near the Detour, distant from thence 36 miles, on the following evening.

In consequence of it having been reported that the enemy had several canoes of Indians with them as a precautionary measure, I acceded to Lieutenant-Colonel McDouall's wishes that a select body of Indian warriors should accompany the expedition, and I feel under great obligation to Mr. Dickson, the head of the Indian Department (who volunteered his services to head them), for the good order and regularity they observed the whole time. On the 3rd instant I went in a canoe for the purpose of reconnoitering the enemy's position, being fearful they might have shifted it during my absence, leaving the boats concealed in a small bay. Being only able to see one of the enemy's schooners which was anchored about 6 miles from us and in mid-channel of the Detour, I conceived it prudent to wait for the cover of night. At 6 p.m. I embarked in my boats and proceeded towards the Detour. The night being favorable, we had approached within ten yards of the enemy's schooner before they hailed us, but before we had time to get alongside, they fired their gun, which providentially missed us, and at the same time opened a smart fire with their small arms with very little effect. We soon got alongside and gained the deck where the contest was short, the enemy being driven below from whence, however, they fired several muskets, which unfortunately killed one of my seamen. She proved to be the United States schooner, Tigress, mounting one long 24-pounder with a complement of 31 men and officers, commanded by Sailing Master Champlin, who, with the rest of his officers, was severely wounded. Their loss was four wounded, one killed and three missing, reported to have been killed and thrown overboard. Our loss in this affair was trifling, having had two seamen killed, Lieutenant Bulger and seven soldiers wounded. Early in the morning of the 4th instant I despatched the prisoners under guard to Michilimackinac and prepared to attack the enemy's other vessel, whcih I understood was anchored some distance from me among the islands. I despatched Lieutenant Livingston in his canoe to look out, who, in two hours, returned and informed me that the enemy's schooner was beating up to me. As I knew from the distance she must have been off that they could not have heard the firing, and consequently must have been ignorant of her consort's having been captured. I determined not to alter the position of the Tigress, but to keep the American pendant still flying. This I did, being aware that if she once had a suspicion of my being an enemy she would escape from her superior sailing. Everything succeeded to my wishes. Unsuspicious of what had taken place, she anchored within two miles of me in the course of the night of the 5th instant I slipped my cable and ran down under my jib and foresail, keeping ten or twelve men on deck, the rest being in the hold or cabin, excepting a few soldiers whom I had covered up with great coats, etc., to prevent anything that could excite suspicion. So little were they apprehensive of our design that they were employed in washing decks, when within about twelve yards of her I fired my long 24-pounder, which was the signal for the soldiers in the hold to board. I immediately ran on board of her when the soldiers fired a volley, and boarded with the whole of my crew. She was immediately carried and the British flag hoisted over the American. She proved to be the United States schooner, Scorpion, commanded by Lieutenant Turner, mounting one long 24-pounder and one long 12-pounder in her hold, and a complement of five officers and 31 seamen. The loss of the enemy on this occasion was two killed and two wounded, that of ours, one wounded.

These vessels had been detached from the American squadron purposely to cut off all communication with Michilimackinac, and to destroy the Uorthwest trade. Several articles of private property plundered from the inhabitants of St. Mary's and St. Joseph's were found on board. They are both fine vessels, well equipped and nearly new, and in my opinion, perfectly calculated for His Majesty's service. It is a pleasing duty to me to point out to you the gallant and steady conduct of all engaged in the affair. To Lieutenants Bulger, Armstrong and Radenhurst, and the gallant detachment of the Royal Newfoundland Regiment, I am highly indebted for their cool and determined conduct which was such as has ever marked the character of that meritorious corps. The two former officers are of long standing in the service. I beg leave to recommend them to you for the information of the Commander of the Forces, for their meritorious conduct on this occasion. I herewith enclose you a list of the killed and wounded, also the dimen-

AN EPISODE OF THE WAR OF 1812. 123

sions of both schooners, which, until your pleasure is known, I have called one the Surprise and the other Confiance. I shall sail from this island for the Nottawasaga River directly. I have had the schooners surveyed and valued for the purpose of bringing up stores and provisions to this island.

(Canadian Archives, Series M, Volume 6, page 202.)

From Captain Sinclair to the Secretary of the Navy.

UNITED STATES SLOOP NIAGARA,
OFF ERIE, October 28th, 1814.

SIR,—I am under the mortifying necessity of stating to you that the report mentioned in my last letter of the vessels left in the upper lake, having been surprised and captured by the enemy, has turned out to be correct. The boatswain and four men from the Scorpion made their escape on their way to Kingston, and crossed Lake Ontario from the Bay of Quinte to the Genesee River, and from thence to this place. The man's story is a most unfavorable one, and such as I am loath to believe, true from the well known character of Lieutenant Turner. He says the blockade of Nottawasaga River was raised a short time after my departure, that the lieutenant who commanded the Nancy (and who escaped in the woods when she was destroyed), had passed up to Mackinac in boats, and it was by him and his crew they were captured. The Tigress had been separated from them five days among the islands, during which time she had been captured. They came in sight of her laying at anchor in the evening; the wind being light they anchored some distance from her without passing signals. In the morning there was only four or five men and no officer on deck. The Tigress got under way, ran down, fired into them and was on board without any report being made to Mr. Turner, nor was there an officer of any grade on deck when she was captured. The wind was light, the Scorpion had the advantage of a long 12-pounder over the other, and could have recaptured her with much ease. The Tigress had made great resistance, but was overpowered by an overwhelming force. Her commander, Sailing Master Champlin, and all her officers were wounded, as were many of her men, and some killed. I had given Lieutenant Turner a picked crew from this vessel with my sailing master, and had added to both their crews, 25 chosen men, borrowed from Colonel Croghan to act as marines, I had also left him a boarding netting, indeed, there was no precaution I did not take in anticipation of every effort. I knew the enemy would make to regain their line of communication on which their very existence depended.

I herewith enclose you my instructions to Lieutenant Turner, After which I cannot express to you, Sir, my chagrin at the little regard which appears to have been paid to them, and the evil consequences growing out of such neglect, consequences, but too well known to you and to the government. You must first believe the infinite interest I had taken in the expedition from the moment I had been entrusted with the conducting it, and the sanguine hope I had formed of its complete success, and the benefits resulting from it to my country to enable you to form an adequate idea of the mortification I now experience.

From Niles' Register, Volume VII, page 173.

ERIE, November 11th, 1814.

Arrived on Sunday last the cartel schooner Union, R. Martin, master, 16 days from Mackinaw, and 3 days from Detroit, with furs and peltry, the property of J. J. Astor. Besides several other passengers, came Sailing Master Champlin, Commander of the Tigress, who, we are happy to learn, is now in a fair way of recovering from the wounds he received in gallantly defending his vessel. Lieutenant Turner and most of the officers and men of the captured schooners have been sent to Quebec. Lieutenant Worsley was at the head of the expedition sent against the Scorpion and Tigress. After the block-house and Nancy were blown up at Nottawasaga, he coasted round from that place in boats and canoes with 22 men, and arrived safe at Mackinaw. He immediately applied to Lieutenant-Colonel McDowell for 100 of the Newfoundland Regiment (mostly fishermen), and said he would bring the two American schooners. Unfortunately he succeeded.

The Union was detained at Mackinaw 38 days until the schooners made a trip to Nottawasaga and returned with provisions. During this time her crew were closely watched. The commanding officer placed sentinels over the vessel, who were permitted to plunder with impunity. When Mr. Champlin and the seamen, all paroled prisoners, were put on board the Union, Lieutenant-Colonel McDowell refused to order on board any provisions, saying he supposed Mr. Astor had a sufficiency.

The passengers from Mackinaw speak in high terms of the humane and gentlemanly conduct of Mr. Robert Dickson; at the same time they depict the conduct of Lieutenant-Colonel McDowell as illiberal, rascally and contemptible. The principal agent of Mr. Astor says that

Lieutenant-Colonel McDowell is unquestionably the greatest savage he saw on the island.

Result of proceedings, and the opinion of a Court of Inquiry, held on board the United States ship Independence, in Boston harbor, by order of the Secretary of the Navy, to investigate the loss, by capture, of the United States schooners Scorpion and Tigress, while under the command of Lieutenant Daniel Turner, of the United States Navy, on Lake Huron, in the month of September, 1814.

All the evidence being thus closed, the Court proceeded to deliberate on the testimony adduced, and having fully considered the same, came to the following result:

That the Scorpion, under the command of Lieutenant Turner, and the Tigress, under the command of Sailing Master (now Lieutenant) Champlin were left on the 16th of August last, in Gloucester Bay, by Commodore Sinclair, to blockade Nottawasaga River; that the Scorpion had thirty men, including her officers and mounted one 24-pounder, and although there was a 12-pounder on board, its carriage had been so much disabled as to render it useless, and Lieutenant Turner had not the means of repairing it. It is in evidence, and fully proved, that the Scorpion had no boarding netting, and that she was deficient in spare cordage; that she had no signals, and that her crew was composed of men of the most ordinary class.

The Court find that the Tigress had twenty-eight men, officers included, and mounted one 24-pounder, that she had neither boarding nettings nor signals, and was deficient in cordage. It does not, however, appear that the armament of these schooners was deficient except in pistols.

The Court are of the opinion that inasmuch as no anchorage was found in Gloucester Bay, and it having become dangerous to remain there any longer from the severity of the gales which were increasing, Lieutenant Turner was perfectly justified in raising the blockade of Nottawasaga River and proceeding to St. Joseph's, that the positions taken by him while at St. Joseph's, and in the neighborhood of French River, were well calculated to annoy the enemy in his line of communication with Mackinac.

The Court find that after Lieutenant Turner had proceeded to cruise off French River on the night of the 3rd of September last, the Tigress was attacked by the enemy in five large boats (one of them mounting a 6-pounder and another a 3-pounder), and by about nineteen canoes, carrying about 300 sailors, soldiers, and Indians, under the command of an English naval officer; that owing to the extreme darkness of the night the enemy were not perceived until they were close on board, nor were they then discovered except by the sound of their oars.

After they were discovered every exertion was made by Lieutenant Champlin, his officers and men to defend his schooner that bravery and skill could suggest, and not until all the officers were cut down, did the overwhelming numbers of the enemy prevail. The enemy having thus captured the Tigress and having mounted on her their 6 and 3-pounders, and having placed on board a complement of between seventy and one hundred men, remained at St. Joseph's until the 5th of September. On the evening of that day the Court find that the Scorpion returned from cruising off French River, and came to an anchor within five miles of the Tigress without any information having been received or suspicion entertained by Lieutenant Turner of her capture. At the dawn of the next day, it appears that the gunner having charge of the watch, passed word to the sailing master that the Tigress was bearing down under American colors. In a few minutes after she ran alongside the Scorpion, fired, boarded, and carried her.

It appears to the Court that the loss of the Scorpion is in a great measure to be attributed to the want of signals, and owing to this deficiency no suspicions were excited as to the character of the Tigress, and from some of the English officers and men on board her being dressed in the clothing of her former officers and men, and the remainder of her crew being concealed, a surprise was effected which precluded the possibility of defence.

The Court are therefore of opinion from the whole testimony that the conduct of Lieutenant Turner was that of a discreet and vigilant officer.

WM. C. AYLWIN, JOHN SHAW,
Judge Advocate. President.
Approved,
B. W. CROWNINSHIELD.

(From Niles' Register, Volume VIII, pages 403-4.)

VIII.

REGISTER OF BAPTISMS, MARRIAGES, AND DEATHS, AT ST. THOMAS, U.C., COMMENCING WITH THE ESTABLISHMENT OF THE MISSION IN JULY, 1824.

This Register is presented to the Mission of St. Thomas by the Reverend A. Mackintosh, its First Missionary.

Register of St. Thomas, 1824.
Alexander Mackintosh,
Rector and Missionary.

Baptism.

St. Thomas, 25th July, 1824—Mary Ann, infant daughter of James Hepburn and Margaret, his wife, Southwold, was baptized by me, this day, by public baptism. Ann Mitchell, Margaret Hepburn, Thomas Ryal, Sponsors.

Marriage.

St. Thomas, 25th July, 1824—Benjamin Petit and Lydia Johnson, both of Southwold, were married by me, this day, by banns. Witnesses —Thomas Talbot, John Warren, Josiah C. Goodhul, Bela Shaw.

Burial.

St. Thomas, 31st July, 1824—Maria Moorehouse, a native of , aged 3 years, was interred by me, this day.

Baptism.

St. Thomas, 1st August, 1824—Thomas, infant son of Phinehas Drake, and Emily, his wife, Yarmouth, was baptised by me, this day, by public baptism. Richard C. Drake, Richard D. Drake, Mary Spades, Sponsors.

Marriage.

St. Thomas, 2nd August, 1824—Samuel Horton, of Southwold, and Catharine Gozorte, of London, were married by me, this day, by banns. Witnesses—John Rolph, Bryant Wade, Abraham Youngs.

Baptism.

St. Thomas, 8th August, 1824—Mary Lawrence, daughter of Daniel Rapelje, and Elizabeth, his wife, Yarmouth, was baptised by me, this day, by public baptism. George Lawrence, Mary Lawrence, Elizabeth Rapelje, Sponsors.

Baptisms.

St. Thomas, 8th August, 1824—Robert, Walter and Mary Ann, children of Benjamin Wilson, and Sarah, his wife, were baptised by me, this day, by public baptism. Daniel Rapelje, George Lawrence, Mary Lawrence, Sponsors.

Burial.

St. Thomas, 20th August, 1824—Alexander Mackintosh, of Mallahide, aged ——, was interred by me, this day.

Marriage.

St. Thomas, 4th September, 1824—James McNaims and Charlotte Schram, both of Western, were married by me, this day, by banns. Witnesses—Mary Dingman, Henry Haigler, Leonard Loomis.

Baptisms.

St. Thomas, 4th September, 1824—Henry B. and Frances Eliza, children of John Bostwick, Esq., and Polly, his wife, Yarmouth, were baptised by me at Vittoria, on 29th August, by public baptism. Joseph Ryerson, Hetty Ryerson, George Ryerson, Hetty Williams, Sponsors.

Baptism.

St. Thomas, 4th September, 1824—Frances Mary, infant daughter of George J. Ryerson, and Sarah, his wife, was baptised by me, at Vittoria, on 29th August, by public baptism. George C. Salmon, Mrs. Rolph, Mrs. Salmon, Sponsors.

Baptism.

St. Thomas, 4th September, 1824—Henry James, infant son of John B. Askin and Elizabeth, his wife, was baptised by me, at Woodhouse, on 31st August, by public baptism. James Hamilton, John B. Muirhead, Cynthia Van Allen, Sponsors.

VITAL STATISTICS AT ST. THOMAS, U.C., COMMENCING 1824.

Baptism.

St. Thomas, 22nd August, 1824—Sarah Jane, infant daughter of James Mitchell and Jane, his wife, Southwold, was baptised, this day, by me, by public baptism. John Mitchell, Ann Mitchell, Sponsors.

Marriage.

St. Thomas, 5th September, 1824—Finlay Grant, of Yarmouth, and Hannah Cheyna, of Westminister, were married by me, this day, by banns. Witnesses—James Hamilton, Bela Shaw, Henry Warren.

Marriage.

St. Thomas, 6th September, 1824—John Evans and Sidney Willoughby, both of London, U.C., were married by me, this day, by banns. Witnesses—Ezekiel Evans, James Little, Michael Murphy.

Baptism.

September 8th, 1824—Sarah Ann, infant daughter of Stephen Backus, and Ann, his wife, Dunwich, was this day baptised by me, by public baptism. Wm. Pearce, Frances Pearce, Catherine Pearce, Sponsors.

Baptism.

8th September, 1824—Mary Ann, infant daughter of John Miles Farland, and Martha, his wife, Dunwich, was this day baptised by me, by public baptism. Lesslie Patterson, Lydia Patterson, Maria Dobbyn, Sponsors.

Baptism.

9th September, 1824—Philip, infant son of George Henry, and Mary, his wife, Dunwich, was this day baptised by me, by public baptism. Walter Story, Joseph Patterson, Mary Story, Sponsors.

Baptisms.

9th September, 1824—William, Mary Ann, Robert, David, Henry, children of Thomas Ford and Altha, his wife, Aldborough, were baptised this day, by me, by public baptism. Thomas Ford, Altha Ford, Sponsors.

Baptisms.

9th September, 1824—Archibald, Duncan, Malcolm, children of Duncan Stewart, and Mary, his wife, Aldboro', were baptised this day, by me, by public baptism. Duncan Stewart, Mary Stewart, Sponsors.

Baptisms.

10th September, 1824—John, Sarah, Sussanah, children of Matthew Stewart ,and Anna, his wife, Orford, W.D., were this day baptised by me, by public baptism. Lesslie Patterson, Lydia Patterson, Sarah Stewart, Sponsors.

Baptism.

10th September, 1824—Alexander, infant son of Robert Stewart, and Marjory, his wife, Orford, W.D., was this day baptised by me, by public baptism. Robert Stewart, Marjory Stewart, Sponsors.

Baptisms.

10th September, 1824—John, Martha, Levi, Richard, children of Freeman Green, and Elizabeth, his wife, Howard, W.D., were this day baptised by me, by public baptism. Freeman Green, Elizabeth Green, Sponsors.

Baptism.

10th September, 1824—Lovel Harrison, an adult, Howard, W.D., was this day baptised by me, by public baptism.

Baptisms.

10th September, 1824—John, Sophia, George, Jane, children of John Parker, and Sarah, his wife, Howard, W.D., were this day baptised by me, by public baptism. Thomas Gardiner, Harriet Parker, Jno. Parker, Sponsors.

Baptism.

12th September, 1824—Clara, infant daughter of William Smith, and Ann, his wife, was this day baptised by me, by public baptism, at Chatham, W.D. Phillis Eberts, Ann Smith, George Kerby, Sponsors.

Baptism.

12th September, 1824— ———, infant son of Peter Traxler, and Rebecca, his wife, Chatham, W.D., was this day baptised by me, by public baptism. Peter Traxler, Jno. Pepte Courtney, Margaret Traxler, Sponsors.

Baptism.

13th September, 1824—Michael, son of John Courtnay, and Christian, his wife, Chatham, W.D., was this day baptised by me, by public baptism. Peter Traxler, Michael Traxler, Madeline Traxler, Sponsors.

Baptisms.

14th September, 1824—Elizabeth, Mary, Nancy, adults, daughters of Joshua Cornwall, Camden, W.D., the first two by Mary, his first wife, and the third by Catherine, his present wife, were this day baptised by me, by public baptism.

Marriage.

St. Thomas, 20th September, 1824—Walter Chase and Ann Secord, both of Yarmouth, were married by me, this day, by banns. Witnesses— Michael McCormick, Stephen Secord, Hannah Merril, David Secord.

Marraiage.

St. Thomas, 22nd September, 1824—Stephen Landan, of Burford, and Anna Sutton, of Westminster, were married by me, this day, by banns. Witnesses—Thomas Evans, Charity Patterson, William Sutton.

Burial.

24th September, 1824—Isaac Copeland, a native of Ireland, was this day interred by me.

Baptism.

26th September, 1824—Thomas, infant son of Charles Golden, and Ann, his wife, was this day baptised by me, by public baptism, in London. Joseph Sifton, Catherine Sifton, Helen Shoebottom, Sponsors.

Baptisms.

26th September, 1824—Mary Ann and Margaret, Children of John Gray, and Mary, his wife, London, were this day baptised by me, by public baptism. William Geary, Eliza Geary, Mary Geary, Sponsors.

Baptisms.

26th September, 1824—Henry and Rebecca, children of Stephen Powell, and Esther, his wife, were this day baptised by me, by public baptism, in London. Stephen Powell, Leonard and John Ardiel Rebecca and Sarah Ardiel, Sponsors.

Baptism.

26th September, 1824—William Nelson, infant son of William Haskett, and Mary, his wife, London, was this day baptised by me, by public baptism. Robert Harden, Mary Haskett, William Geary, Sponsors.

Baptism.

26th September, 1824—Charles, infant son of Charles Sifton, and Esther, his wife, London, was this day baptised by me, by public baptism. James Golden, Eliza Talbot, C. Sifton, Sponsors.

Baptism.

26th September, 1824—John, infant son of John Ardiel, and Lary, his wife, London, was baptised by me, this day, by public baptism. William Fitzgerald, John Ardiel, Mary Ardiel, Sponsors.

Baptism.

26th September, 1824—Robert, infant son of John Turner, and Margaret, his wife, London, was this day baptised by me, by public baptism. Wm. Guess, John Turner, Ellen Guess, Sponsors.

Baptisms.

26th September, 1824—The following children were baptised by me, this day, by public baptism, in London, as underneath, viz:—

James, infant son of Jacob Fralick, of London, and Anne, his wife. Charles Sifton, Esther Sifton, Jacob Fralick, Sponsors.

Benjamin, infant son of Francis Lewis, of London, and Sarah, his wife. Stephen Powell, Francis Lewis, Esther Powell, Sponsors.

Thomas, infant son of Samuel Howard, and Ann, his wife, of London. Frederick Fitzgerald, S. Howard, Ann Howard, Sponsors.

Richard and William, children of John Hayes, of London, and Mary, his wife. Charles Golden, Margaret Shoebottom, Ann Golden, John Shoebottom, Sponsors.

John, infant son of Robert Rolph, of London, and Elizabeth, his wife. John Geary, R. Rolph, Sarah Geary, Sponsors.

Baptisms.

26th September, 1824—The following children were baptised by me, this day, by public baptism, in London, as underneath :—

James, infant son of James Shoebottom, of London, and Ellen, his wife. James Hayes, Francis Lewis, Mary Hayes, Sponsors.

Thomas, infant son of Thomas Harrison, of London, and Catherine, his wife. John Fralick, James Golden, Caroline Fralick, Sponsors.

Rebecca, infant daughter of Joseph O'Brien, of London, and Charlotte, his wife. John Ardiel, Jos. O'Brien, Mary Ardiel, Sponsors.

Phila, daughter of Isaiah Carter, and Desire, his wife, of London. Ann Geary, Desire Carter, George Geary, Sponsors.

Baptisms.

The following by public baptism, viz.—Lucy Ann, Ira Palmer, Lancaster, Amelia, William, George Peter, children of Ira Schoffield, Esq., of London, and Ruth, his wife. Ira Schoffield, Richard Talbot, William Gearry, Lydia Talbot, Martha Maria Schoffield, Sponsors.

Burial.

St. Thomas, 13th October, 1824—Mr. William Hambley, a native of England, aged 78, was interred by me, this day.

Marriage.

St. Thomas, 18th October, 1824—Thomas Dickison, and Elizabeth Sells, both of Southwold, were married by me, this day, by banns. Witnesses—John Dougherty, Sarah Sells, Abraham Youngs.

Marriage.

St. Thomas, 19th October, 1824—David Brooks, and Charlotte Chase, both of Mallahide, were married by me, this day, by banns. Witnesses—Daniel Brooks, Hiram Corless, Nancy Brooks.

Marriage.

St. Thomas, 20th October 1824—William Robb, and Hannah Zaviz, both of Yarmouth, were this day married by me, by banns. Witnesses—Joseph Smith, Thomas Zavitz, Robert Nelson.

Baptisms.

9th November, 1824—The following children were baptised by me this day, by public baptism, in London, as underneath:—

Ezekiel Evans, infant son of James Tennant, and Elizabeth, his wife, William Hodgson, Elizabeth Tennant, Sponsors.

—————, infant child of Joseph Hughes, and Alice, his wife. Sponsors.

—————, infant child of Henry O'Niel, and Mahaly, his wife. Sponsors.

Marriage.

St. Thomas, 15th November, 1824—John Rhodes and Abigail Secord, both of Yarmouth, were this day married by me, by banns. Witnesses—Stephen Secord, Peter Secord, Michael McCormick.

Marriage.

St. Thomas, 16th November, 1824—John Ransom Herman, and Elsa Hull, both of Westminster, were this day married, by me, by banns. Witnesses—Josiah C. Goodhue, Catherine Goodhue, Anna Hunt, J. Pattys.

Marriage.

St. Thomas, 6th December, 1824—Moses Warner and Amanda Robinson, both of Dunwich, were this day married by me, by banns. Witnesses—Oliver Warner, Lessin Robinson, Lydia Warner.

Burial.

St. Thomas, 7th December, 1824—Charles Dougherty, a native of Ireland, aged 32, was this day interred by me.

Marriage.

St. Thomas, 13th December, 1824—Isaac Trerice and Effie McGillup, both of Port Talbot, Dunwich, were this day married by me, by banns. Witnesses—Wm. Buchannan, Jacob Hunter, Col. Talbot.

Marriage.

St. Thomas, 10th January, 1825—William Russell, and Rhode Eliza Duncombe, both of St. Thomas, Yarmouth, were this day married by me, by banns. Witnesses—David Duncomb, Robert Nelson, Archd. Chisholm.

Marriage.

17th January, 1825—Peter Peer, and Nancy Birch, both of Southwold, were this day married by me, by banns. Witnesses—Abraham Young, Peter Horton, Samuel Horton.

Baptisms.

11th February, 1825—At Aldborough. The following children were baptised by me, this day, by public baptism, as underneath:—

Roger and Rebecca, children of James Dickson and Isabella, his wife. James Dickson, Isabella Dickson, Sponsors.

Elizabeth, infant daughter of James Scafe, and Eliza, his wife. James Scafe, Eliza Scafe, Sponsors.

Edmund and William, children of Edmund Mitton, and Mary, his wife. Edmund Mitton, Mary Mitton, Sponsors.

Marriage.

17th February, 1825—John Stafford and Margaret Nicolls, both of Southwold, were this day married by me, by license. Witnesses—Arthur Nicolls, John Hamilton, Caleb Stafford.

Baptism.

20th February, 1825—Ann Caroline, daughter of George D. Spades, and Mary, his wife, was this day baptised by me, by public baptism. Mary Spades, Rhoda Eliza Russell, William Russell, Sponsors.

Marriage.

2nd March, 1825—John Hunt and Charity Patterson, both of the township of Westminster, were this day married by banns. Witnesses—T. Hunt, T. Pattys, W. Hunt.

Burial.

3rd March, 1825—Jane Scaine (wife of Thomas Scaine, of Dunwich, a native of England) died 1st March, aged 59, was this day interred by me.

Marriage.

7th March, 1825—Matthew Peer, of London, and Dorothy House, of Yarmouth, were this day married by me, by banns. Witnesses—John Bostwick, Abraham House, Abraham [his X mark] House, Senr.

Marriage.

9th March, 1825—James Brown and Lydia Kipp, both of the township of Yarmouth, were this day married by me, by banns. Witnesses—Enoch Moore, Lindley Moore, Jonathan Steele, W. T. Pruynn.

Baptism.

9th March, 1825—Hannah, wife of William Robb, of Yarmouth, was this day baptised by me, by public baptism. William Robb, Robt. Nelson, Witnesses.

Baptism.

9th March, 1825—Thomas Bissland, infant son of William Robb and Hannah, his wife, of Yarmouth, was this day baptised by me, by public baptism. Robt. Nelson, William Robb, Hannah Robb, Sponsors.

Baptism.

27th March, 1825—Charlotte Augusta, daughter of John Bostwick and Polly, his wife, of Yarmouth, was this day baptised by me, by public baptism. Joseph Smith, Hannah Smith, Hetty Williams, Sponsors.

Baptism.

27th March, 1825—Sarah Ann, daughter of Thomas Zavitz, of Yarmouth, and Mary, his wife, was this day baptised by me, by public baptism. William Robb, Hannah Robb, Mary Zavitz, Sponsors.

Baptism.

27th March, 1825—Henry, son of Edmund Morgan of Yarmouth, and Catherine, his wife, was this day baptised by me, by public baptism. Joseph Smith, Hannah Smith, Edmund Morgan, Sponsors.

Baptism.

27th March, 1825—Allan and William, sons of Ewen Cameron, of Southwold, and Ellen, his wife, were this day baptised by me, by public baptism. Ewen Cameron, William Chisholm, Frances Chisholm, Sponsors.

VITAL STATISTICS AT ST. THOMAS, U.C., COMMENCING 1824.   137

Baptism.

27th March, 1825—Mary Jane, daughter of William Parker, of Yarmouth, and Nancy, his wife, was this day baptised by me, by public baptism. Jarvis Thayer, Junr., Nancy Parker, Anne Parker, Sponsors.

Baptism.

27th March, 1825—Patrick and Jesse, sons of George Parker, of Yarmouth, and Hannah, his wife, were this day baptised by me, by public baptism. William Parker, Nancy Parker, Jesse Page, Betsey Page, Sponsors.

Marriage.

30th March, 1825—Abraham Miller and Mary Walters, both of Westminster, were this day married by me, by banns. Witnesses—Walter Walters, Edward [his X mark] Hunt, Anna Hunt, William Mandeville.

Marriage.

4th April, 1825—Michael Murphy, of Yarmouth, Blacksmith, and Mary McNeal, of Parmouth, spinster, were this day married by me, by license. Witnesses—Patrick Burns, Hugh McNeal, Jnd. Davis.

Marriage.

10th April, 1825—Erastus Westover, farmer, and Mary Ann Jewell, spinster, both of the Township of Mallahide, were this day married by me, by banns. Witnesses—Josiah C. Goodhue, Archibald Chisholm, George Caughell.

Baptism.

13th April, 1825—Catherine, infant daughter of William Eldridge and Amy, his wife, was this day baptised by me, by private baptism. The Mother, Amy Eldridge, Sponsors.

Marriage.

18th April, 1825—Elijah Gregory, of Southwold, Farmer, and Ann Elizabeth, Slott, spinster, of Westminster, were this day married by me, by banns. Witnesses—William T. VanAllan, William Deeow, John Routledge.

Marriage.

20th April, 1825—David Cummings and Elizabeth House, both of the Township of Yarmouth, were this day married by me, by banns. Witnesses—Matthew House, Nancy [her X mark] House, Margaret [her X mark] House.

Baptism.

26th April, 1825—John Cockroft, infant son of John Kirkpatrick, of Windham, and Maria, his wife, born 17th January, 1825, was this day baptised by me by public baptism. R. L. Cockroft, Alexander Kirkpatrick, per proxy, J. K., Cynthia Street, per proxy, R. E. C. Sponsors.

Marriage.

2nd May, 1825—Israel Doane and Sarah Mills, both of the Township of Yarmouth, were this day married by me, by license. Witnesses—Harvy Bryant, James Canberes, Jane Sands.

Marriage.

4th May, 1825—Joseph Steinhoff and Elizabeth Van Velsor, the former of the Township of Yarmouth, and the latter of Southwold, were this day married by me, by license. Witnesses—William Vanvelsor, William Decow, Sally McIntyre.

Marriage.

9th May, 1825—Orrin Ladd and Lucinda Young, both of the Township of Dunwich, were this day married by me, by banns. Witnesses—James Young, Jefferson Blake, Miriam Wiley.

Baptism.

15th May, 1825—Lydia, infant daughter of Lesslie Paterson, Esq., of Dunwich, and Lydia, his wife, was this day baptised by me, by public baptism. Sarah Stewart, Catherine Pearce, Lesslie Pearce, Sponsors.

Baptism.

15th May, 1825—Henry, infant son of Richard Dobbins, of Dunwich, and Maria, his wife, was this day baptised by me, by public baptism. Thomas Moorhouse, Richard Dobbins, Maria Dobbins, Sponsors.

VITAL STATISTICS AT ST. THOMAS, U.C., COMMENCING 1824. 139

Baptism.

15th May, 1825—Elizabeth Ann, infant daughter of Gregory Bobier, of Dunwich, and Sarah, his wife, was this day baptised by me, by public baptism. Margaret Bobier, Sarah Bobier, Gregory Bobier, Sponsors.

Baptism.

15th May, 1825—Alexander George, infant son of George Crane, of Dunwich, and Isabella, his wife, was this day baptised by me, by public baptism. William Crane, George Crane, Isabella Crane, Sponsors.

Marriage.

22nd May, 1825—Samuel Harper, of Mallahide, farmer, and Mira Hay, of Mallahide, spinster, were this day married by me, by banns. Witnesses—Caleb Burdich, Jacob Hoffman, Cornelius Bowen.

Baptism.

24th May, 1825—Alexander, infant son of Duncan McKenzie, of London, and Margaret, his wife, was this day baptised by me, by public baptism, in London. Duncan McKenzie, Thomas Laurieson, Margaret McKenzie, Sponsors.

Baptisms.

24th May, 1825—Robert and Elizabeth, children of George Rutledge, of London, and Jane, his wife, were this day baptised by me, by public baptism, in London. Thomas Rutledge, William Armstrong, Elizabeth Sommers, Mary Sommers, Sponsors.

Baptisms.

24th May, 1825—William and Deborah, children of John Turner, and Margaret, his wife, of London, were this day baptised by me, by public baptism, in London. John Turner, Margaret Turner, William Gerry, Elizabeth Gerry, Sponsors.

Baptism.

24th May, 1825—Mary Jane, infant daughter of James Shoebottom, and Helen, his wife, was this day baptised by me, by public baptism, in London. Jas. Shoebottom, Helen Shoebottom, Rebecca Sifton, Sponsors.

Baptism.

24th May, 1825—Margaret Ann, infant daughter of Leonard Ardiel and Rebecca, his wife, was this day baptised by me, by public baptism, in London. Jas. Fitzgerald, Leonard Ardiel, Rebecca Ardiel, Sponsors.

Baptism.

24th May 1825—William Lewis, infant son of John Macleod, of London, and Elizabeth, his wife, was this day baptised by me, by public baptism, in London. John Gray, John McLeod, Eliza McLeod, Sponsors.

Baptism.

24th May, 1825—Jane, infant daughter of Felix McLaughlin and Jane, his wife, of London, was this day baptised by me, by public baptism, in London, John Gerry, Sarah Gerry, Jane McLaughlin, Sponsors.

Baptism.

24th May, 1825—Mary, infant daughter of George Carter, of London, and Desire, his wife, was this day baptised by me, by public baptism, in London. George Carter, Ann Gerry, Elizabeth Gerry, Sponsors.

Baptism.

18th June, 1825—Benjamin Wilson, of Yarmouth, adult, was this day baptised by me, by public baptism. George Crane, Sarah Wilson, Witnesses.

Marriage.

23rd June, 1825—Samuel Guernsey, of Southwold, widower, and Rhoda Duncombe, of St. Thomas, widow, were this day married by me, by banns. Witnesses—E. E. Duncombe, Archibald Chisholm, Samuel Garnsey.

Marriage.

23rd June, 1825—Timothy Burwell, of Southwold, yeoman, and Margaret Wallace, of the same township, spinster, were this day married by me, by banns. Witnesses—John Wallace, Alexa Moore, John Burwell, Anna [her X mark] Burwell.

On Sunday, the 19th of June, the Sacrament of the Lord's Supper was administered in the Church of St. Thomas (for the first time) by the Honorable and Reverend Dr. Stewart, assisted by the Reverend A. M. ——————. Number of communicants 12.

On Tuesday, the 21st of June, the Sacrament of the Lord's Supper was administered in the House of Lesslie Patterson, Esq., of Dunwich, by the Honorable and Reverend Dr. Stewart, assisted by the Reverend A. M. ——————. Number of communicants 39.

Baptism.

21st June, 1825—Stephen, infant son of Stephen Backus, of Dunwich and Anne, his wife, was this day baptised by me, by public baptism, in Dunwich. Walter Story, Lesslie Pearce, Sarah Stewart, Sponsors.

Marriage.

3rd July, 1825—John Delorier, of Mallahide, Carpenter, and Lucinda Loucks, of the same township, spinster, were this day married by me, by banns. Witnesses—John Graves, Jacob Hoffman, N. B. Millard.

Marriage.

4th July, 1825—Ambrose Tyrrel, of the Township of Mallahide, yeoman, and Catherine Clarke, of the same township, spinster, were this day married by me, by banns. Witnesses—Benjamin Clark, Enos Call, John Nickel.

Marriage.

10th July, 1825—Joshua Chapel and Maria Vanalstine, both of Yarmouth, were this day married by me, by banns. Witnesses—Archibald Chisholme, Joseph Lyons, John Ellwood, Mercy Lyons.

Baptism.

10th July, 1825—James, infant son of John Scatcherd, of Missouri, and Ann, his wife, was this day baptised by me, by public baptism, in Southwold. John Scatcherd, Ann Scatcherd, Sponsors.

Baptism.

17th July, 1825—George, infant son of Josiah C. Goodhue, of St. Thomas, and Catherine, his wife, born 2nd April last, was this day baptised by me by public baptism. George I. Goodhue, Lucius Bigelow, Elizabeth Mitchell, per proxy, Mrs. Shaw, Sponsors.

Marriage.

20th August, 1825—Benajah Brown, of the Township of Walsingham, merchant, and Elizabeth Partlo, of Mallahide, spinster, were this day married by me, by license. Witnesses—Stephen Randal, A. H. Burwell, Ely Brown.

Marriage.

12th September, 1825—Jefferson Blake, of the Township of Dunwich, yoeman, and Miriam Willey, of the same place, spinster, were this day married by me, by banns. Witnesses—Lemuel Ladd, Orrin Ladd, Glbt. Young.

Marriage.

13th October, 1825—Alvaro Ladd, of the Township of Westminster, merchant, and Nancy Shotwell, of the same township, spinster, were this day married by me by banns. Witnesses—Jefferson Blake, Henry Scheneck, L. Ladd, Michael McLaughlan.

Marriage.

17th October, 1825—Thomas Williams, of the Township of Southwold, yeoman, and Martha White, of the same township, spinster, were this day married by me, by banns. Witnesses—William White, Samuel Garnsey, George Harvey.

Marriage.

17th October, 1825—James Peppin, of the Township of Yarmouth, shoemaker, and Hannah Strawn, of the same township, spinster, were this day married by me, by banns. Witnesses—Abner Strawn, Elijah Osborn, Daniel W. Stockton.

Marriage.

6th November, 1825—Peter Graves, of the Township of Southwold, shoemaker, and Mary Mann, of Yarmouth, spinster, were this day married by me, by banns. Witnesses—J. Nevills, John Marlatt, Lymon Mann.

Burial.

9th November, 1825—Matthew Stewart, of Orford, aged 30, was this day buried by me, in Dunwich.

Marriage.

10th November, 1825—Joseph Atwood, of Mallahide, farmer, and Mary Smith, of the same township, spinster, were this day married by me, by banns. Witnesses—Ira Whitcomb, John [his X mark] Rokes, Ira [his X mark] Atwood.

Burial.

28th October, 1825—Abigail, wife of John Rhodes, of Yarmouth, was this day interred in the Churchyard of St. Thomas.

Baptism.

13th November, 1825—Henry Lesslie, infant son of John Miles Farland, of Dunwich, and Martha, his wife, was this day baptised by me, by public baptism. Lesslie Paterson, Wm Buchanan, Lydia Paterson, Sponsors.

Baptism.

13th November, 1825—Annabella, infant daughter of William Buchanan, of Dunwich, and Annabella, his wife, was this day baptised by me, by public baptism. John M. Farland, Catherine Pearce, Annabella Buchanan, Sponsors.

Marriage.

28th November, 1825—John Elliott, of Carradoc, yeoman, and Dorothy Bateman, of the same township, spinster, were this day married by me, by banns. Witnesses—Stephen Randal, William Bateman, Jane Elliott.

Marriage.

7th December, 1825—William Decow, of Southwold, Yeoman, and Sarah McIntyre, of the same township, spinster, were this day married by me, by banns. Witnesses—Henry Hamilton, Samuel Garnsey, William Tanelson.

Marriage.

15th December, 1825—Isaac Culver and Jane Little, both of Yarmouth, were this day married by me, by banns. Witnesses—William J. Collver, James Stokes, John Learn.

Burial.

12th December, 1825—Eleanor Drake, daughter of William Drake, of Yarmouth, aged 13 years, died on 11th inst., and was buried by me, this day in the Churchyard of St. Thomas.

Burial.

13th December, 1825—Richard Ellison, of Southwold, farmer, aged 24 years, died on 11th inst., and was this day buried by me, in Southwold.

Marriage.

15th December, 1825—Philip Kilmore, of Mallahide, farmer, and Hannah Kilmore, of the same township, spinster, were this day married by me, by banns. Witnesses—Philip Kilmore, Martha [her X mark] Kilmore, John Rokes.

Burial.

18th December, 1825—Sarah, wife of Adam Burwell, of Southwold, aged 69 years, died on 16th inst., and was this day interred by me, in the Churchyard of St. Thomas. She was mother to Colonel Burwell of Port Talbot.

Marriage.

21st December, 1825—Harvey Kipp, of Yarmouth, farmer, and Susan Macklem, of the same township, spinster, were this day married by me, by banns. Witnesses—T. Itell, Jane Doan, Hiram Kipp.

Marriage.

21st December, 1825—Hiram Kipp, of Yarmouth, farmer, and Sarah Harvey, of the same township, spinster, were this day married by me, by banns. Witnesses—T. Itell, Jane Doan, Harvey Kipp.

Baptism.

20th December, 1825—Ann Melissa (aged 2 years and 3 1-2 months), daughter of Richard D. Drake, of Southwold, and Elizabeth, his wife, was this day baptised by me, by private baptism. Margaret Drake, Elizabeth Drake, Richard D. Drake, Sponsors.

Marriage.

25th December, 1825—Jarvis Thayer, of Yarmouth, farmer, and Nancy Parker, of the same township, spinster, were this day married by me, by banns. Witnesses—William Parker, Nahum P. Thayer, Charles McGaw.

Marriage.

28th December, 1825—Abraham Backhouse, of Mallahide, yeoman, and Amelia Alway, of Yarmouth, spinster, were this day married by me by banns. Witnesses—William Alway, John Backhouse, Robt. Alway.

Marriage.

24th January, 1826—John Campbell, of Eckfrid, farmer, and Jane Elliott, of Carradoc, spinster, were this day married by me by license. Witnesses—Malcolm Campbell, Joseph Elliott, George Elliott.

Marriage.

26th January, 1826—George Mitchell, of Southwold, yeoman, and Margaret Mitchell, of the same township, spinster, were this day married by me, by license. Witnesses—John Mitchell, John Elliot, Samuel Glass, Thomas Ryal, Barbara Mackintosh.

Baptisms.

26th January, 1826—Catherine Amelia, infant daughter of James Hamilton, Esq., of Southwold, and Catherine Jane, his wife, born 15th August, 1825, was this day baptised by me, by public baptism. Mary Waddel as proxy for Amelia Jackson, Eliza Warren as proxy for Jane Grant, Edmund Edward Warren, Sponsors.

Baptism.

Henry, infant son of James Hamilton, Esq., of Southwold, and Catherine Jane, his wife, born 15th August, 1825, was this day baptised by me by public baptism. John Warren, John Waddel as proxy for James B. Ewart, Catherine Goodhue as proxy for Maria L. Hamilton, Sponsors.

Baptism.

26th January, 1826—Amelia Maria, infant daughter of John Waddel, of Southwold, and Mary, his wife, was this day baptised by me, by public baptism. Catherine Jane Hamilton, Eliza Warren, as proxy for Henry B. Warren, Sponsors.

Marriage.

31st January, 1826—Montgomery Smith, of Dunwich, yeoman, and Elizabeth Watson, of Southwold, spinster, were this day married by me, by banns. Witnesses—Allen Watson, Thomas Williams, John Gibson, John Barber.

Marriage.

31st January, 1826—Henry Hamilton, of Southwold, yeoman, and Ruth Lumley, of Dunwich, spinster, were this day married by me, by banns. Witnesses—Thomas Lumley, John Gibson, Thomas Williams, John Rokes, Lewis Freeman.

Marriage.

14th February, 1826—Patten Atwood, of Dunwich, yeoman, and Anna Brookes, of the same township, spinster, were this day married by me, by banns. Witnesses—A. H. Burwell, O. Warner, M. E. Smith.

Marriage.

15th February, 1826—John W. Beemer, of Mallahide, yeoman, and Mary McKenney, of the same township, spinster, were this day married by me, by license. Witnesses—Matthew McKenney, Abram Beemer, R. W. Paddleford, Daniel Davis.

Marriage.

16th February, 1826—Samuel Glass, of Westminster, yeoman, and Eliza Owray, of the same township, spinster, were this day married by me by banns. Witnesses—James Little, Samuel Smith, James Williams, William Orr.

Marriage.

St. Thomas, 19th February, 1826—John Dean, of Dearham, yeoman, and Mary Ann Jones, of Bayham, spinster, were this day married by me, by banns. Witnesses—Stephen Randal, Lambert Jones, David Cascadden.

Marriage.

23rd February, 1826—John Spitler, of Southwold, yeoman, and Sarah Ann Steinhoff, of the same township, spinster, were this day married by me, by banns. Witnesses—James McAffee, Thomas Petit, John Ebenly.

Marriage.

2nd March, 1826—Daniel Bowlby, of Southwold, yeoman, and Sarah Herrot, of Mallahide, spinster, were this day married by me, by liense. Witnesses—John Boughner, Samuel Smith, Charles Hannan.

Marriage.

St. Thomas, 7th March, 1826—Isaac Bowlby, of Southwold, yeoman, and Hannah Boughner, of the same township, spinster, were this day married by me, by banns. Witnesses—A. H. Burwell, Garret Smith, Charles Hannan.

Marriage.

8th March, 1826—Oliver Warner and Irene Attwood, both of the Township of Dunwich, were this day married by me, by banns. Witnesses—Jefferson Blake, Duncan McGregor, Patten Attwood, Trueman Waters.

Burial.

24th March, 1826—William Hutchinson, Esq., aged 86, a half pay Revolutionary Captain, died 20th inst., and was this day interred by me in Walsingham.

Baptism.

26th March, 1826—John, infant son of Thomas Ryal, of Yarmouth, and Rachel, his wife, was this day baptised by me, by public baptism. James Mitchell, Thomas Ryall, Jane Mitchell, Sponsors.

Baptism.

St. Thomas, 26th March, 1826—John, infant son of James Mitchell, and Jane, his wife, was this day baptised by me, by public baptism. James Mitchell, Thomas Ryall, Rachel Ryall, Sponsors.

Baptisms.

26th March, 1826—Eliza Ann and Maria, children of James Fitzsimmons and Margaret, his wife (Roman Catholics), were this day baptised by me, by public baptism. William Ryall, Ann Mitchell, Margaret Fitzsimmons, Sponsors.

Baptism.

11th April, 1826—Isaac Newton, infant son of Thomas Dickison, of Southwold, Cooper, and Elizabeth, his wife, was this day baptised by me, by public baptism. Thomas Dickison, Elizabeth Dickison, Sponsors.

Baptisms.

11th April, 1826—John Fletcher, and Mary Ann, children of Joseph Little, of Southwold, yeoman, and Jane, his wife, were this day baptised by me, by public baptism. John Fletcher, Joseph Little, Jane Little, Sponsors.

Baptisms.

St. Thomas, 11th April, 1826—William Augustus and Mary Ellen, children of the late William Hambly Glover, of Dundas Street, and Mary, his wife (now wife of John Fletcher, of Southwold), were this day baptised by me, by public baptism. John Fletcher, Mary Fletcher, Sponsors.

Marriage.

11th April, 1826—John Fletcher, of Southwold, yeoman, and Mary Glover, of the same place, widow, were this day married by me, by banns. Witnesses—John Dougherty, Charles Fuller, Thomas Dickison.

Baptism.

16th April, 1826—Mary, infant daughter of James Ferguson, of Southwold, yeoman, and Sarah, his wife, was this day baptised by me, by public baptism. Joseph Smith, Anna Smith, Hannah Robb, Sponsors.

Marriage.

18th April, 1826—Samuel Crawford, of Howard, W.D., yeoman, and Sophronia Smith, of Dunwich, spinster, were this day married by me, by banns. Witnesses—Orrin Ladd, Montgomery Smith, Willis Smith.

Burial.

22nd April, 1826—Wm. Sturges (father-in-law to Wm. Lee, of Southwold), aged 69 years, 11months, 2 days, died on 19th inst., and was this day buried by me, in the Churchyard of St. Thomas.

VITAL STATISTICS AT ST. THOMAS, U.C., COMMENCING 1824.

Burial.

28th April, 1826—Christian Zavitz, of Yarmouth, aged about 80, died on 27th inst., was this day burried by me, in Yarmouth, near the School House at Page's.

Baptism.

2nd May, 1826—Thomas, infant son of James Parkinson, and Sarah, his wife, was this day baptised by me, by public baptism, in London. Thos. Parkinson, Jas. Parkinson, Sarah Parkinson, Sponsors.

Baptism.

2nd May, 1826—Mary Jane, infant daughter of James Golden and Jane, his wife, was this day baptised by me, by public baptism, in London. James Baillie, Elizabeth Baillie, Jane Golden, Sponsors.

Baptism.

2nd May, 1826—Rebecca Elizabeth, infant daughter of Joseph Sifton and Catherine, his wife, was this day baptised by me, by public baptism, in London. Mary Shoebottom, Catherine Sifton, Joseph Sifton, Sponsors.

Baptism.

2nd May, 1826—Thomas, infant son of Anthony Hughes and Jane, his wife, was this day baptised by me, by public baptism, in London. James Orrum, Anthony Hughes, Alice Orrum, Sponsors.

Baptism.

2nd May, 1826—Mary Ann, infant daughter of Joseph Hughes and Alice, his wife, was this day baptised by me, by public baptism, in London. James Hughes, Alice Hughes, Anthony Hughes, Sponsors.

Baptism.

2nd May, 1826—Maria, infant daughter of Thomas Shoebottom and Eliza, his wife, was this day baptised by me, by public baptism, in London. Margaret Shoebottom, Eliza Shoebottom, Thos. Shoebottom, Sponsors.

Baptism.

2nd May, 1826—Mary Ann, infant daughter of Robert Ralph and Elizabeth, his wife, was this day baptised by me, by public baptism, in London. Esther Sifton, Elizabeth Ralph, Charles Sifton, Sponsors.

Baptism.

2nd May, 1826—Mary Talbot, infant daughter of Philip Hardings and Esther, his wife, was this day baptised by me, by public baptism, in London. Mary Hardy, Ann Geary, Joseph Hardy, Sponsors.

Baptism.

2nd May, 1826—Henry, infant son of Richard Ferguson and Margaret, his wife, was this day baptised by me, by public baptism, in London. Harry Ferguson, John Ferguson, Elizabeth Ferguson, Sponsors.

Baptism.

2nd May, 1826—Rebecca, infant daughter of Charles Sifton and Esther, his wife, was this day baptised by me, by public baptism, in London. Eliza Talbot, Esther Talbot, John Talbot, Sponsors.

Baptism.

2nd May, 1826—George, infant son of William Guest and Ellen, his wife, was this day baptised by me, by public baptism, in London. Casar McLeod, George Guest, Lucy Ann Schofield, Sponsors.

Baptism.

2nd May, 1826—Maria, infant daughter of John Hayes and Mary, his wife, was this day baptised by me, by public baptism, in London. Ann Shoebottom, Mary Hayes, Thos. Shoebottom, Sponsors.

Baptism.

2nd May, 1826—Barnard, infant son of James Stanley and Margaret, his wife, was this day baptised by me, by public baptism, in London. Thos. Shoebottom, James Stanley, Mary Shoebottom, Sponsors.

Baptism.

2nd May, 1826—Benjamin, infant son of Jacob Frelick and Nancy, his wife, was this day baptised by me, by public baptism, in London. William Geary, Jacob Frelick, Elizabeth Geary, Sponsors.

Baptism.

2nd May, 1826—Frances, infant daughter of John Turner and Margaret, his wife, was this day baptised by me, by public baptism, in London. William English, Mary Gray, Margaret Turner, Sponsors.

Baptism.

2nd May, 1826—James, infant son of John Evans and Sidney, his wife, born 5th December, 1825, was this day baptised by me, by public baptism, in London. William Geary, George Shoebottom, Sarah Geary, Sponsors.

Baptism.

2nd May, 1826—Thomas, infant son of John Gray and Mary, his wife, was this day baptised by me, by public baptism, in London. William Powell, John Gray, Barbara Powell, Sponsors.

Baptism.

4th May, 1826—Margaret, infant daughter of Duncan MacKenzie and Margaret, his wife, was this day baptised by me, by public baptism, in London. Duncan MacKenzie, Margaret MacKenzie, Sponsors.

Baptism.

St. Thomas, 7th May, 1826—Eleanor, infant daughter of George D. Spades and Mary, his wife, born 4th March, was this day baptised by me, by public baptism. Richard D. Drake, Mary Spades, Margaret Drake, Sponsors.

Baptism.

St. Thomas, 7th May, 1826—Elizabeth, daughter of the late Leonard Hutson, of the Township of Woodhouse, and Sarah, his wife, born 16th August, 1807, was this day baptised by me, by public baptism. Mary Spades, Ann Drake, Adam H. Burwell, Sponsors.

Burial.

8th May, 1826—Catherine, wife of Joseph Marlatt, of Yarmouth, died 7th inst., aged 24 years, and was this day buried by me, in the Churchyard of St. Thomas.

Marriage.

10th May, 1826—Reuben Covill, of Yarmouth, yeoman, and Philenia Turrill, of the same township, spinster, were this day married by me, by banns. Witnesses—Alonso Turrill, Elizabeth [her X mark] Tuttle, Simon Nicolls.

Marriage.

18th May, 1826—William Mandeville, of Southwold, yeoman, and Ann Ellison, of the same township, spinster, were this day married by me, by license. Witnesses—Luke Ellison, John Ellison, Henry Mandaville.

Marriage.

24th May, 1826—Lieut. William Windham Phelan, h.p., 89th Foot, now residing in Yarmouth, and Eliza Moore, of the same township, spinster, were this day married by me, by license. Witnesses—Edward T. Phelan, Lindley Moore, Martha Phelan.

Marriage.

25th May, 1826—Joseph Lawrason, of London, yeoman, and Lemantha Curtis, of Westminster, spinster, were this day married by me, by license. Witnesses—Silas E. Curtis, Lawrence Lawrason, Thomas Lawrason.

Marriage.

St. Thomas, 29th May, 1826—Crowell Wilson, of Dunwich, yeoman, and Jane Mitten, of the same township, spinster, were this day married by me, by banns. Witnesses—Benjamin Willson, William Crane, Peter Parker.

Marriage.

29th May, 1826—Hiram Coress and Ann Brookes, both of the Township of Mallahide, were this day married by me, by banns. Witnesses—John VanPatter, David [his X mark] Coress, Sally [her X mark] Tuttle.

Burial.

17th June, 1826—Daniel Springer, Esq., aged 63 1-2, Lt.-Col. 4th Regt., Middlesex Militia, died on 15th inst., and was this day interred by me, with Masonic honors, in Delaware.

Baptism.

St. Thomas, 20th June—Cynthia Winnifred, infant daughter of John B. Askin, Esq., of Woodhouse, and Elizabeth, his wife, born 2nd February, 1826, was this day baptised by me, by public baptism. Elizabeth Askin, as proxy for Catherine Jane Hamilton, Eliza Warren, as proxy for Cynthia VanAllan, Edmund Edward Warren, Sponsors.

Baptism.

22nd June, 1826—Henry, son of John Davis, of Yarmouth, and Margaret, his wife, born 26th May, 1821, was this day baptised by me, by public baptism. Archibald McNeale, John Davis, Margaret Davis, Sponsors.

Baptism.

22nd June, 1826—John, son of John Davis, of Yarmouth, and Margaret, his wife, born 28th February, 1824, was this day baptised by me, by public baptism. John McNeale, Archibald McNeale, Margaret Davis, Sponsors.

Baptism.

22nd June, 1826—William Augustus, infant son of John Davis, of Yarmouth, and Margaret, his wife, born 8th January, 1826, was this day baptised by me, by public baptism. Archibald McNeale, John Davis, Abigail McNeale, Sponsors.

Baptism.

St. Thomas, 22nd June, 1826—Phebe, daughter of Hugh McNeale, of Yarmouth, and Abigail, his wife, born 10th December, 1821, was this day baptised by me, by public baptism. Archibald McNeale, Hugh McNeale, Abigail McNeale, Sponsors.

Baptism.

22nd June, 1826—Archibald, son of Hugh McNeale, of Yarmouth, and Abigail, his wife, born 29th March, 1823, was this day baptised by me, by public baptism. Archibald McNeale, John McNeale, Abigail McNeale, Sponsors.

Baptism.

22nd June, 1826—Matilda Ann, daughter of Hugh McNeale, and Abigail, his wife, born 3rd December, 1825, was this day baptised by me, by public baptism. Hugh McNeale, Archibald McNeale, Abigail McNeale, Sponsors.

Baptism.

22nd June, 1826—Abigail, wife of Hugh McNeale, of Yarmouth, was this day baptised by me, by public baptism. Archibald McNeale, John Davis, Margaret Davis, Sponsors.

Baptisms.

St. Thomas, 27th June, 1826—Joseph William, born 19th November, 1822, Benjamin, born 8th March, 1824, David, born 26th December, 1825, children of William Watterworth, of Southwold, yeoman, and Ann, his wife, were this day baptised by me, by public baptism. William Watterworth, Ann Watterworth, Sponsors.

Marriage.

27th June, 1826—George Teeple, of Yarmouth, yeoman, and Frances Drake, of the same township, spinster, were this day married by me, by banns. Witnesses—Abram Eveland, John Littell, Edward Teeple.

Marriage.

28th June, 1826—David Kelley, of Southwold, yeoman, and Irene Young, of the same township, spinster, were this day married by me, by banns. Witnesses—John Willson, Thomas Lumley, Jonas Clark.

Marriage.

11th July, 1826—Isaac Hunt, of Westminster, yeoman, and Rachel Howie, of the same township, widow, were this day married by me, by banns. Witnesses—Edward Hunt, Jesse Bennet, Wm. Hunt.

Baptisms.

10th July, 1826—Mary, daughter of Alexander Macpherson, of Dunwich, and Isabel, his wife, born 8th March, 1824, and Alexander, son of Alexander Macpherson, of Dunwich, born 13th April, 1825, were this day baptised by me, by public baptism. Alexander Macpherson, Isabel Mackay, parents, Sponsors.

Marriage.

13th July, 1826—Israel Waters, of the Township of Yarmouth, yeoman, and Elizabeth Wedge, spinster, were this day married by me, by license. Witnesses—Lemuel Ladd, Ira Whitcomb, Pherney Jones.

Marriage.

St. Thomas, 19th July, 1826—John C. Macpherson, of Westminster, yeoman, and Harriet Cheyna, of the same township, spinster, were this day married by me, by banns. Witnesses—D. Mcpharson, Garner Ellwood, Thomas McPherson.

Baptism.

22nd July, 1826—Eliza Ann, daughter of Enos Call and Ann, his wife, was this day baptised by me, by private baptism. Enos Call, Ann Call, parents, Emma Eldridge, Sponsors.

Marriage.

St. Thomas, 19th August, 1826—James Carsout, of the Township of London, yeoman, and Melissa Farrow, of the same township, spinster, were this day married by me, by license. Witnesses—Abraham King, Christopher Carsout, Mary King.

Baptisms.

19th August, 1826—Charles, born 12th April, 1824, and David, born 20th August, 1825, children of Abraham King, of Southwold, and Mary, his wife, were this day baptised by me, by public baptism. Abraham King, Christopher Corsaut, Mary Ward, Sponsors.

Marriage.

23rd August, 1826—Duncan MacGregor, Esq., merchant, Chatham, Western District, and Cynthia VanAllen, of Woodhouse, London District, spinster, were this day married by me, by license. Witnesses—William VanAllen, Robert Nelson, Peter Rapelje.

Baptism.

2nd October, 1826—Lucius Lyman, son of Ira Whitcomb, of St. Thomas, and Jemima, his wife, born 3rd September, 1825, was this day baptised by me, by private baptism. Ira Whitcomb, Jemima Whitcomb, parents, Sponsors.

Baptism.

St. Thomas, 26th September, 1826—Erasmus Aeneas, infant son of James Mitchell, Esq., of Charlotteville (Co. Norfolk), and Elizabeth T., his wife, born 3rd June, 1826, was this day baptised by me, by public baptism. James Mitchell, Marcus E. Ryerson, Margaret Mitchell, Sponsors.

Marriage.

4th October, 1826—Charles Fuller, of the Township of Southwold, yeoman, and Matilda Bodoin, of the same township, spinster, were this day married by me, by banns. Witnesses—John [his X mark] Doherty, Hugh Howell, Ludwick Sells.

Burial.

3rd October, 1826—Elijah Witt, of Southwold, aged —— years, died on 2nd inst., and was this day interred in the Churchyard of St. Thomas.

Burial.

5th October, 1826—John Burwell, of Southwold, yeoman, aged 35 years and 10 months, died on 3rd inst., and was this day interred in the Churchyard of St. Thomas.

Burial.

5th October, 1826—Lucius Lyman Whitcombe, infant son of Ira Whitcomb, of St. Thomas, died 4th inst., aged 3 months, and was this day interred by me, in the Churchyard of St. Thomas.

Burial.

5th October, 1826—Walter Murphy, infant son of Michael Murphy, of St. Thomas, died 4th inst., aged 8½ months, and was this day interred in the Churchyard of St. Thomas.

Burial.

6th October, 1826—John Elliot, of St. Thomas, Cooper, a native of Scotland, died 5th inst., aged 26 years, 5 months, and was this day interred by me, in the Churchyard of St. Thomas.

Baptism.

St. Thomas, 14th October, 1826—William, son of William Williams, of Yarmouth, and Sarah, his wife, born ————, 1824, was this day baptised by me, by public baptism. John Matthews, Rachel Hughes, Sarah Williams, Sponsors.

On Sunday the 15th Otober, 1826, the Sarament of the Lord's Supper was administered by me to eight persons.

Marriage.

17th October, 1826—Jeston Robinson, of Dunwich, yeoman, and Lydia Warner, of the same township, spinster, were this day married by me, by banns. Witnesses—Hiram [his X mark] Warner, Moses [his X mark] Warner, Philip [his X mark] Brookes.

On Thursday, 19th October, I administered the Sacrament of the Lord's Supper to Benjamin Bowbeer, who lay very sick.

Marriage.

19th October, 1826—Jesse Bennet, of Westminster, yeoman, and Margaret Lockwood, of Carradoc, spinster, were this day married by me, by banns. Witnesses—Daniel Lockwood, Edna Hunt, Wm. McDavid.

Marriage.

19th October, 1826—John Graves and Elizabeth Eveland, yeoman, and spinster, of the Township of Yarmouth, were this day married by me, by banns. Witnesses—O'Neal Claes, Hiland Ward, Abram Eveland.

Marriage.

19th October, 1826—Jeronimus Rapelje, of Yarmouth, yeoman, and Jennetta Best, of the same township, spinster, were this day married by me, by license. Witnesses—Daniel Rapelje, Charles Conrade, John Rapelje.

Burial.

St. Thomas, 30th October, 1826—Ezekiel Evans, of Westminster, yeoman, died on 29th inst., aged 41 years, and was this day interred by me, in the Churchyard of St. Thomas.

Marriage.

31st October, 1826—Abraham Huff, of the Township of Yarmouth, yeoman, and Rachel Heaton, of the same township, spinster, were this day married by me, by banns. Witnesses—John Huff, Jane Willson, Benjamin C. Doan.

Baptisms.

6th November, 1826—Ann Eliza, born 24th September, 1810, William Henry, born 3rd January, 1813, Jane Maria, born 3rd October, 1818, Mary Lee, born 27th July, 1823, children of John W. Clark and Anne, his wife, now residing in Southwold, were this day baptised by me, by public baptism. Wm. H. Lee, Phebe Lee, Wm. B. Lee, Mary Lee, Sponsors.

Burial.

St. Thomas, 13th November, 1826—Ann Clark, wife of John W. Clark, of Southwold, died 11th inst., in the 32nd year of her age, and was this day interred by me, in the Churhyard of St. Thomas.

Marriage.

14th November 1826—Isaac Hunt, of Mallahide, yeoman, and Amy Baker, of the same township, spinster, were this day married by me, by banns. Witnesses—David Hunt, John Laur, Lydia Baker.

Marriage.

29th November, 1826—Garret Smith, of Southwold, yeoman, and Sarah Sells, of the same township, spinster, were this day married by me, by banns. Witnesses—Charles Hannan, Joseph Smith, Thomas Dickeson.

Baptisms.

3rd December, 1826—George John, born 26th October, 1823, Grace, born 15th July, 1825, children of the late John Elliot, of St. Thomas, cooper, and Ann, his wife, were this day baptised by me, by public baptism. John Mackintosh, Barbara Mackintosh, Margaret Campbell, Sponsors.

Marriage.

5th December, 1826—James Hamilton of Southwold, yeoman, and Anne Daer, of Mallahide, widow, were this day married by me, by banns. Witnesses—Mary Davis, William Davis, Asahel Barnes.

Baptisms.

6th December, 1826—John, born 17th October, 1824, Robert, born 10th October, 1826, children of James Hepburne, of Southwold, and Margaret, his wife, were this day baptised by me, by public baptism. James Hepburn, John Mitchell, Lucy Williams, for John James Hepburn, Robt. Mitchell, Sarah Williams, for Robert, Sponsors.

Marriage.

St. Thomas, 11th December, 1826—Elijah Osborne, of Yarmouth, and Anne Scott, of the same township, spinster, were this day married by me, by banns. Witnesses—H. Scott, D. W. Stockton, Applonia [her X mark] Osborne.

Burial.

13th December, 1826—Robert, infant son of James Hepburne, of Southwold, died 12th inst., aged 2 months, and was this day interred by me, in the Churchyard of St. Thomas.

Marriage.

25th December, 1826—John Jones, of Westminster, yeoman, and Maria Ayres, of the same township, spinster, were this day married by me, by banns. Witnesses—Garner Ellwood, John Bostwick, Daniel Corson.

Marriage.

St. Thomas, 25th December, 1826—John Smith, of Westminster, yeoman, and Sarah Jones, of the same township, spinster, were this day married by me, by banns. Witnesses—John Bostwick, Garner Ellwood, Daniel Corson.

Sacrament.

On Sunday, 31st December, I administered the Sacrament of the Lord's Supper, in the Church of St. Thomas,—number of communicants, twenty-three.

88 marriages recorded this year.

Marriage.

St. Thomas, 4th January, 1827—Joseph Pettys, adopted son of Daniel Pettys, of Westminster, and Lucy Williams, of the same township, spinster, were this day married by me, by banns. Witnesses—James Little, John Corsen, David Morden Garner Ellwood.

Marriage.

4th January, 1827—Amasa Wood, of Southwold, widower, and Mary Kelley, of the same township, widow, were this day married by me, by banns. Witnesses—Wm. Howard, Robert Burwell, John Lipscott, Wm. Burwell.

Baptism.

7th January, 1827—Elizabeth Ann, infant daugher of Wm. Parker, of Yarmouth, and Ann, his wife, was this day baptised by me, by public baptism. Jesse Page, Elizabeth Page, Ann Parker, Sponsors.

Baptism.

St. Thomas, 7th January, 1827—Nahum Pond, infant son of Jarvis Thayer, of Yarmouth, and Ann, his wife, born ——————, was this day baptised by me, by bublic baptism. William Parker, Jarvis Thayer, Ann Parker, Sponsors.

Baptism.

7th January, 1827—Margaret, infant daughter of William Robb, of London, and Hannah, his wife, born ——————, was this day baptised by me, by public baptism. Thomas Hardison, Anna Smith, Elizabeth Hardison, Sponsors.

Marriage.

8th January, 1827—James Beattie, of Westminster, yeoman, and Sarah Schram, of the same township, spinster, were this day married by me, by banns. Witnesses—Peter C. Schram, James Uptigrove, William Schram.

Marriage.

St. Thomas, 8th January, 1827—Robert Guy, of Southwold, widower, and Ann Lodge, of the same township, widow, were this day married by me, by banns. Witnesses—John Lee, Abraham King, Silas Toles.

Baptisms.

8th January, 1827—Margaret, Elizabeth Ann, and Thomas, children of the late Thomas Lodge, of Southwold, and Ann, his wife, were this day baptised by me, by public baptism. Margaret was born 14th February, 1816; Elizabeth Ann, 8th July, 1819, and Thomas, 28th February, 1826. Robert Guy, Jane Hogle, Margaret Toles, Sponsors.

Marriage.

30th January, 1827—John Louckes, of Malahide, farmer, and Susan Thomson, of the same township, spinster, were this day married by me, by banns. Witnesses—John Bostwick, Melinda Louckes, Jacob Louckes.

Marriage.

29th January, 1827—Jacob Johnstone and Irene Bissel, both of Southwold, were this day married by me, by banns, according to the rites and ceremonies of the Church of England. Witnesses—William Burwell, Sarah Bissel, Lydia Bissell.

Marriage.

10th February, 1827—John Stiles, of London, yeoman, and Elizabeth Kent, of the same township, spinster, were this day married by me, by banns, according to the rites and ceremonies of the Church of England. Witnesses—John Kent, Mary Kent, John Kent, Jr., Stephen Stiles.

Baptism.

10th February, 1827—Sarah Ann, daughter of John Kent, of London, and Mary, his wife, born 30th January, 1826, was this day baptised by me, by bublic baptism. Mary Kent, Elizabeth Stiles, John Stiles, Sponsors.

Sacrament.

St. Thomas.—On Sunday, 11th February, 1827—I administered the Sacrament of the Lord's Supper, in London. The number of communicants was twenty-eight.

Baptism.

11th February, 1827—Elizabeth, daughter of George Nealan, of London, and Margaret, his wife, born 27th November, 1826, was this day baptised by me by public baptism. Bridget Orme, Margaret Nealan, Thomas Orme, Sponsors.

Baptism.

11th February, 1827—Ely Talbot, son of William Fitzgerald, of London, and Sarah, his wife, born 2nd July, 1826, was this day baptised by me, by public baptism. Joseph Sifton, William Fitzgerald, Catherine Sifton, Sponsors.

Baptism.

11th February, 1827—Frances, daughter of William Haskett, of London, and Mary, his wife, born 20th July, 1826, was this day baptised by me, by public baptism. Alicia Gray, Mary Haskett, James Shoebottom, Sponsors.

Baptism.

St. Thomas, 18th February, 1827—William Campbell, infant son of Henry Buskirk, of Yarmouth, and Ruth, his wife, born 7th, May, 1826, was this day baptised by me, by public baptism. Henry Buskirk, Jesse Page, Ruth Buskirk, Sponsors.

Marriage.

21st February, 1827—Stephen Raymond, of Southwold, Farmer and Francis Smith, of the same township, spinster, were this day married by me, by banns. Witnesses—William Vanwicken, Abraham Griffin, John Holmes, John Steinhoff.

Marriage.

1st March, 1827—Anson Simons, of Westminster, cloth manufacturer, and Lavinia McMillen, of the same township, spinster, were this day married by me, by banns. Witnesses—Archibald McMillen, Caleb Reynolds, Solomon Monroe, John Fitch.

Marriage.

St. Thomas, March 7th, 1827—George Harvey, of Southwold, yeoman, and Mary White, of the same township, spinster, were this day married by me, by banns. Witnesses—William White, George R. Williams, Sarah West.

Marriage.

8th March, 1827—William Burwell, of Southwold, yeoman, and Sarah Bissel, of the same township, spinster, were this day married by me, by banns. Witnesses—Jacob Johnstone, Timothy Culver, Adam Burwell.

Marriage.

15th March, 1827—Robert Johnson, of Malahide, yeoman, and Frances Evans, alias Robinson, of Southwold, widow, were this day married by me, by banns. Witnesses—James Little, James Hepburne, Edward Johnson.

Baptism.

St. Thomas, 18th March, 1827—Colin, son of George Henry, of Dunwich, and Mary, his wife, born 18th March, 1826, was this day baptised by me, by public baptism. Margaret McIntyre, George Henry, Walter Patterson, Sponsors.

Marriage.

25th March, 1827—William Searles, of the Township of Townsend, yeoman, and Lorenzo Ross, of the Township of Southwold, spinster, were this day married by me, by license. Witnesses—Wm. W. Ross, Francis A. Ross, William Ross, Jun.

Baptisms.

26th March, 1827—William, born 5th June, 1821, John, born 8th June, 1823, Jane, born 7th January, 1826, children of William Partridge, of Southwold, and Anne, his wife, were this day baptised by me, by public baptism. John Partridge, Anne Partridge, Hannah Burwell, Samuel Burwell, Sponsors.

Marriage.

St. Thomas, 29th Farch, 1827—John Routledge, of the Township of Westminster, yeoman, and Nancy Morden, of the same township, spinster, were this day married by me, by banns. Witnesses—David Morden, James Parkinson, George Routledge, James Beattie, Thomas Parkinson.

Marriage.

2nd April, 1827—Amos McNames, of Oxford, yeoman, and Sarah Ann Thomson, of Westminster, spinster, were this day married by me, by banns. Witnesses—Peter Schram, Enoch Bundick, Abram McNames.

Marriage.

9th April, 1827—Asa B. Lewis, of Malahide, yeoman, and Alma Hopkins, of Southwold, spinster, were this day married by me, by banns. Witnesses—William B. Lee, Archibald Chisholm, Samuel Ellison, John Lee.

Baptism.

St. Thomas, 16th April, 1827—John, infant son of Benjamin Willson, of Yarmouth, and Sarah, his wife born 5th March, 1827, was this day baptised by me, by public baptism. William Pearce, Lesslie Pearce, Catherine Pearce, Sponsors.

Marriage.

19th April, 1827—John B. Graves, of Ekfrid, yeoman, and Catherine Hardy, of Mosa, spinster, were this day married by me, by banns. Witnesses—Elijah Mann, Peter Graves, Mary Graves.

On Sunday, 15th April, 1827, the Sacrament of the Lord's Supper was adminisered by me, in the Church of St. Thomas, to twenty-two persons (Easter Sunday).

Burial.

27th April, 1827—Ann, daughter of widow Ann Mitchell, of Southwold, died on 25th inst., aged 9 years and 5 months, and was this day interred by me, in St. Thomas.

Marriage.

St. Thomas, 30th April, 1827—Charles Whitsell, of Malahide, yeoman, and Sarah Bentley, of the same township, spinster, were this day married by me, by banns. Witnesses—Gilbert Mitten, Daniel Dreadwell, Elisha R. Smith.

Marriage.

1st May, 1827—John Kilmer, of Malahide, farmer, and Deborah Barss, of the same township, spinster, were this day married by me, by banns. Witnesses—Stephen Holland, Peter Laur, Asa Learn.

Baptism.

19th May, 1827—William, infant son of Lovell Harrison, of Howard, Margaret, his wife, born 22nd October, 1826, was this day baptised by me, by public baptism. William Riddle, Lovell Harrison, Margaret Harrison, Sponsors.

Marriage.

St. Thomas, 2nd May, 1827—George R. Williams, of Southwold, Farmer, and Ann Nicholls, of the same township, spinster, were this day married by me, by banns. Witnesses—John Holmes, John Nicolls, Thomas Williams.

Marriage.

19th May, 1827—David Palmer, of Howard, Westminster District, widower, and Sarah Watson, of Southwold, widow, were this day married by me by banns. Witnesses—Allen Watson, James Watson, George Ironside, James Richardson.

Marriage.

21st May, 1827—Lawrence Lawrason, of London, merchant, and Abigail Lee, of Southwold, spinster, were this day married by me by license. Witnesses—Archibald Chisholm, Wm. B. Lee, John Lee.

Marriage.

22nd May, 1827—John Mackintosh, of Southwold, yeoman, and Margaret Campbell, of the same township, spinster, were this day married by me, by banns. Witnesses—John Campbell, Dugald Campbell, Alexander Campbell.

Baptisms.

8th June, 1827—David, born April, 1823, and Rachel, born 17th October, 1825, children of David Morgan, of London, and Sarah, his wife, were this day baptised by me, by public baptism. John Matthews,

David Morgan, Rachel Hughes, Sarah Morgan, Catherine Hughes, Sponsors.

On Sunday, 10th June, being Trinity Sunday, I administered the Sacrament of the Lord's Supper to twenty-four persons, in London.

Baptism.

10th June, 1827—Mary, daughter of William English, of London, and Ann, his wife, born 15th January, 1826, was this day baptised by me, by public baptism. Samuel Dickson, Mary Wilson, Ann English, Sponsors.

Baptism.

10th June, 1827—Rebecca, daughter of Francis Lewis, of London, and Sarah, his wife, born 19th June, 1826, was this day baptised by me, by public baptism. Francis Lewis, Catherine Ardiel, Sarah Lewis, Sponsors.

Baptism.

10th June, 1827—Elizabeth, infant daughter of Charles Sifton, of London, and Esther, his wife, born 27th March, 1827, was this day baptised by me, by public baptism. John Talbot, Elizabeth Talbot, Esther Sifton, Sponsors.

Baptism.

10th June, 1827—Sarah, infant daughter of John Hayes, of London, and Mary, his wife, born 26th March, 1827, was this day baptised by me, by public baptism. Thomas Shoebottom, Mary Shoebottom, Mary Hayes, Sponsors.

Baptism.

10th June, 1827—Mary, infant daughter of John Harding, of London, and Jane, his wife, born 1st February, 1827, was this day baptised by me, by public baptism. Robt. Harding, Elizabeth Hardy, Ann Talbot, Sponsors.

Baptism.

10th June, 1827—Maria, daughter of Thomas W. Howard, of London, and Mary, his wife, was this day baptised by me, by public baptism. Thomas W. Howard, Mary Howard, Mary Howard, Sponsors.

VITAL STATISTICS AT ST. THOMAS, U.C., COMMENCING 1824.

Marriage.

27th June, 1827—Henry McAllister, of Yarmouth, yeoman, and Elizabeth Schaffe, of the same township, widow, were this day married by me, by license. Witnesses—John Van Sickle, David Burgess, Josiah Moorehouse.

Baptism.

28th June, 1827—Isabella Pherney Jones, daughter of Giles Jones, of Stanstead, L.C., and Jemima, his wife, born 27th May, 1807, was this day baptised by me, by public baptism. Catherine Goodhue, Stephen Randal, Witnesses.

Baptism.

30th June, 1827—David Freeman, son of Prince Freeman and Elizabeth, his wife, of Detroit, Mich., United States, born 12th April, 1809, was this day baptised by me, by public baptism. Stephen Radal, James Nevills, Gilbert Dumont, Anne Elliott, Witnesses.

Marriage.

18th July, 1827—John Carey, of Munsey Town, Methodist, schoolmaster, and Lydia Woodhull, of Lobo, spinster, were this day married by me by banns. Witnesses—William Hough, John Matthews, Josiah Woodhull.

Baptism.

19th July, 1827—Richard Talbot, born 19th September, 1826, son of Philip Harding, of London, and Esther, his wife, was this day baptised by me, by public baptism. John Harding, Joseph Hardy, Eliza Geary, Sponsors.

Baptism.

19th July, 1827—William Henry, born 11th August, 1826, son of Jacob Fraelick, of London, and Anne, his wife, was this day baptised by me, by public baptism. Joseph Sifton, Catherine Sifton, Anne Fraelick, Sponsors.

Baptism.

19th July, 1827—Mary Ann, born 28th May, 1827, infant daughter of Felix McLaughlin, of London, and Jane, his wife, was this day baptised by me, by public baptism. Thomas T. Howard, Caroline Fraelick, Jane McLaughlin, Sponsors.

Baptism.

19th July, 1827—Esther, born 19th September, 1807, daughter of Richard Talbot, of London, and Lydia, his wife, (and wife of Philip Harding) was this day baptised by me, by public baptism. Margaret Talbot, Jane Harding, Philip Harding, William Geary, Sponsors.

Marriage.

25th July, 1827—Nelson Perkins, of London, yeoman, and Melinda Lord, alias Caryl, of the same township, widow, were this day married by me by license, according to the rites and ceremonies of the Church of England. Witnesses—James Givins, Silas E. Cunks, Maria Curtis.

Marriage.

St. Thomas, 29th July, 1827—Alpheus Burch, of Mallahide, yeoman, and Elizabeth White, of Bayham, spinster, were this day married by me, by banns, according to the rites and ceremonies of the Church of England. Witnesses—Jacob Huffman, Isaac White, J. Nevills, James Givins, Stephen Randal.

Marriage.

30th July, 1827—Robert McKenney, of the Township of Mallahide, yeoman, and Catharine Nickerson, of the same township, spinster, were this day married by me, by banns. Witnesses—Matthew McKenney, James McKenney, Levi Nickerson, Thomas Hodgkinson.

On Thursday, 2nd August, 1827, the Lord Bishop of Quebec, held a confirmation in London, when the following thirty persons were confirmed: John Harding, Jane Harding, Philip Harding, Esther Harding, Sarah Geary, Anne Geary, Lucy Ann Schofield, William Gray, Margaret Talbot, Maria Sifton, Jane Wilkins, Elizabeth Orme, Catharine Sifton, Alicia Gray, Stephen Powell, Ambrose Powell, Margaret Shoebottom, Thomas Shoebottom, Jeremiah Robson, Isabella Robson, John Kent, Jr., Elizabeth Stiles, William Robert Talbot, Eliza Talbot, Esther Sifton, William Baillie, Mary Gray, Margaret Robson, Jane Robson, John Stiles.

VITAL STATISTICS AT ST. THOMAS, U.C., COMMENCING 1824. 169

N.B.—The following marriage and baptisms are from the list of the Hon. and Rev. Dr. Stewart, while visiting missionary in the years 1820-1822—Marked thus X.

Marriage.

X. William Ostrander, of Majorage, bachelor, and Sarah Ryckman, minor, spinster, both of the Township of Yarmouth, were this day married by the Honorable and Reverend C. Stewart, D.D., by banns. at Port Talbot, in the presence of the Honorable Thomas Talbot, Messrs. Lesslie Patterson and John Conrad.

Baptisms.

At Port Talbot, by Dr. Stewart, 16th April, 1820.

X. Olivia, daughter of Lesslie Patterson and Lydia, his wife, born 3rd January, 1818. Stephen Backus, Elizabeth Stewart, Sarah Stewart, Sponsors.

X. John, son of John Pearce and Frances, his wife, born 14th November, 1818. Lesslie Patterson, Stephen Backus, Susan Stewart, Sponsors.

X. Thomas, born September 28th, 1816, and Mary, born June 28th, 1818, children of Stephen Backus and Anne, his wife. Lesslie Patterson, John Pearce, Elizabeth and Sarah Stewart, Sponsors.

Baptisms.

By the Honorable and Reverend Dr. Stewart, visiting missionary, at Port Talbot, 16th April, 1820.

X. John, son of Andrew Weldon and Jane, his wife, deceased, born 19th November, 1816. John Pearce, Lesslie and Lydia Patterson, Sponsors.

John, son of Richard and Maria Dobbyn, born 8th November, 1819. Henry Dobbyn and Martha Bobier, Sponsors.

At Port Talbot, 17th April, 1820.

X. Samuel Burwell (adult), born in February, 1793. Thomas Talbot (Honorable), Mahlon Burwell, Hannah Burwell, Sponsors.

X. Charlotte, born 4th April, 1819, daughter of Samuel Burwell and Hannah, his wife. Thomas Talbot (Honorable), and Maria Dobbyn, Sponsors.

At De Fields House (Otter Creek), in the Township of Bayham, 19th April, 1827.

X. John Martin, son of Anson Treadwell and Nancy, his wife (deceased), born 7th June, 1815. Joseph De Fields, Elizabeth De Fields, Henry Metcalf, Sponsors.

Baptisms.

St. Thomas, 19th April, 1820.

By the Honorable and Reverend Dr. Stewart, visiting missionary, continued, at Otter Creek, in Bayham, 19th April, 1820.

X. Mary Jane, born 5th October, 1816, daughter of James Howe (deceased), and Catharine, his wife. Elijah McKenney and Mary Bristol, Sponsors.

X. Harriet Augusta, born 28th November, 1816, daughter of Richard and Mary Bristol. Elijah McKenney and Catharine Howe, Sponsors.

In Dunwich, 26th June, 1822.

X. Catherine, born 23rd August, 1820, Hugh, born 4th December, 1821, children of James and Margaret Trainer. Lesslie and Lydia Patterson, Thomas and Barbara Matthews, Sponsors.

X. Elizabeth, born 1st May, 1821, daughter of Richard and Maria Dobbyn. John and Martha Farland and Mary Story, Sponsors.

X. Lesslie, born May 11th, 1820, Frances, born June 7th, 1822, children of Lesslie and Lydia Patterson. Stephen Backus, John M. Farland, Elizabeth and Sarah Stewart, Sponsors.

X. William, born 2nd October, 1819, Elizabeth, born 14th June, 1822, children of Benoni and Susannah Hill. George Henry and Catharine McCallum, Sponsors.

X. Anne, born April 19th, 1822, daughter of Henry and Anne Coyne. Parents and Mary Coyne, Sponsors.

X. Olivia, daughter of Stephen and Anne Backus, born May 22nd, 1821. Walter Story, Mary Story and Elizabeth Stewart, Sponsors.

X. William, born 20th December, 1807, Hannah, 10th May, 1818, Susan, born 25th February, 1820, Jane, born 4th January, 1822, children of George and Isabella Crane. Parents, John M. Farland and Lydia Patterson, Sponsors.

X. Caroline, born 20th September, 1819, Jane, born 9th October, 1820, James, 1st May, 1822, children of Henry and Eliza Dobbyn. Alexander Weldon, John M. Farland and Martha Bowbeer, Sponsors.

X. Sally, born 9th January, 1820, daughter of Alexander and Catharine McCallum. Archibald McIntyre, Susannah Hill, Sponsors.

X. Anne Backus, born 17th April, 1817, daughter of John and Euphemia Parker. Stephen and Anne Backus, Sponsors.

X. Isaac, son of Henry and Anne Coyne, born 27th June, 1818. Walter Story, George Gibb and Mary Story, Sponsors.

X. Mary, daughter of Duncan and Flora McLellan, born 19th November, 1820. George and Mary Gibb, Margaret Gray, Sponsors.

In Southwold, 23rd June, 1822.

Adam Hood, adult son of Adam and Sarah Burwell, born 4th June, 1790. James Hamilton and John Warren, Sponsors.

X. Sally, born 9th January, 1820, daughter of Alexander and Catharine McCallum. Archibald McIntyre, Susannah Hill, Sponsors.

X. Anne Backus, born 17th April, 1817, daughter of John and Euphemia Parker. Stephen and Anne Backus, Sponsors.

X. Isaac, son of Henry and Anne Coyne, born 27th June, 1818. Walter Story, George Gibb and Mary Story, Sponsors.

X. Mary, daughter of Duncan and Flora McLellan, born 19th November, 1820. George and Mary Gibb and Margaret Gray, Sponsors.

In Southwold, 23rd June, 1822.

Adam Hood, adult son of Adam and Sarah Burwell, born 4th June, 1790. James Hamilton and John Warren, Sponsors.

24th June, 1822—Alma, adult daughter of William Hopkins, deceased, and Sarah Freeman, born 11th March, 1806. Francis Siddal and Mercy N. Martin, Sponsors.

X. Amelia, daughter of James and Margaret Hepburne, born 27th May, 1820. James Mitchell, Rachel Mitchell, Sarah Siddal, Sponsors.

X. John, born 17th January, 1818, Rhoda Emma, born 30th March, 1819, Anne, born 23rd November, 1821, children of Francis and Sarah Siddal. James Hamilton, James Mitchell, Diana Mandeville and Margaret Hepburne, Sponsors.

In London, 28th July, 1822.

X. Catherine, daughter of Thomas and Mary Howard, born 3rd July, 1822. Parents and Catharine Harrison, Sponsors.

X. Elizabeth, daughter of Thomas and Catharine Harrison, born 22nd January, 1821. Thomas and Mary Howard, Sponsors.

X. Mary, born 31st August, 1819, Esther, born 19th September, 1821, children of Charles and Anne Goulding. William and Elizabeth Geary, Anne Geary and James Goulding, Sponsors.

X. John, son of Joseph and Catharine Sifton, born 16th January, 1821. Charles Sifton, Elizabeth Woomack, Sponsors.

X. John Wright, son of Charles and Esther Sifton, born 20th April, 1822. John Talbot, James Goulding, Catharine Sifton, Elizabeth Geary, Sponsors.

X. William, son of Thomas and Anne Bailey, born 10th October, 1821. John Scatcherd, James Farley, Anne Farley, Sponsors.

VITAL STATISTICS AT ST. THOMAS, U.C., COMMENCING 1824.   173

X. James, son of James and Sarah McFadden, born 25th April, 1821. Thomas and Anne Bailey and John Scatcherd, Sponsors.

X. Hiram, born 11th March, 1798, Martha Maria, born 23rd May, 1803, adults, children of Ira and Ruth Schofield. Simeon Bullen and Margaret Talbot, Sponsors.

X. Thomas, son of Thomas T. and Esther Howard, born 10th May, 1820. Parents and Thomas Shoebottom, Sponsors.

X. Charles, son of John and Elizabeth Freligh, born 22nd June, 1822. Charles and Anne Goulding, Sponsors.

X. John George, son of Duncan and Margaret Mackenzie, born 29th April, 1822. Thomas Routledge, John Donaldson, Elizabeth Keys, Sponsors.

X. Edward, son of Samuel and Anne Howard, born 19th October, 1821. George Fitzgerald, Mary Howard, Sponsors.

X. Anne Jane, born 4th June, 1820, Thomas Valentine, born April 6th, 1822, children of Thomas and Elizabeth Guest. Leonard and Rebecca Ardiel, Sponsors.

X. Samuel, son of John and Anne Neill, born 5th July, 1819. Thomas Harrison, Catharine Harrison, Felix McLaughlin, Sponsors.

X. John, son of Jacob and Nancy Freligh, born 15th July, 1821. John and Elizabeth Freligh and Jeremiah Schram, Sponsors.

X. James, son of Robert and Elizabeth Ralph, born 29th December, 1821. John Ardiel and Mary Green, Sponsors.

X. John, son of Felix and Jane McLaughlin, born 1st January, 1821. Parents and Thomas Shoebottom, Sponsors.

X. Michael, born 12th July, 1818, John, born 25th April, 1820, children of William and Bridget Colbart. Thomas and Elizabeth Guest. Duncan Mackenzie, Sponsors.

X. Nancy, wife of Jacob Freligh, parents deceased, born 28th November, 1798. Felix McLaughlin, Mary Getty, Catharine Harrison, Sponsors.

Here end the baptisms by the Honorable and Reverend Dr. Stewart.

Burial.

St. Thomas, 20th August, 1827—Timothy Burwell, of Southwold, yeoman, aged 26 years, died on 19th inst., and was this day interred by me, in the Churchyard of St. Thomas.

Baptism.

21st August, 1827—William Sewell, born January, 1827, infant son of Josiah C. Goodhue and Catharine, his wife, was this day baptised by me, by public baptism. Isabella P. Jones, Josiah C. Goodhue, per A. M., Alexander Mackintosh, Sponsors.

Baptism.

21st August, 1827—Alma, born December, 1812, daughter of James Nevills of Yarmouth, and Elizabeth, his wife, was this day baptised by me, by public baptism. James Nevills, Margaret Rapelje, Elizabeth Rapelje, Sponsors.

Baptism.

23rd August, 1827—Gilman Willson, of Dunwich, an adult, born 17th ———, was this day baptised by me, by public baptism. John Bostwick, Benjamin Willson, Hannah Willson, Sponsors.

Confirmation by the Lord Bishop of Quebec, on Tuesday, the 21st of August, the following persons were confirmed in Dunwich:—William Pearce, Richard Pearce, Lesslie Pearce, Catherine Pearce, Mary Anne Pearce, Stephen Backus, Anne Backus, Andrew Backus, Anne Morehouse, Lydia Patterson, Walter Patterson, Mary Patterson, Hannah Patterson, Joseph Patterson, Charles Crane, Benjamin Siddall, Martha Farland—17 in number.

At St. Thomas, on Thursday, the 23rd of August, the following persons were confirmed:—Jeronymus Rapelje, Senr., Jeronymus Rapelje, Jr., Daniel P. Rapelje, Elizabeth Rapelje, Elizabeth Ann Rapelje, Benjamin Willson, Sarah Willson, Mary Hughes, David, Hughes, Richard Hughes, Isabella P. Jones, Sarah Smith, Eliza Smith, Hetty Bostwick, Joseph Bostwick, Maria Williams, George Williams, Alma Nevills, David Freeman, Hercules Burwell, Isaac Brock Burwell, Sarah Burwell, Hannah H. Haun, Lucinda Spades, George D. Spades, Catharine Hamilton, Anne Chisholme, Margaret Hepburne, Anne Srake, Margaret Srake, Christina Baillie, James Mitchell, Robert Mitchell, Gilman Willson, Hannah Willson, John Bostwick, William Parker, Anne Parker, George Parker, Jesse Page, Benjamin Page, Elizabeth Page, ———— Mandeville—44 in number.

Marriage.

27th August, 1827—Harden Ellsworth, of Mallahide, widower, and Margaret Hickey, of Bayham, spinster, were this day married by me, by banns. Witnesses—Isaac Hunt, John Van Patter, Elisha R. Smith.

Marriage.

27th August, 1827—Elisha R. Smith, of Mallahide, yeoman, and Christina Hutcheson, of the same township, spinster, were this day married by me, by banns. Witnesses—Elias B. Smith, Isaac Hunt, John Van Patter, Harden Ellsworth.

Baptism.

21st August, 1827—Robert, son of Stephen Backus and Anne, his wife, born 15th June, 1827, was this day baptised by the Reverend Crosbie Morgell, Chaplain to the Bishop of Quebec. ————, Sponsors.

Marriage.

St. Thomas, 28th August, 1827—William H. Savis, of Mallahide, yeoman, and Hannah Crane, of the same township, spinster, were this day married by me, by banns. Witnesses—Jehiel Mann, Jacob M. Crane, Rhoda Mann, Eliza Davis.

30th August, 1827—Ira Whitcomb, an adult, born 28th September, 1793, Jemima Whitcomb, an adult, his wife, born 16th October, 1796, were this day baptised by me by public baptism. James Givins, Catharine Goodhue, Isabella P. Jones, Witnesses.

Baptisms.

30th August, 1827—Catharine Malvina, born 30th October, 1815, Nathan Wesson, born 25th January, 1821, Jason Wright, born 12th June, 1823, were this day baptised by me, by public baptism. James Givins, Ira Whitcomb, Isabella P. Jones, Catharine Goodhue, Sponsors.

Burial.

St. Thomas, 1st September, 1827—Margaret, daughter of John Book, of Southwold, died 31st August, aged 5½ years, and was this day buried by me, in the Churchyard of St. Thomas.

Marriage.

2nd September, 1827—Magnus Crawford, of Howard, W.D., yeoman, and Margaret Kelley, of the same township, spinster, were this day married by me, by banns. Witnesses—Samuel Craford, Thomas Craford, Cynthia Crawford.

Marriage.

4th September, 1827—Jehiel Mann, of Yarmouth, widower, and Hannah Decow, of Souhwold, spinster, were this day married by me, by banns. Witnesses—Abraham Griffin, Moses Willey, Alfred Hamilton.

Marriage.

4th September, 1827—Joseph Marlatt, of Yarmouth, widower, and Elizabeth Coughel, of the same township, spinster, were this day married by me, by banns. Witnesses—David S. Coughel, John Marlatt, John Coughel, Jas. Givens.

Marriage.

4th September, 1827—James Reynolds, of Westminster, yeoman, and Almira Wells, of the same township, spinster, were this day married by me, by banns. Witnesses—Timothy Kilbourn, Riley Wells, Horace Kilbourn, Jas. Givins.

Burial.

—— September, 1827—Michael McCormack, of St. Thomas, wheel-Wright, a native of Ireland, died on the —— inst., and was this day interred in the Churhyard of St. Thomas.

VITAL STATISTICS AT ST. THOMAS, U.C., COMMENCING 1824.   177

Burial.

St. Thomas, 8th October, 1827—John, son of John Eslick and his wife, died 6th inst., aged 4 years and 11 months, was this day interred in the Churchyard of St. Thomas.

Marriage.

10th October, 1827—Peter Schram, of Westminster, yeoman, and Margaret Beattie, of the same township, spinster, were this day married by me, by banns, according to the rites and ceremonies of the Church of England. Witnesses—James Beattie, Sarah Beattie, Simon Nicholls.

Burial.

21st October, 1827—Sarah Ann, daughter of Samuel N. York, of Yarmouth, and Lucy, his wife, died, 19th inst., aged 11 months, and was this day interred in the Churchyard of St. Thomas.

On Sunday, the 28th of October, I performed Divine Service in Dunwich, to continue regularly every 6th Sunday till their church is finished, then the first Sunday of each month.

Marriage.

St. Thomas, 30th October, 1827—Matthias B. Millard, of the Township of Malahide, yeoman, and Dorothy Schoffe, of the same township, spinster, were his day married by me, by banns. Witnesses—Cornelius Bowen, Philo Burch, John Dougharty.

Marriage.

30th October, 1827—Cornelius Bowen, of the Township of Malahide, yeoman, and Belinda Brooks, of the same township, spinster, were this day married by me, by banns. Witnesses—M. B. Millard, John Dougharty, Philo Burtch.

Marriage.

St. Thomas, 1st November, 1827—Peter Caughell, of the Township of Yarmouth, yeoman, and Mary Culver, of the same township, spinster, were this day married by me, by banns. Witnesses—John Caughell, Joseph Marlatt, David Caughell.

Marriage.

6th November, 1827—Lyman Mann, of Yarmouth, yeoman, and Betsy Ann Vroman, of the same township, spinster, were this day married by me, by banns. Witnesses—Rhoda Mann, Daniel Mann, Elizabeth Mann.

Marriage.

12th November, 1827—John O'Reilly, of the Township of Yarmouh, farmer, and Diana With, of the same township, widow, were this day married by me, by banns. Witnesses—R. C. Drake, Abel Bigsley, Benjamin C. Doan.

St. Thomas, 15th November, 1827—John Fitch, of the Township of Westminster, Tanner, and Getty Carrol, of the Township of London, spinster, were this day married by me, by banns. Witnesses—Silas E. Curtis, Eli Trowbridge, Abraham Carrol, John Ewart.

Marriage.

22nd November, 1827—Archibald McNeal, of Yarmouth, yeoman, and Anne Rowland, alias Beman, of the Township of Southwold, widow, were this day married by me, by license. Witnesses—Lemuel Ladd, Garret Smith, William Broderick.

Marriage.

28th November, 1827—Thomas Pettit, of the Township of Southwold, yeoman, and Huldah Gilbert, of the same township, spinster, were this day married by me, by banns. Witnesses—Alfred Hamilton, Z. Gillies, I. Stafford.

Marriage.

St. Thomas, 21st December, 1827—Gilbert Demont, of the Township of Yarmouth, cooper, and Amelia Murray, of the same place, spinster, were this day married by me, by license. Witnesses—John Robert Murray, Anne Elliott, Margaret Mackintosh.

Marriage.

24th December, 1827—Clarke Gardiner, of the Township of Yarmouth, yeoman, and Anne House, of the same township, spinser, were this day married by me, by banns. Witnesses—Matthew House, Joseph Allway, Abram House.

VITAL STATISTICS AT ST. THOMAS, U.C., COMMENCING 1824. 179

Sacrament.

On Tuesday, 25th December, 1827, being Christmas day, the Sacrament of the Lord's Supper was administered by me, in the Church of St. Thomas to 21 communicants.

Marriage.

St. Thomas, 26th December, 1827—William Pace, of the Township of Yarmouth, yeoman, and Paulina Chapel, of the same township, spinster, were his day married by me, by banns. Witnesses—Noah Brookfield, John Van Sickle, Josiah Morehouse, John Pace.

Marriage.

27th December, 1827—Joseph Hodgson, of the Township of London, widower, and Charity Patterson, of the Township of Westminster, widow, were this day married by me, by banns. Witnesses—John Sutton, John Hunt, Thomas P. Cheyna.

Sacrament.

On Sunday, 30th December, the Sacrament of the Lord's Supper was administered by me, in Dunwich, to 24 communicants.

Marriage.

St. Thomas, 1st January, 1828—Robert Nelson, of the Township of Howard, Western District, merchant, and Frances Dragon, of the Township of Raleigh, W.D., spinster, were this day married by me, by license. Witnesses—E. E. Warren, William McCrae, Duncan McGregor, Thomas Williams.

Marriage.

8th January, 1828—David Cascadden, of the Township of Malahide, yeoman, and Ann Gustin, of the same township, spinster, were this day married by me, by banns. Witnesses—Francis Moore, William Cascadden, Alexander Moore.

Burial.

9th January, 1828—Christian Long, of the Township of Southwold, yeoman, died 7th January inst., aged 69 years, and was this day interred in the Churchyard of St. Thomas.

Marriage.

St. Thomas, 9th January, 1828—Samuel Stephenson, of Malahide, yeoman, and Sarah Ann Sibley, of Bayham, were this day married by me, by banns. Witnesses—William Davis, David Sibley, Frances McGaffee.

Marriage.

24th January, 1828—John Welter, of Southwold, yeoman, and Christina Bastedo, of the same township, spinster, were this day married by me, by banns. Witnesses—David Welter, Levi Fowler, Thomas Fowler.

Burial.

24th January, 1828—John, son of John Davis, of Yarmouth, and Margaret, his wife, died 23rd January, aged 3 years, 11 months, and was this day interred by me, in the Churchyard of St. Thomas.

Marriage.

St. Thomas, 24th January, 1828—Daniel Brookes, of the Township of Dorchester, yeoman, and Mary Chase, of the Township of Malahide, spinster, were this day married by me, by banns. Witnesses—William McIntosh, James Henderson, Archibald McLachlin.

Marriage.

27th January, 1828—John Hess, of Yarmouth, yeoman, and Permit Maria Batchelor, of the same township, spinster, were this day married by me, by banns, according to the rites and ceremonies of the Church of England. Witnesses—Richard Nicolls, William Drake, Abraham Smith, Ilosia Baker.

Burial.

28th February, 1828—This day a child of John Welter, of Southwold, who died unbaptised, aged about 2 weeks, was interred in the Churchyard of St. Thomas.

Marriage.

St. Thomas, 28th January, 1828—Walter Ward, of the Township of Malahide, yeoman, and Sarah Leek, of the same township, widow, were this day married by me, by banns. Witnesses—Daniel McKenney, Hyland Ward, Chancey Burgess, Warren Davis.

Marriage.

28th January, 1828—Harvey Bryant, of the Township of Yarmouth, yeoman, and Jane Doane, of the same township, spinster, were this day married by me, by banns. Witnesses—Chancey Burgess, Jonathan Steel, Maria Kipp.

Burial.

29th February, 1828—This day a male child, aged twelve days, son of John Mackintosh, of Southwold, who died unbaptised, was this day interred in the Churchyard of St. Thomas.

Marriage.

St. Thomas, 28th January, 1828—Abraham House, of the Township of Yarmouth, widower, and Anne Gardiner, of the same township, spinster, were this day married by me, by banns. Witnesses—Henry House, Garret Oakes, David Cummings.

Marriage.

28th January, 1828—Harvey Bryant, of the Township of Yarmouth, yeoman, and Amy Simons, of the same township, spinster, were this day married by me, by banns. Witnesses—Daniel W. Stockton, Elijah Osborn, Eliza [her X mark] Leper.

Marriage.

21st February, 1828—Christopher Minor, of the Township of Yarmouth, yeoman, and Elizabeth Van Sickle, of the same township, spinster, were this day married by me, by banns. Witnesses—Asa Fordyyce, Silas Gavitz, James Van Sickle.

Marriage.

St. Thomas, 5th March, 1828—Benjamin Davis, of the Township of Westminster, yeoman, and Eliza Wilson, of the same township, spinster, were this day married by me, by banns. Witnesses—D. MacPherson, Amos Davis, Thomas Macpherson.

On Thursday, the 6th March, I performed Divine Service in London, and baptised the following children:—

6th March, 1828—Jane, daughter of James and Sarah Parkinson, of London, born 4th October, 1827, was this day baptised by me, by public baptism. Parents and Mary Brown, Sponsors.

Mary Jane, daughter of Richard and Margaret Ferguson, of London, born 5th September, 1827, was this day baptised by me, by public baptism. Richard Ferguson, Elizabeth Ferguson, Margaret Ferguson, Sponsors.

Baptisms in London, 6th March, continued.

Hannah Rosanna, daughter of John Talbot, of London, and Elizabeth, his wife, born 22nd December, 1817. Joseph Sifton, Esther Sifton, Anne Geary, Sponsors.

John, son of Thomas and Eliza Shoebottom, of London, born 18th October, 1827. John Shoebottom, James Shoebottom, Mary Shoebottom, Sponsors.

Helen, born 4th November, 1827, daughter of Thomas and Mary Hodgeons, of London. Anne Shoebottom, George Shoebottom, Mary Hodgeons, Sponsors.

George, born 29th August, 1827, son of James and Helen Shoebottom, of London. Thomas Shoebottom, Foliot Gray, Eliza Shoebottom, Sponsors.

Francis Henry, born 1st August, 1827, son of John and Elizabeth Ferguson, of London. John Ferguson, Elizabeth Ferguson, parents, Francis Walden.

Mary, daughter of Stephen and Mary Powell, of London, born 15th June, 1826. Stephen Powell (father), Mary Hardinge, Sarah Gearry, Sponsors.

Jane, daughter of John and Mary Gray, of London, born 20th October, 1827. John Gray, Mary Gray, parents, Eliza Talbot, Sponsors.

Robert, son of Robert and Elizabeth Ralph, of London, born 15th June, 1827. John Talbot, Elizabeth Talbot, Elizabeth Ralph (mother), Sponsors.

St. Thomas, 1828.

Baptisms in London on 6th March, continued.

Eleanor, born 29th November, 1827, daughter of William and Eleanor Guest, of London. George Guest, Mary Jones, Judith Ardiel, Sponsors.

Marriage.

17th March, 1828—Nicholas Westbrooke, of Westminster, yeoman, and Hannah Patrick, of the same township, spinster, were this day married by me, by banns. Witnesses—Timothy Kilbourn, D. H. Cutten, Stephen Malatt.

Marriage.

Gilbert Miller, of the Township of Mallahide, yeoman, and Wilmot Van Patten, of the same township, spinster, were this day married by me, by banns. Witnesses—M. B. Millard, Dorothy Millard, Mary Spades.

Burial.

St. Thomas, 14th March, 1828———————, child of Thomas Hardison, of Yarmouth, and ———, his wife, dièd on the 12th inst., aged 13 months, and was this day interred by me, in Yarmouth.

Baptism.

23rd March, 1828—John Henry, infant son of Samuel Mason, of Yarmouth, and Alice, his wife, born 23rd January, 1828, was this day baptised by me, by public baptism. Joseph Smith, John Mason and Anna Smith, Sponsors.

Baptism.

24th March, 1828—Charles Augustus, infant son of Ira Whitcomb, of Yarmouth, and Jemima, his wife, born 1st January, 1828, was this day baptised by me, by public baptism. James Givins, Ira Whitcombe, Isabella P. Jones, proxy of the mother, Sponsors.

Marriage.

St. Thomas, 27th March, 1828—Levi Harris, of Bayham, yeoman, and Margaret Willis, of Malahide, spinster, were this day married by me, by banns. Witnesses—Henry Willis, Samuel H. Anderson, Septimus Davis.

Marriage.

30th March, 1828—Abel Bigsby, of St. Thomas, carpenter, and Harriet Sampson, of the Township of Yarmouth, spinster, were this day married by me, by banns. Witnesses—Barzillai Sampson, Enos Call, John Farnham.

Marriage.

1st April, 1828—Richard Hayes, of the Township of London, yeoman, and Rebecca Wallace, of the same township, widow, were this day married by me, by banns. Witnesses—Joseph Sifton, Maria Sifton, William Fassett.

Marriage.

St. Thomas, 2nd April, 1828—Jonathan Steel, of the Township of Yarmouth, yeoman, and Maria Kipp, of the same township, spinster, were this day married by me, by banns. Witnesses—James Brown, Harvey Kipp, Benjamin Doan, Jr.

Sacrament.

6th April, 1828—Easter Sunday—On this day the Sacremant of the Lord's Supper was administered by me, to eighteen persons.

Sacrament.

13th April, 1828—On this day the Sacremant of the Lord's Supper was administered by me, in Dunwich, to 22 persons.

Baptism.

13th April, 1828—Margaret, daughter of John Miles Farland. of Dunwich, and Martha, his wife, was this day baptised by me, by public baptism. Walter Patterson, Mary Patterson, Margaret Bobier, Sponsors.

VITAL STATISTICS AT ST. THOMAS, U.C., COMMENCING 1824.

Baptism..

14th April, 1828—Donald, son of William Macpherson of Dunwich, and ————, his wife, born ————, was this day baptised by me, by public baptism. The Parents, Sponsors.

Baptism..

14th April, 1828—James, son of Alexander Macpherson, of Dunwich, and Isabel, his wife, born ————, was this day baptised by me, by public baptism. The Parents, Sponsors.

Marriage.

17th April, 1828—Thomas Drake, of the Township of Yarmouth, yeoman, and Vashti Wood, of the Township of Southwold, spinster, were this day married by me, by license. Witnesses—Phineas Drake, James McQueen, Amos M. Barnes, George D. Spades.

Marriage.

St. Thomas, 13th May, 1828—Daniel Stockton, of the Township of Yarmouth, yeoman, and Eliza Leper, of the same township, spinster, were this day married by me, by banns. Witnesses—John Huff, Jacob F. Scott, Mahlon Stockton.

Baptism..

14th October, 1828—Charles Henry, son of Dr. Charles Duncomb, of St. Thomas, and Nancy, his wife, born 21st May, 1822, was this day baptised by me, by public baptism. George D. Spades and Parents, Sponsors.

Baptism.

St. Thomas, 21st October, 1828—Anne, born 18th August, 1802, wife of Mr. Hiram D. Lee, of Westminster, was this day baptised by me, by public baptism. George J. Goodhue, Catherine Goodhue, Abigail Lawreson, Witnesses.

Baptisms.

Westminster, 21st October, 1828—Elvira, born 12th February, 1820, William Edward, born 3rd November, 1822, John Rolph, born 10th October, 1824, and Hiram Chisholm, born 14th September, 1826, children of Mr. Hiram D. Lee, of the Township of Westminster, and Anne, his wife, were this day baptised by me, by public baptism. The Parents, Lawrence Lawrason, Abigail Lawrason, Sponsors.

N.B.—The Visiting Missionary (Mr. Archibald), visited this place on the 29th October. I accompanied him to London, where he preached twice on Sunday, the 2nd November.

Burial.

St. Thomas, 21st October, 1828—Maria, wife of George J. Goodhue, of London, merchant, died 20th inst., aged 28 years and six months, and was this day interred by me, in the burying ground in the Town of London.

Baptism.

21st October, 1828—Maria Fullerton Norton, infant child of George J. Goodhue, of London, and Maria, his wife, born 4th July, 1828, was this day baptised by me by public baptism. Catherine Goodhue, Hiram D. Lee, as proxy for Wm. Henry, Anne Lee, as proxy for Catherine Fullerton, Sponsors.

Marriage.

St. Thomas, 3rd November, 1828—Thomas Pennington, of the Township of Malahide, yeoman, and Laura Dewey, of the same township, spinster, were this day married by me, by banns. Witnesses—John Caray, William Drake, Morris Sovereign, George D. Spades.

Marriage.

St. Thomas, 11th November, 1828—Hammond Oakes, of the Township of Charlotteville, yeoman, and Isabella Phillips, of the Township of Southwold, spinster, were this day married by me, by banns. Witnesses—C. Youmans, Lad. Sells, A. W. Steres.

Marriage.

23rd November, 1828—Edmund Smith, of Southwold, yeoman, and Almiro Thayer, of the Township of Yarmouth, spinster, were his day married by me, by banns. William Parker, Jarvis Thayer, William Smith, John Thayer, Witnesses.

Marriage.

24th November, 1828—Daniel Lockwood, of the Township of Carradoc, yeoman, and Hester Bateman, of the same township, spinster, were this day married by me, by banns. Witnesses—Jesse Bennett, Andrew Nevills, Andrew Fortner.

Marriage.

24th November, 1828—William Bryant, of the Township of Westminster, widower, and Lavinia Macaulay, of the same township, spinster, were this day married by me, by banns. Witnesses—Andrew Beattie, Richard Tunks, Calvin Burtch, William Walters.

Baptism.

St. Thomas, 24th November, 1828—Jane Thomson, born 23rd April, 1828, infant daughter of Peter Schram, of Westminster, and Margaret, his wife, was this day baptised by me, by public baptism. The Parents, Margaret Schram, the older, Sponsors.

Baptism.

24th November, 1828—Susan Gilbert, born 16th June, 1823, daughter of James McNames, of Westminster, and Charlotte, his wife, was baptised by me, this day, by public baptism. Andrew Beattie, Charlotte McNames, Margaret Schram, the older, Sponsors.

Burial.

3rd December, 1828—Adam Burwell, of Southwold, yeoman. (the father of Col. Burwell), died on the 1st inst., aged —— years, and was this day interred by me, in the Churchyard of St. Thomas.

Marriage.

St. Thomas, 22nd January, 1828—Thomas Culver, of the Township of Southwold, yeoman, and Hannah Pettit, of the same township, spinster, were this day married by me, by banns. Witnesses—Joseph Spitler, Adam Burwell, Clark Collven.

Marriage.

St. Thomas, 15th February, 1829—Timothy Kilburn, of the Township of Delaware, yeoman, and Delight Wells, of the Township of West-

minster, spinster, were this day married by me, by banns. Witnesses—
Riley Wells, Gilbert Strong, Cyrus McMillen, Peter Schram.

Burial.

16th February, 1829—John Robert Dumont, child of Gilbert Dumont, and Amelia, his wife, born 21st September, 1828, died 15th inst., ——— was this day buried by me, in the Churchyard of St. Thomas.

Marriage.

17th February, 1829—John Burgess, of the Township of Yarmouth, yeoman, and Hannah Ryckman, of the same township, spinster, were this day married by me, by banns. Witnesses—Alexander Bryce, J. B. Hawkin, Wm. Ostrander, Minor Barnes.

Marriage.

St. Thomas, 18th February, 1829—William Hartwell, Esq., of Pittsford, Monroe Co., N.Y., United States, and Martha Maria Schofield, daughter of Ira Schofield, Esq., of London, U.C., were this day married by me, by license. Witnesses—M. Burwell, James Givins, Geo. J. Goodhue, Edward E. Warren.

Marriage.

25th February, 1829—Abraham Griffin, of Southwold, yeoman, and Eliza Young, of Dunwich, spinster, were his day married by me, by banns. Witnesses—Elliott Young, Russel Young, Ezekiel McIntire.

Marriage.

St. Thomas, 1st March, 1829—John Sutton, of the Township of Southwold, yeoman, and Cynthia Phillips, of the same township, spinster, were this day married by me, by banns. .Witnesses—Amariah Sutton, Jackson Stafford, Isaac Phillips.

2nd March, 1829—Daniel Treadwell, of the Township of Malahide, yeoman, and Sarah Willis, of the same township, spinster, were this day married by me, by banns. Witnesses—Edward Griffin, J. Davis, S. Davis.

Marriage.

12th March, 1829—John Bobier, of the Township of Dunwich, yeoman, and Jane Wellwood, of the Township of Southwold, spinster, were this day married by me, by license. Witnesses—Daniel Wellwood, Joshua Bobier, Richard Milligan, William Crane.

Baptism.

St. Thomas, 1st March, 1829——————, infant child of James Ferguson, of Southwold, and Sarah, his wife, born ————, 1828, was this day baptised by me, by public baptism. ———— Meek and the Parents, Sponsors.

Burial.

5th March, 1829—Eliza, daughter of Calvin Witt, of Southwold, and ————, his wife, died on the 3rd inst., aged —— years, and was this day interred by me, in the Churchyard of St. Thomas.

Marriage.

12th March, 1829—William Crane, of the Township of Dunwich, yeoman, and Margaret Bobier, of the same township, spinster, were this day married by me, by license. Witnesses—John Bobier, Joshua Bobier, Daniel Wellwood, Richard Milligan.

Burial.

22nd March, 1829—Eleanor Spades, daughter of Geo. D. Spades and Mary, his wife, died 21st inst., aged 3 years, was this day interred in the Churchyard of St. Thomas.

Marriage.

St. Thomas, 17th March, 1829—Amos Barnes, of the Township of Yarmouth, yeoman, and Elizabeth Spittler, of the Township of Southwold, spinster, were this day married by me, by banns. Witnesses—Joseph Spittler, Jonas Barnes, Levi Fowler, David Conrad.

Marriage.

24th March, 1829—John Dougherty, of the Township of Southwold, yeoman, and Susannah Ellis, of the same township, spinster, were this day married by me, by banns. Witnesses—James Jackson, Hugh Sharon, Jacob Bodoin, James Little, ———— Clark.

Marriage.

St. Thomas, 24th March, 1829—Alexander Ironside, Esq., of St. Thomas, medical practitioner, and Margaret Rapelje, of the Township of Yarmouth, spinster, were this day married by me, by license. Witnesses—James Givins, James Nevills, Jeronimus Rapelje, Jr.

Marriage.

26th March, 1829—Jacob Preffer, Jun., of the Township of Yarmouth, yeoman, and Agnes Best, of the same township, spinster, were this day married by me, by license. Witnesses—Jacob Preffer, Sen., James Brown, James Givins, Robert Nelson.

Marriage.

St. Thomas, 31st March, 1829—Nathaniel Bryant, of the Township of Yarmouth, yeoman, and Jane Wilson, of the same township, spinster, were this day married by me, by banns. Witnesses—Benjamin Doans, Thomas Sprague, Matilda Willson.

Burial.

1st April, 1829—William Lee, Sen., of Southwold, died 30th March, ult., aged 69 years, and was this day interred by me in the Churchyard of St. Thomas.

Marriage.

St. Thomas, 27th April, 1829—Joseph Smith, of the Township of Southwold, bachelor, and Sarah Williams, of the Township of Westminster, spinster, were this day married by me, by banns. Witnesses—Ganer Ellwood, Samuel Smith, Garet Smith.

Marriage.

4th May, 1829—John Coughel, of the Township of Yarmouth, bachelor, and Abigail Hughes, of the same township, spinster, were this day married by me, by banns. Witnesses—Charles Conrad, Joseph Marlatt, David Caughel.

Marriage.

St. Thomas, 4th May, 1829—Henry Welter, of the Township of Southwold, Bachelor, and Christina Bawtinham, of the same township, spinster, were this day married by me, by banns. Witnesses—Thomas Fowler, Christopher Long, David Welter.

VITAL STATISTICS AT ST. THOMAS, U.C., COMMENCING 1824.   191

Marriage.

St. Thomas, 17th August, 1829—Jacob Hull, of the Township of Westminster, in the London District, and Province of Upper Canada, was married after publication of banns, to Euphemia Lochler, of the same place, on this day, by me. Witnesses—John R. Harman, Jonathan [his X mark] Smith. Given away by Isaac Hunt.

Marriage.

17th August, 1829—Frederick Lown, of the Township of Westminster, in the London District, and Province of Upper Canada, was married after publication of banns, to Polly Dingman, of the same place, on this day, by me. Witnesses—Thomas Pool, and Benjamin Schram. Given away by Thomas Pool.

Burial.

28th August, 1829—Silas Zavitz, commonly called Savage, youngest son of Christie Zavitz and ———, his wife, was buried on this day by me.

Baptism.

20th August, 1829—Andrew, son of Frederick Lown and Polly, his first wife, of the Township of Westminster, born 17th July, 1827, was this day baptised, by public baptism, by me. John Dingman, Thos. Pool, Catherine Pool, Sponsors.

Marriage.

4th September, 1829—Thomas Thomas, of the Township of Southwold, in the district of London, in the Province of Upper Canada, was married by license to Elizabeth Maccormick, of the same place, widow, on this day, by me. Witness—Ann Thomas. Given away by John Holden.

Burial.

September 7th, 1829—James Wilson, from Banbridge, County of Down, in Ireland, died on Sunday, the 6th ult., at Port Stanley, and was buried on Mr. Jos. Smith's farm on this day, by me.

Burial.

September 7th, 1829—Jemima Whitcomb, wife of ———— Whitcomb, age 31 years, 10 mos., and 21 days, died yesterday, Sunday, the 6th, and was buried at St. Thomas, on this day, by me.

Baptism.

October 4th, 1829—Maria, daughter of John Miles Farland, of Dunwich, and Martha, his wife, born on the 20th July, 1829, was publicly baptised on this day, by me. Jane Bobier, Lydia Patterson, John Bobier, Sponsors.

Marriage.

St. Thomas, Oct. 5th, 1829—William Millard, of the Township of Malahide, was married, by banns, to Pamela Martin, of the same place, spinster, on this day, by me. Given away by James Summers. Witnesses—James Burdick, George Gillet.

Marriage.

October, 26th, 1829—Thomas Williams, of the Township of Southwold, widower, was married, by banns, to Mary Nash, of the Township of Dunwich, on this day, by me. Given away by Sylvester [his X mark] Nash. Witnesses—John Robert Murray, Henry S. Lawson, Robert Clark.

Marriage.

October 26th, 1829—Nathan Brown, of the Township of Yarmouth, was married, by banns, to Catherine Gawse, on this day, by me. They are both colored persons. Witnesses—Archibald [his X mark] Lewis, Richard [his X mark] Woods.

Marriage.

St. Thomas, November 8th, 1829—Samuel McDowell, of the Township of Yarmouth, was married, by license, to Aner McCall, of the same place, widow, on this day, by me. Given away by John [his X mark] Storms. Witnesses—Daniel [his X mark] Hendershot, Henry [his X mark] Storms.

Marriage.

November 8th, 1829—James Vansickle, of the Township of Yarmouth, was married, by license, to Susan Minor, of the same place, on this day, by me. Given away by Christian Minor. Witnesses—Joseph M. Moore, Isaac Minor.

Marriage.

November 30th, 1829—Matthias Sutton, of Niagara, was married by license, to Hannah Patterson, of the Township of Westminster, on this day, by me. Given away by Andrew Fortner. Witnesses—Garner Ellwood, Joseph Hodgson.

St. Thomas, December 8th, 1829—William Kelley, of the Township of Southwold, was married, by banns, to Margaret Burwell, of the same place, widow, on this day, by me. Given away by David Kelly. Witnesses—John D. Lawson, Elliot Young.

Marriage.

December 15th, 1829—William C. Mcpherson, of the Township of Westminster, was married, by banns, to Abigail Bruce, of the same place, spinster, on this day, by me. Given away by D. Mcpherson. Witnesses—Garner Ellwood, John Corson.

Marriage.

St. Thomas, December 22nd, 1829—Duncan McLarty, yeoman, and Sarah McIntire, spinster, both of the Township of Southwold, were this day married by me, by banns. Witnesses—John Leitch, Colin Leitch, John Munro.

Marriage.

December 24th, 1829—Phineas Drake, yeoman, and Catharine Hughes, spinster, both of the Township of Southwold, were this day married by me, by license. Witnesses—Wm. Drake, Margaret Drake.

Marriage.

December 29th, 1829—Jacob Pace, cooper, and Margaret McLean, spinster, both of the Township of Yarmouth, were this day married by me, by banns. Witnesses—John Pace, Wm. Parker, Henry Petty.

Burial.

St. Thomas, December 31st, 1829—James Hepburne, of Southwold, died, 29th December, aged —— years, and was this day interred by me in the Churchyard of St. Thomas.

Marriage.

31st December, 1829—Joseph King, of the Township of Yarmouth, and Dorothy Ferguson, of the Township of Malahide, were this day married by me, by banns. Witnesses—Thomas Matthews, Peter Matthews, John Ferguson.

Marriage.

January 12th, 1830—Thomas Meek, of the Township of Southwold, yeoman, and Mary S. Owrey, of the Township of Westminster, were married by me, this day, by license. Witnesses—Richard Nicolls, Archibald Owrey, Wm. Owrey.

Baptism.

18th January, 1829—John, son of Francis and Sarah Johnston, born January, 1830, was this day baptised by me, by public baptism. Wm. Pearce, Joseph Patterson, Catharine Pearce, Mary Patterson, Sponsors.

Marriage.

St. Thomas, January 19th, 1830—Stephen Wilcox, yeoman, and Margaret Wismer, spinster, both of the Township of Yarmouth, were married by me, this day, by banns. Witnesses—David Caughill, Jacob Wismer, John Wismer.

Marriage.

19th January, 1830—George Brown, of the Township of Yarmouth, yeoman, and Sade Thurstin, of the Township of Malahide, were married by me, this day, by banns. Witnesses—Joel Davis, Robert McKeney, Alexander Bryce.

Marriage.

19th January, 1830—Wm. Smith, of the Township of Walsingham, yeoman, and Mary Bowen, of the Township of Bertie, spinster, were married by me, this day, by license. Witnesses—Samuel Smith, Daniel Davis, Jacob Davis.

Marriage.

St. Thomas, 19th January, 1830—Reuben Lamb, yeoman, and Ann Huffman, spinster, both of the Township of Malahide, were this day married by me, by banns. Witnesses—Winslow Hayward, Jacob Huffman, Charles McArthy.

VITAL STATISTICS AT ST. THOMAS, U.C., COMMENCING 1824.

Marriage.

20th January, 1830—John Hunt, yeoman, and Hannah Marr, spinster, both of the Township of Southwold, were this day married by me, by license. Witnesses—Charles Hannan, Thomas Marr, Daniel Smith.

Baptism.

21st January, 1830—Mary, infant daughter of David J. and Jane Bowman, born November 23rd, 1829, was this day baptised by me. Margaret Warren, Archange Warren, Robert Warren, Sponsors.

Marriage.

January 25th, 1830—James Doying, yeoman, and Maria Sampson, spinster, both of the Township of Yarmouth, were married by me, this day, by banns. Witnesses—James Nevills, Henry W. Woods, Peter Secords.

Marriage.

January 28th, 1830—Francis Crane, carpenter, and Esther Philpots, widow, both of the Township of Southwold, were married by me, this day, by banns. Witnesses—Elliot Young, Alfred Hamilton, Rufus Lumley.

Marriage.

February, 22nd, 1830—Wm. Stuart, yeoman, and Sophia Long, spinster, both of the Township of Southwold, were married by me, this day, by banns. Witnesses— ———.

Marriage.

February 22nd, 1830—Thomas Lumley, yeoman, and Christiana Willey, spinster, both of the Township of Dunwich, were this day married by me, by banns. Witnesses— ———.

Marriage.

February 25th, 1830—Aaron Van Pater, yeoman, and Elizabeth Harvey, spinster, both of the Township of Malahide, were this day married by me, by banns. Witnesses—John Harvey, Andrew McCausland, Simon Van Pater.

Baptisms.

1st March, 1830—This day were baptised by me, by public baptism, Wm. King, born January 2nd, 1816, Gilman Wilson King, born July 26th, 1818, John King, born April 28th, 1821, Elias Edwy. King, born September 9th, 1829. Alexander Hamilton, Hooper King, Elizabeth Hamilton, Sponsors.

Eliza King, born October 26th, 1823, and Rosanna King, April 28th, 1826. Elizabeth Hamilton, Elizabeth King, Alexander Hamilton, Sponsors.

The above named are the children of Hooper King and Elizabeth, his wife.

Baptism.

7th March, 1830—Egerton LeRoy Mason, infant son of Samuel Mason, and Alice, his wife, born 24th November, 1829, was this day baptised by me, by public baptism. George R. Williams, Joseph R. Bostwick, Maria L. Williams.

Publications of the Ontario Historical Society.

Vol. I.—pp. 140. Royal 8vo. (Out of print.)

Rev. John Langhorn—Personal Note.
Marriage Record of Rev. John Langhorn, No. 1.
Rev. G. O'Kill Stuart's Register at St. John's Church, Bath.
Marriage Register of St. John's Church, Ernest Town, No. 2.
Langhorn's Book No. 3.
In the Parish Register of St. George, Kingston.
A Register of Baptisms for the Township of Fredericksburgh.
Rev. John Langhorn's Records, 1787-1813—Burials.
Rev. John Langhorn's Register of St. Paul's Church, Fredericksburgh.
Rev. Robert McDowall—Personal Note.
McDowall Marriage Register.
A Register of Baptisms by the Rev. Robert McDowall.
Marriage Register of Stephen Conger, J. P., Hallowell.
Some Descendants of Joseph Brant.
Remarks on the Maps from St. Regis to Sault Ste. Marie.
Sketch of Peter Teeple, Loyalist and Pioneer, 1762-1847.
The Cameron Rolls, 1812.
The Talbot Settlement and Buffalo in 1816.

Vol. II.—pp. 128. Royal 8vo. $1.00.

The United Empire Loyalist Settlement at Long Point, Lake Erie.

Vol. III.—pp. 199. Royal 8vo. $1.00.

Early Records of St. Mark's and St. Andrew's Churches, Niagara. By Janet Carnochan.
    Baptisms in Niagara by Rev. Robert Addison.
    Weddings at Niagara, 1792.
    Burials, Niagara, 1792.
    Register of Baptisms, commencing 29th June, 1817, Township of Grimsby.
    Register of Marriages, Township of Grimsby, U.C., commencing August, 1817.
    Register of Burials in the Township of Grimsby.
    Register of Christenings in the Presbyterian Congregation, Township of Newark, Upper Canada.
    Register of Births and Baptisms, St. Andrew's Church, Niagara.
    Marriages celebrated by Rev. Robert McGill.

Vol. III.—*Continued.*

German-Canadian Folk Lore. By W. J. Wintemberg.
The Settlers of March Township. By Mrs. M. H. Ahearn.
The Settlement of the County of Grenville. By Mrs Burritt.
Recollections of Mary Warren Breckenridge, of Clark Township. By Catherine F. Lefroy
A Relic of Thayendanegea (Capt. Joseph Brant). By Mrs. M. E. Rose Holden.
Some Presbyterian U. E. Loyalists. By D. W. Clendennan.
The Migration of *Voyageurs* from Drummond Island to Penetanguishene in 1828. By A. C. Osborne.
List of the Drummond Island *Voyageurs.*
Portrait of Father Marquette.
A Brief History of David Barker, a United Empire Loyalist. By J. S. Barker.
The Old "Bragh" or Hand Mill. By Sheriff McKellar.
The Ethnographical Elements of Ontario. By A. F Hunter, M.A.

Vol. IV.—pp. 115. Royal 8vo, $1.00.

Exploration of the Great Lakes, 1669-1670. By Dollier de Casson and de Bréhant de Galinée.
Galinée's Narrative and Map, with an English Version, including all the Map Legends. Translator and Editor, James H. Coyne.

Vol. V.—pp. 236. Royal 8vo. $1.00.

I. Discovery and Exploration of the Bay of Quinte. James H. Coyne, B.A.
II. The Origin of our Maple Leaf Emblem. The Editor
III. The Count de Puisaye. A Forgotten Page of Canadian History. Miss Janet Carnochan.
IV. Historical Notes on Yonge Street. Miss L. Teefy.
V. Presqu'isle. I. M. Wellington, with Notes by C. C. James.
VI. Genealogical List of the Bull Family. Dr. A. C. Bowerman.
VII. A Record of Marriages and Baptisms in the Gore and London District, by the Rev. Ralph Leeming, from 1816-1827. With Introduction by H. H. Robertson, Barrister, Hamilton. Ont.
VIII. Ancaster Parish Records, 1830-1838, from the Register of the Rev. John Miller, M.A.
IX. Sketch of the Rev. William Smart, Presbyterian Minister of Elizabethtown. Holly S. Seaman.
X. Record of Marriages and Baptisms from the Registers of the Rev. William Smart, Elizabethtown, 1812-1842.

Vol. VI.—pp. 170. Royal 8vo. $1.00.

I. The Coming of the Mississagas. J. Hampden Burnham.
II. The First Indian Land Grant in Malden. C. W. Martin.
III. Journal of a Journey from Sandwich to York in 1806, Charles Aikens.
IV. The John Richardson Letters. Col. E. Cruikshank.
V. Ontario Onomatology and British Biography. H. F. Gardiner.
VI. The Origin of "Napanee." C. C. James.
VII. Napanee's First Mills and their Building. Thomas W. Casey.
VIII. Local Historic Places in Essex County. Miss Margaret Claire Kilroy.
IX. Notes on the early History of the County of Essex. Francis Cleary.
X. Battle of Queenston Heights. Editor.
XI. Battle of Windsor. John McCrae.
XII. The Western District Literary and Agricultural Association. Rev. Thomas Nattress.
XIII. Battle of Goose Creek. John S. Barker.
XIV. McCollom Memoirs. W. A. McCollom.
XV. Breif Sketch of a Canadian Pioneer. (Reprint.)
XVI. The Switzers of the Bay of Quinte. E. E. Switzer.
XVII. The State Historian of New York and the Clinton Papers—A Criticism. H. H. Robertson.
XVIII. Anderson Record from 1699 to 1896. Mrs. S. Rowe.
XIX. Lutheran Church Record, 1793-1832.
XX. Assessment of the Township of Hallowell for 1808.

Vol. VII.—pp. 236. Royal 8vo. $1.00.

The First Chapter of Upper Canadian History. By Avern Pardoe.
In the Footsteps of the Habitant on the South shore of the Detroit River. By Margaret Claire Kilroy.
Births, Marriages and Deaths recorded in the Parish Registers of Assumption, Sandwich, By Francis Cleary.
The Pennsylvania Germans of Waterloo County, Ontario By Rev. A. B. Sherk.
Black List.
An Old Family Account Book. By Michael G. Sherk.
The Origin of the Maple Leaf as the Emblem of Canada. By Miss Janet Carnochan.
Testimonial of Mr. Roger Bates, of the Township of Hamilton, District of Newcastle, now living on his farm near Cobourg.
Reminiscences of Mrs. White, of White's Mills, near Cobourg, Upper Canada, formerly Miss Catherine Chrysler, of Sydney, near Belleville, aged 79.
Memoirs of Colonel John Clark, of Port Dalhousie, C.W.
The Origin of the Names of the Post Offices in Simcoe County. By David Williams, B.A.

Vol. VIII.—pp. 228. Royal 8vo. $1.00.

I. The Insurrection in the Short Hills in 1838. Lt.-Col. E. Cruikshank.
II. The Hamiltons of Queenston, Kingston and Hamilton. H. F. Gardiner.
III. The Petuns. Lt.-Col. G. W. Bruce.
IV. The Nottawasaga River Route. G. K. Mills, B.A.
V. The First Commission of the Peace for the District of Mecklenburg R. V. Rogers, LL.D.
VI. Some Events in the History of Kingston. W. S. Ellis, B.A.
VII. Early History of the Anglican Church in Kingston. Rev. Archdeacon McMorine, D.D.
VIII. Some Epochs in the Story of Old Kingston. Miss Agnes Maule Machar ("Fidelis")
IX. The Navies on Lake Ontario in the War of 1812. Notes from the Papers of a Naval Officer then serving on His Majesty's Ships. Barlow Cumberland, M.A.
X. Cataraqui. Charles MacKenzie.
XI. Captain William Gilkinson. Notes from a Paper prepared by Miss Augusta Isabella Grant Gilkison.
XII. Early Churches in the Niagara Peninsula, Stamford and Chippewa, with Marriage Records of Thomas and James Cummings, J.P., and Extracts from the Cummings Papers. Miss Janet Carnochan.

Vol. IX.—pp. 200. Royal 8vo. $1.00.

I. Fort Malden or Amherstburg. By Francis Cleary.
II. Thamesville and the Battle of the Thames. By Katherine B. Coutts.
III. The Highland Pioneers of the County of Middlesex.
IV Centenary of the Death of Brant. By Herbert F. Gardiner, M.A.
V. The Pioneers of Middlesex.
VI. The Beginning of London. By Col. T. Campbell, M.D.
VII. An Episode of the War of 1812. The Story of the Schooner "Nancy."
VIII. Register of Baptisms, Marriages and Deaths, at St. Thomas, U.C., Commencing with the Establishment of the Mission in July, 1824.

Ontario Historical Society

PAPERS AND RECORDS

VOL. X.

TORONTO
PUBLISHED BY THE SOCIETY
1913

OFFICERS, 1912-13.

Honorary President:
THE HONORABLE THE MINISTER OF EDUCATION.

President:
JOHN DEARNESS, M.A., London.

1st Vice-President:
CLARANCE M. WARNER, Napanee.

2nd Vice-President:
SIR EDMUND WALKER, Toronto.

Secretary and Acting Treasurer:
ALEXANDER FRASER, LL.D., Toronto.

Auditors:
J. J. MURPHY, Toronto.   FRANK YEIGH, Toronto.

Councillors:
A. F. HUNTER, M.A.   D. S. WALLACE, M.A.
J. STEWART CARSTAIRS, B.A.   W. L. GRANT, M.A.
ALEXANDER FRASER, LL.D.

CONTENTS.

CHAP.		PAGE
I.	Major-General Sir Isaac Brock, K.B. J. A. Macdonell, K.C.	5
II.	Romantic Elements in the History of the Mississippi Valley. Reuben Gold Thwaites, LL.D.	33
III.	Collections of Historical Material Relating to the War of 1812. Frank H. Severance, L.H.D.	43
IV.	Despatch from Colonel Lethbridge to Major-General Isaac Brock. Lieut.-Col. Cole	57
V.	Military Movements in Eastern Ontario during the War of 1812. Lieut.-Col. W. S. Buell	60
VI.	Defence of Essex during the War of 1812. Francis Cleary.	72
VII.	The Economic Effect of the War of 1812 on Upper Canada. Adam Shortt, C.M.G., M.A., F.R.S.C.	79

NOTE.

The Editorial Committee assumes no responsibility for the accuracy of statements made, or for opinions expressed in the Papers contained in this volume.

ALEXANDER FRASER, *Secretary.*

I.

MAJOR-GENERAL SIR ISAAC BROCK, K.B.*

(Born 6th October, 1769; died 13th October, 1812.)

By J. A. MACDONELL, K.C., GLENGARRY.

"We are engaged in an awful and eventful contest. By unanimity and despatch in our councils and by vigour in our operations, we will teach the enemy this lesson: that a country defended by free men, enthusiastically devoted to the cause of their King and constitution, can never be conquered."

It was with these glorious and inspiring words that Major-General Brock, then Lieutenant-Governor of the Province of Upper Canada, concluded the speech with which on the 27th July, 1812, he opened the extra session of the Legislature of the Province, which he had summoned immediately following the declaration of war by the United States on the 18th of June.

He had been appointed Administrator, or President, as the office was then styled, on the 30th of September, 1811, assuming his government on the 9th of October, in the absence of Lieutenant-Governor Gore, who had left York (now Toronto) on the day previous. It was his fate nobly to fall at Queenston Heights on the 13th of the same month in the following year; he therefore held office for but a few days over a year. But that short time was sufficient to obtain for his name immortality, so long as the English language can narrate what in that brief period he accomplished, and to hold forth for succeeding generations of British subjects in Canada and throughout the Empire, the bright example of his genius and his gallantry, his indomitable spirit and extraordinary fertility of resource.

Isaac Brock was the eighth son of John Brock, Esquire, a gentleman of Guernsey, of good family and independent means, who, in his youth, had been a midshipman in the

*Read at the meeting of the Ontario Historical Society at Napanee, Ont, 1912.

Royal Navy, by Elizabeth De Lisle, his wife. He was born at St. Peter's Port, Guernsey, on the 6th of October, 1768, the same memorable year which gave birth to Wellington and Napoleon; and was thus but forty-three years of age at the time of his death. Singularly, and sadly enough, of all the eight brothers who reached maturity, no male descendant is now in existence to bear that honoured name. Brock is described as being always tall and robust for his age; with strength and determination, the best boxer and swimmer of his set, yet at the same time always of the most gentle and kindly nature. In more mature years he was a man of towering frame and commanding aspect. From a primary school at Southampton he was sent to complete his education and perfect his knowledge of the language, to a French pastor at Rotterdam. He entered the 8th Regiment as an ensign, when but little over fifteen; raising an independent company, he was gazetted captain, but shortly afterwards was placed on half-pay. In 1791, by purchase, he exchanged into the 49th Regiment, with which he was destined to be so long and honourably associated, and which took part in the Battle of Queenston Heights, when he died. He served with that regiment in Barbadoes and Jamaica, becoming major in 1795, and lieutenant-colonel in 1797, while yet but twenty-eight years of age. The regiment had fallen into bad habits and worse discipline, but under his command it soon regained its good character; the Duke of York, then Commander-in-Chief, declaring that Lieut.-Colonel Brock, from one of the worst, had made the 49th one of the best regiments in the service. While he exercised his command with vigour and strictness, his discipline was tempered by reason and justice. He possessed that happy quality which the French call "camaraderie," which has always been found in really great soldiers and than which nothing more endears a commanding officer to the men who are fortunate enough to serve under him— indeed, the secret of Brock's influence and success was that he really cared for his men, and that they recognized that such was his guiding principle. Under his command, the 49th served under Sir Ralph Abercrombie, and subsequently Sir John Moore, in North Holland, in 1799, where Colonel Brock greatly distinguished himself. The regiment suffered severely at Egmont-op-Zee, where Brock himself was wounded.

In 1801, he was second in command of the land forces in the celebrated attack on Copenhagen by Lord Nelson.

In 1802, he came with his regiment to Canada, and Canada was happily destined to benefit by his untiring services for the following ten years, while here it was his lot to achieve imperishable renown. The first three years he spent on regimental duty, being quartered at different times with the 49th at Montreal, York, Fort George (Niagara-on-the-Lake), and Quebec. In 1805 he became a full colonel and returned to England on leave of absence. While there he laid before the Commander-in-Chief the outline of a plan for the formation of a veteran battalion to serve in Canada. *1802. His advent to Canada.* *1805. Full Colonel.* *Recommends formation of veteran battalion.*

The Royal Canadian Volunteer Regiment of Foot, of two battalions, which had been raised and placed in 1796 on the regular establishment of the army, and the first battalion of which under Lieut.-Colonel the Baron de Longueuil had garrisoned the posts of Lower Canada, and the second battalion under Lieut.-Colonel Macdonell those of the Upper Province, had, together with all Fencible corps in the army, been disbanded in 1802, during the short-lived Peace of Amiens. Both Provinces were therefore practically without regular local forces. But Britain at this time had her hands full with Napoleon; every available man was required in the Peninsula, and the British Government, seeing no reason or occasion for war with the United States, did not believe that war would take place, and Colonel Brock did not therefore succeed in convincing the Home authorities of the necessity of establishing such a corps at the time. He received, though, the thanks of H.R.H. the Duke of York, Commander-in-Chief, for his communication and his very sensible and valuable observations respecting the distribution of troops in Canada, and the promise that his recommendations would be taken into consideration at a seasonable opportunity. In the light of events which transpired in the near future, the wisdom of Colonel Brock's proposal is apparent. His suggestion was that detachments of the proposed corps should be stationed at St. John's and Chambly in Lower Canada, (now the Province of Quebec), Kingston, York (now Toronto), Fort George (Niagara), Amherstburg, and St. Joseph's Island, in the Upper Province.

While on a visit to his family and friends in Guernsey, Colonel Brock deemed the intelligence from the United *1806. Last visit home.*

States to be of so warlike a character that he resolved upon returning to Canada before his leave had expired; and such was his anxiety to be at his post that he overtook, at Cork, the *Lady Saumaurez,* a German vessel, well manned and armed as a letter of marque, bound for Quebec, and left London on the 26th of June, 1806, never to return or to see home and kindred again.

Very soon after his arrival in Canada Colonel Brock succeeded to the command of the troops in both Provinces, with the pay and allowances of a brigadier. He resided in Quebec until the arrival in October, 1807, of that renowned soldier, Sir James Craig, as Governor-General and Commander-in-Chief, who appointed him a brigadier, which appointment was subsequently confirmed by the King.

1806. Warns British Govt. of hostility of U. S.

In September, 1806, ever zealous, alert and watchful, he had deemed it his duty, immediately upon his return to Canada and on ascertaining the precarious and critical position of affairs, to address an urgent letter to the Imperial authorities in which he stated that it was impossible to view the late hostile measures of the American Government towards Britain, without considering a rupture between the two countries as probable to occur, if not indeed inevitable and imminent, and that he was in consequence most anxious that such precautionary measures should be taken as the exigencies seemed not only to justify, but to demand.

He warned the Government that even then the Americans were busily engaged in establishing and drilling their militia, and openly declared their intention of entering Canada, while the defenseless state of our frontiers constituted the strongest possible inducement to them so to do. He stated that the means at his disposal were too limited to enable him to oppose them with effect, and that unless he received assistance he would be obliged to confine himself to the defence of the Citadel of Quebec.

1807. Recommends formation of Glengarry Fencible Regt. on proposal of Col. Macdonell.

Again in 1807 he returned to the subject, when forwarding to the War Office the proposal of Colonel Macdonell, formerly commanding the 2nd Battalion R. C. V. (which had been disbanded as we have seen in 1802), for the formation of a corps of Glengarry Fencibles. He strongly urged the establishment of such a regiment, to be raised among the Highland people in Glengarry. His wise suggestion was not at the time carried into effect, but when a few years afterwards our relations with the United States had arrived at a crisis, the British Government hastened to adopt his plan, and the "Glengarry Light Infantry Regiment" was raised and placed upon the establishment of the army, that ubiquitous regiment which was to take part in almost every battle for the defence of the country in the War of 1812-14, and to amply justify Brock's selection of the Glengarry Highlanders as the men to face the emergency and rally to the defence of the country—and largely to save it.

But his efforts extended in all directions. The naval force and craft in Canada were then in an incipient and exceedingly unsatisfactory condition. General Brock was firmly impressed with the absolute necessity of our holding the control of the River St. Lawrence and the Great Lakes in the event of war, and shortly after taking over the command of the forces he turned his attention to that urgent and important subject and directed that the following number of boats, independent of those required for the Commissariat, should be kept in constant repair at the several posts for military service, viz: Quebec 6, Three Rivers 2, William Henry (Sorel) 1, Montreal 7, St. John 2, Kingston 4, Fort George 12, York 3, and Amherstburg 4, a total of 41. *Prepares naval craft on river and lakes.*

In 1808 General Brock appears to have been stationed at Montreal, where, as elsewhere in Canada, he was a great social favourite. People instinctively recognized his worth, his work, his zeal and ability, and appreciated to the fullest extent the wholehearted manner in which he threw himself into the discharge of his every duty. Then, too, whatever the views and misconceptions of English statesmen, as to what was coming in the comparatively near future, there was no doubt whatever upon the part of the leading, observant and influential men in Canada. For years before war was actually declared by the United States, they were able to read the signs of the times and were convinced that Brock was the man for the occasion when we had to face the inevitable. These gentlemen, therefore, were naturally desirous of showing their appreciation of the services he was rendering in advance to face this great emergency and to forestall a dire catastrophe. These were the palmy days of the celebrated North-West Company, which for years "held a lordly *1808. Montreal. Intimacy with the partners of the North-West Company. Important services of the latter during war. The great North-West Company.*

sway" over the wintry lakes and the boundless forests of the Canadas, almost equal to that of the East India Company over the voluptuous climes and magnificent realms of the Orient. The principal partners, Scotsmen, and mostly Highland gentlemen at that, resided at Montreal, where they formed a commercial aristocracy, and lived in a generous and most hospitable manner. Few distinguished travellers visited Canada, or leading military men stationed here, at this period, in the days of the MacGillivrays, the MacTavishes, the Mackenzies, the Frobishers and the other magnates of the North-West, when the company was in the zenith of its influence and activity, but must have often recalled in after years, the round of feasting and revelry kept up by those hyperborean nabobs. Then, too, they were at the head of what was practically an army of six hundred voyageurs, hardy, serviceable, intrepid, inured to danger, amenable to discipline and obedient to instructions. With these merchant princes, General Brock lived on terms of intimacy, and that intimacy was afterwards to be productive of the most important results. Not only did the North-West Company, when war occurred, immediately constitute themselves into one of the most useful, active and efficient regiments, the *Corps de Voyageurs Canadien,* in which, with scarcely an exception, the officers were Highland Scotsmen, partners and officers of the company, and every voyageur a French-Canadian, but also that Sir George Prevost, then Governor-General (and unfortunately Commander-in-Chief in Canada), was able to write a despatch informing Lord Liverpool that hostilities had commenced, was due to the zeal and patriotism of the principal partners of the North-West Company, who, foreseeing the inevitable, had taken extraordinary precautions and means to obtain early information of the declaration of war by the American Government.

War declared by U. S. 18th June.
Prevost so advised by British chargé d'affaires on 26th July.

War was declared on the 18th of June. It seems almost incomprehensible that Prevost, then at Montreal, did not receive official intelligence of this momentous fact from Mr. Foster, who, up to that date, was British chargé d'affaires at Washington, until the 26th of July, fourteen days after General Hull's army had actually invaded Upper Canada, and equally incredible that Mr. Foster did not see fit to find some means of conveying, also, official intelligence to General Brock, in command in that Province, and so hard beset there, leaving him to learn the news by the roundabout way of Montreal, when, with the greatest despatch, a fortnight further must in those days have elapsed for the intelligence by this channel to reach Fort George, the military headquarters, or York, then the seat of Civil Government. Thanks, however, to Brock's personal friends of the North-West Company, six days after the declaration of war at Washington (on the 18th of June), on the 24th day of that month, it was made known, both to Sir George Prevost at Montreal, and to General Brock at Fort George, when Prevost wrote a despatch to Lord Liverpool, and Brock took time by the forelock, with the result that in a very short space of time Hull's invading force of 2,500 men was being marched to Montreal, ragged and dejected prisoners of war, and Brock was in possession of Detroit and the whole State of Michigan, and had captured sufficient arms to arm the militia of Upper Canada. This prompt and invaluable service was rendered possible by the wise precautions and statesmanlike prescience of the North-West Company, who had despatched their own trusted emissaries to Washington with instructions to watch events, and had made all necessary arrangements so that the very moment war was declared, intelligence of that pregnant fact should immediately be rushed through to Canada by their voyageurs and Indian runners. It was due to them and thanks to them alone, that the first knowledge of actual hostilities was not conveyed at the cannon's mouth. Brock made no mistake in the selection of his friends! It was by vigour in our operations that the country was to be saved and not by the mere writing of despatches, and seldom indeed was more vigour shown or greater and more conspicuous service rendered than on this momentous and memorable occasion.

24th June both Prevost and Brock advised by North-West Company.

In 1810 Brigadier-General Brock was stationed as Commandant at Quebec, where he enjoyed the whole confidence of Sir James Craig, who, like himself, was every inch a soldier, though embarrassed with the difficult and unwelcome functions of Civil Government; but so thoroughly did Sir James trust and rely upon him, that, strongly impressed with

1810. Assumes command in Upper Canada.

the absolute necessity of having a military man of the first character and reputation take charge of affairs in the Upper Province, he despatched General Brock to Fort George with that object, and with the exception of a few months in 1811, during which he visited Lower Canada on duty, Brock continued in command of the troops in Upper Canada until his death, Lieutenant-Governor Gore at first administering the Government of the Province.

Applies for active service in the Peninsula.

But during all this time great events were transpiring elsewhere. The Peninsula was the theatre of the greatest war in which Great Britain had ever been involved, and against the greatest leader the world had ever produced; honour and glory and professional reputation were there to be obtained; military advancement to a man of Brock's capacity was a certainty. Little wonder, therefore, that with the accounts of Ciudad Rodrigo, Badajos and Salamanca ringing in his ears, he found Fort George, its inactivity, its sombre life and dull environment, irksome in the extreme.

He had long wished for and sought active employment in the field, and looking with envy upon those gaining laurels for themselves and shedding lustre upon British arms in Portugal and Spain, had frequently applied to Sir James Craig for leave of absence. He had absolute assurance too from those who spoke with knowledge and authority, that his name had been mentioned at the Horse Guards in such a way as to indicate that no officer of his rank in the service stood higher in the estimation of the Commander-in-Chief and his military entourage.

Sir James Craig, however, wrote to him from Quebec, on the 4th of March, 1811, to say that though far from being indifferent to forwarding his interests and his wishes for active employment, he felt that, from the necessity of retiring from Canada himself, owing to the precarious condition of his health (which shortly after resulted in his death), it was indispensably necessary to leave this country in the best state of security he could, and that under existing circumstances he

Sir James Craig presents him with his charger, " Alfred."

was obliged to decline Brock's request for leave; that he regretted extremely the disappointment General Brock would thus experience, but requested him to do him the honour to accept, as a legacy and as a mark of his sincere esteem and regard, his favorite charger, "Alfred," satisfied that not elsewhere in America could he procure so safe and excellent a horse, and this war-horse met the fitting fate of a war-horse shortly after the death of his illustrious owner, as we will afterwards see.

At the close of the year His Royal Highness the Duke of York expressed his readiness to gratify General Brock's wishes for more active employment in Europe should he be still of the same mind, and Sir George Prevost was authorized to replace him by another officer. But when the permission reached Canada early in 1812, war with the United States was evidently near at hand, and Brock, with such a prospect, even a certainty, and with all the instincts of a soldier, was retained by honour, duty, and inclination, in this country. *[Now declines offer of service in Peninsula.]*

On the 11th June, 1811, he had been promoted by the Prince Regent, to serve from that day as a Major-General on the staff of North America. Sir James Craig had left on the 19th of the same month, and after an interregnum of nearly three months, Sir George Prevost arrived at Quebec in September, to assume the Government and the chief command of the forces in British North America. I fear it is as a writer of despatches, disingenuous at that, that Sir George Prevost is best known to us. *[Appointed Major-General 11th June, 1811, and Lieutenant-Governor of Upper Canada, 30th Sept., 1811.]*

As previously stated, Major-General Brock was appointed Administrator of Upper Canada, taking over the office on the 9th October. In addition to his pay as Officer Commanding in Upper Canada he had a salary of £1,000 a year as Administrator, but to add to the other embarrassments with which he now had to contend, at the very time he was appointed, he became involved in most serious monetary difficulties through the failure of a firm of London bankers and merchants of which his elder brother, Mr. William Brock, was senior partner. Mr. William Brock had advanced his brother Isaac at different times £3,000 for the purchase of his commissions in the 49th Regiment; but being then in affluent circumstances and having no children of his own, he had intended the money as a gift *[Becomes financially involved by failure of his brother's firm in London. His honourable conduct.]*

to a favorite and most promising brother. It had, however, been charged in the books of the firm, and Major-General Brock was now called upon by the creditors to repay the amount. He was a man of generous disposition, dispensing somewhat extensive hospitality, especially of recent years, since his appointment to his important military command in Canada, and had saved nothing. It came as a great blow. The high position to which he had just been elevated necessitated considerable outlay to keep up its proper dignity. But Brock was, above all things, a man of the most scrupulous honour, and immediately and instinctively determined upon the proper course, forwarding a power of attorney to London to enable his whole official salary as Lieutenant-Governor to be appropriated towards the liquidation of the debt, though he was aware that it would, to some extent, necessitate a loss of popularity, and, that people unacquainted with the circumstances would attribute the consequent and unavoidable frugality of his establishment to motives of parsimony and not to rectitude of principle and the dictates of the nicest and most chivalrous sense of honour.

Approach of war.
Unpreparedness of British Government.
But events were hurrying on and all tending in the direction of war with our neighbors, who were evidently bent upon it. It is unnecessary now to discuss the pretext upon which they eventually declared it. It is sufficient to state that with Great Britain the war was purely defensive. She fought not for new conquests or to establish new claims, but for the protection of her colonies and the maintenance of rights which had received the solemn confirmation of time, while the Canadians fought for the protection of their hearths and homes and for the retention of those institutions which were inexpressibly dear to them; and those objects were completely secured; the ratification of the Treaty of Ghent by America was a tacit abandonment of every assumption against which the Government of Britain had contended; while Canada lost not one foot of soil and Canadians rejoiced in their self-respect and their connection with the Mother Land, with all which that implied.

The difficulties which now confronted General Brock and with which he had to contend and overcome as best he could, were sufficient to appal a heart even as stout and to tax to the utmost a mind as versatile and resourceful as his. When we calmly consider them all it seems nothing short of marvellous, that any man should have been equal to circumstances so adverse, labour so incessant and arduous, anxieties so great and constant, perplexities and complications so manifold, and able to meet and overcome them all.

Pressed by European embroilments, fighting on the Continent with her back to the wall, pouring out her blood and treasure in her gigantic struggle with Napoleon, his marshals and his legions, Britain was naturally desirous of avoiding war with the United States, nor could its Government, failing to recognize any sufficient cause or justification for it, be brought to recognize and understand that war was inevitable, that the American President and Government were determined upon it, and only waited until Britain's embarrassments seemed such that the time was opportune to strike the blow.

In May, a month before the declaration of war, Prevost was informed that the Government apprehended no immediate hostilities, while even in July, Lord Liverpool wrote, acknowledging an address of the Legislature of Lower Canada, expressing the willingness of the people of that Province to defend their country, that he hoped there would be no necessity for the sacrifices which so willingly would be made, directed that all extraordinary precautions for defence should be suspended, and that the arrangements for the raising of the Glengarry Regiment should be abandoned; while further to show how great was their miscalculation of events, the Duke of York, as Commander-in-Chief, recommended that the 41st and 49th Regiments, then stationed in Canada, the latter Brock's own corps, brought by him to the highest state of efficiency, having had ten years' continuous service in Canada, and therefore thoroughly acquainted and acclimatized, should return to England and be replaced by one of the foreign regiments (then in the pay and service of the British Government), and one of the line.

In July, 1812, Home Govt. orders stoppage of all his preparations.

War had even then been declared and an American army had actually landed and taken post in Canada—temporarily, however, for they had not reckoned upon Major-General Brock.

<small>Sir George Prevost a blight upon him.</small> Then, too, Sir George Prevost was a positive blight upon him. He was upon the ground and knew, or should have known, the circumstances, the position of affairs, the temper of the American people, and the intentions of their Government, unless wilfully blind to all the signs of the times, or utterly lacking in all those statesmanlike and military qualities and attributes so essential to the dual position he occupied as Governor-General of Canada and Commander-in-Chief of the Forces.

On the 2nd of December, 1811, General Brock wrote him: " I cannot conceal from your Excellency that unless a strong regular force be sent to this Province, to animate the loyal and overawe the disaffected, nothing effectual can be expected." Prevost answered, in February, that he could send him no reinforcement to Upper Canada, adding somewhat inconsequently, " Though anxious to afford you every efficient support in my power."

In the same month of December Brock communicated to him his plan of campaign, urged that on the commencement of war active operations should immediately be taken against Detroit, pointed out that Michillimackinac should also be attacked and taken, and had the sagacity to foresee and foretell that an overwhelming force would enter Canada, or attempt to do so, by crossing the Niagara River, and that the next invasion of the Province would take place from Ogdensburg, with a view to the descent of the St. Lawrence, and the attack and probable capture of Montreal; Prevost replied recommending precaution, acknowledged the advantage of striking rather than awaiting and receiving the first blow, but gave neither encouragement nor assistance to Brock's wise and timely suggestions. He derived consolation from the opinion conveyed to him by Mr. Foster, British chargé d'affaires at Washington, that war after all might possibly be avoided, and declared to Brock that it warranted him in recommending the most rigid economy in carrying on the King's service and in avoiding all expense that was not absolutely necessary.

Even when war had actually been declared, writing to Brock on the 10th of July, 1812, he held that offensive measures should not be speedily adopted and ventured upon the prediction that the attempt of the Americans on the Province would be but feeble, while two days afterwards Hull began the invasion of Canada (time and again to be renewed with unceasing vigour and larger force), at the head of 2,500 men and, as President Madison somewhat inaptly expressed it, "With the prospect of easy and victorious progress." Here again the President failed to take Major-General Brock into his calculations, or was unaware of the vigour with which that enterprising officer carried on his operations.

But it was not only the fact that the British Government was unprepared for war with the United States and had taken no precautions against it, and the supineness of Sir George Prevost, who disapproved of all energetic measures, that caused General Brock so much embarrassment, anxiety, care and trouble, in the grave emergency which he was now called upon to face. *[Traitors within the gates.]*

He had also to contend with traitors within his gates; internal disaffection, disloyalty, treason and treachery were rampant in many parts of the Province of Upper Canada.

A large proportion of its population even then were long known as "Proclamation men," Yankee settlers, who had taken advantage of Governor Simcoe's liberal system of land grants, and had come to Canada from purely mercenary motives, bringing with them their republican sentiments and anti-British proclivities, amounting in many instances to hatred.

This disloyal element was much more extensive than is now generally known or supposed, and came nigh to the undoing of the country. Brock's letters and despatches are replete with reference to the anxiety which their machinations and ill-concealed hostility caused him. After war had broken out he was obliged to issue a proclamation ordering all persons suspected of traitorous intercourse with the enemy to be apprehended and treated according to law; those who had not taken the oath of allegiance were ordered to do so or leave the Province. Many were sent out of the country, large numbers left of their own accord; those who refused the oath or to take up arms to defend the country and remained in the Province after a given date, were declared to be enemies and spies, and treated accordingly; a large number of this disloyal element were arrested and imprisoned early in the war, as on the day of the battle of Queenston, October 13th, 1812, the jail and courthouse at Niagara as well as the blockhouse at Fort George were filled with political prisoners, over 300 aliens and traitors being in custody, some of whom were tried and sentenced to death during the war, and others sent to Quebec for imprisonment; indeed, even the militia were in some parts tampered with and disaffected. On the 3rd of August, Brock was compelled to declare to his Executive Council that " the enemy had invaded and taken post in the Western district, the militia in a perfect state of insubordination had withdrawn from the ranks on active service, had insulted their officers and some, not immediately embodied, had manifested, in many instances, a treasonable spirit of mutiny and disaffection, that in the Western and London districts several persons had negotiated with the enemy's commander, hailing his arrival and pledging their support, while the Indians on the Grand River had been tampered with, had withdrawn from their voluntary service and declared for a neutrality."

Disloyalty in the Legislature. This disloyal element, too, was not without representation even in the Legislature of the Province, and there they endeavored to thwart all those prompt and effective measures which in the crisis were essential to the preservation of the country and were submitted to and urged upon it by Brock as Administrator. "The many doubtful characters in the militia," he stated in one of his despatches, "made me anxious to introduce the oath of abjuration into the bill. It was lost by the casting vote of the chairman. The great influence which the numerous settlers from the United States possess over the decisions of the Lower House is truly alarming and ought immediately by every practicable means to be diminished." The bill for the suspension of the Habeas Corpus Act was also defeated in the session which opened on the 4th of February, 1812. The leaders of this disloyal faction in the Legislature were three men whose names should go down to posterity with infamy: Joseph Willcocks, the leader of the Opposition; Benjamin Mallory and Abraham Markle. At the next session Willcocks and Markle, who were still members, were expelled from the House "for their disloyal and infamous conduct." Mallory had not been re-elected in 1812. Willcocks was killed at Fort Erie in 1814, in command of a regiment in the American army; Mallory served throughout the war as major in the same regiment.

After Hull had invaded the Province, Brock summoned the Legislature and on the 27th of July opened an extra session. In his speech he stated " a few traitors have already joined the enemy; have been suffered to come into the country with impunity and have been harboured and concealed in the interior. To protect and defend the loyal inhabitants from their machinations is an object worthy of your most serious deliberation." ✗ *[margin: Legislature summoned upon declaration of war, and proves recalcitrant. House dissolved and martial law proclaimed.]*

But notwithstanding that the state of the country required urgent and decisive measures, many members of the House of Assembly, under the baneful influence of the disloyal element, were seized with apprehension and endeavored to avoid incurring the indignation of the enemy. They again refused to repeal or suspend the Habeas Corpus Act, and in consequence of these difficulties, Brock, knowing that General Hull's emissaries throughout the country were both numerous and active, called together his Executive Council. So serious and grave were the circumstances in which he felt himself placed, and feeling that but little could be expected from a prolonged session, he asked his constitutional advisers whether it would not be expedient to prorogue the Legislature and proclaim martial law. The Council adjourned until the next day, the 4th of August, for deliberation, and then unanimously adopted the legal opinion of Attorney-General Macdonell, and gave it as their advice that under the circumstances of the Province, the House of Assembly should be prorogued and that the General should proclaim and exercise martial law under authority of his commission from the King. Accordingly on the 5th, Brock prorogued the House and martial law prevailed.

This brought the traitors to time; large numbers immediately decamped to the States, among them Willcocks, Mallory and Markle; the atmosphere was cleared and Brock became master of the situation. But what a situation!

Overwhelming odds against him. Militia without arms or clothes.

Now let us consider for a moment Brock's position. For the defence of this Province his entire forces consisted, all told, regulars and militia, of 1,500 men.

In Lower Canada Sir George Prevost had about 3,000 regular troops. The total number of men capable of bearing arms in Upper Canada was about 11,000, the proportion available for constant, active service was 4,000.

Against this, at the beginning of 1812, the United States had a regular army of 5,500 men. On the 11th of January, 1812, five months before the declaration of war, an act of Congress was passed for raising 25,000 men for five years. In the next month an act was passed to organize 50,000 volunteers, and in April, 100,000 militia were called into active service. During the whole war the United States' regular army amounted to about 30,000. The whole militia force raised during the war was 471,622, making a grand total of over half a million men engaged in the effort to conquer Provinces containing a total population of 300,000.

Another great difficulty was the lack of military stores and supplies; Brock was obliged to ask the militia to clothe themselves; many of them were actually drilling in their naked feet. He was without a military chest, without money to buy provisions, blankets, or shoes. He had to borrow the money to fit out the expedition to Detroit. The militia were practically without arms until the capture of Detroit placed at his disposal 2,500 muskets of General Hull's army, and there he also captured a number of pieces of artillery which were of service in subsequent operations.

Proclamation of martial law the turning-point.

The proclamation of martial law was the turning-point; indeed it may be said to have been the salvation of the Province. It would seem probable that Brock's intention to proclaim it had become known to the Legislature, for on the very day of prorogation the loyal party in the House succeeded in carrying a most spirited and patriotic address in which they called upon the people of Upper Canada to deem no sacrifice too costly which secured to them their happy constitution.

The change in the prospects within a few days was almost miraculous. The stirring address of the House of Assembly went forth to the people of the Province on the 5th of August, and on the 6th Brock left for Amherstburg accompanied by Attorney-General Macdonell, who now became his Military Secretary and Provincial aide-de-camp. They had with them some 40 regular soldiers and 260 militia.

Sets off on his campaign. Capture of Detroit and State of Michigan.

Hostilities had actually commenced on the 12th of July, when General Hull crossed the Detroit River to Sandwich, invading the Province with an army of 2,500 men and a blood-curdling proclamation. This fulmination was promptly answered by General Brock. The two productions might well be placed in parallel columns so that the vulgarity and fanfarronade of the one and the dignified and resolute tone of the other might be fully understood and appreciated.

General Hull had the insolence to announce to the Canadian people that "he was in possession of their country," to inform them that an ocean and wilderness isolated them from Great Britain, "whose tyranny he knew they felt," that his army was ready and anxious to release them from oppression, that they must choose between liberty and security as offered by the United States, and war and annihilation, the penalty of refusal.

Brock, in his counter-manifesto, properly characterized Hull's invitation to Canadians to seek protection from Britain under the flag of the United States as an insult. He cited the advantages of British connection and warned our people that secession meant the restitution of Canada to France, which was the price to be paid by America to that country for the aid given to the revolting colonies during the Revolutionary War. He reminded them of the constancy of their fathers, and urged upon them to repel the invaders and thus give their children no cause to reproach them with sacrificing the richest inheritance upon earth, participation in the name, character and freedom of Britons.

Upon his arrival at Amherstburg, Brock, for the first time, met Tecumseh, who was to prove such an invaluable ally, and soon so nobly to die! At the conclusion of their interview, the great Indian showed his estimate and appreciation of him when he turned to his warriors and declared to them, " This is a man!"

Nor was General Brock long in determining on his course. The Americans had evacuated Amherstburg and retired to their own side of the river, to Detroit, which was strongly fortified. His entire force now consisted of 330 regulars, 400 militia, and 600 Indians—Sioux, Wyandots and Dacotahs. " My force," he wrote to General Hull, " warrants my demanding the immediate surrender of Fort Detroit," and knowing Hull's dread of the Indians he warned him that they might possibly get beyond his control. Colonel Macdonell and Captain Glegg carried this summons across the river under a flag of truce, and shortly returned with the assurance from General Hull that " he was prepared to meet any force brought against him and accept any consequences." Brock thereupon issued orders to cross the river at dawn, while the Indians crossed under cover of the night. Upon landing, Brock mustered his men, deploying the Indians in the shelter of the woods, skirmishing to effect a flank movement, and advanced to the attack, while the battery of Sandwich threw a few shells into the American fort.

It seems almost incredible, particularly when we think of the proclamation! With the odds about ten to one in his favour, Hull's heart now failed him when he saw the advance of the British, and their field pieces trained upon the fort; the gunners awaited but the final command, when an officer bearing a white flag emerged from the fort, while a boat with another flag of truce was seen crossing the river to the Sandwich battery. Macdonell and Glegg galloped out to meet the messenger and returned with a despatch from Hull to General Brock, as follows: " The object of the flag which crossed the river was to propose a cessation of hostilities for an hour, for the purpose of entering into negotiations for the surrender of Detroit."

Again Macdonell and Glegg rode out and returned with the terms of capitulation signed by General Hull.

One general officer and 3,500 men of all ranks, who were to have conquered Canada, surrendered as prisoners of war, while with them were handed over 2,500 stand of arms, 33 pieces of cannon, the *Adams* brig of war, stores, and munitions of war to the value of £40,000, and Detroit and 59,700 square miles of American territory—the whole State of Michigan—passed into the possession of General Brock.

Brock believed that it was by vigour in our operations that the war was to be won.

In nineteen days he had met and prorogued the Legislature, transported his small force 300 miles, 200 of which was by open boat, captured an army three times his strength, strongly entrenched in a well-protected fort, and 60,000 square miles of that enemy's territory.

By a strange coincidence his despatches with the colours he had taken reached London on the morning of the 5th of October, the anniversary of his birth. The despatches were immediately published in a "Gazette Extraordinary" and the clangour of bells and the booming of guns announced his victory. The Prince Regent expressed his appreciation of Brock's "able, judicious and decisive conduct" and bestowed upon him an extra Knighthood of the Order of the Bath in consideration "of all the difficulties with which he was surrounded during the invasion of the Province and the singular judgment, firmness, skill and courage with which he surmounted them so effectually."

But he never saw the insignia of his rank or learnt of the Sovereign's approbation. Ere that reached Canada, he had fought his last fight. The Battle of Queenston Heights was won, and all that was mortal of Sir Isaac Brock lay under a cavalier bastion in Fort George.

Having brought affairs to so satisfactory a conclusion in this quarter, and completed all necessary arrangements, Brock lost not a moment in returning to York to carry on that plan of campaign upon which he had determined. Quite apart, however, from the high considerations of public duty by which he was always animated, there may have been another reason why he and his Attorney-General, now associated with him in his capacity as military secretary and aide-de-camp, may have been desirous of reporting themselves at York. Both were young, Brock in the prime of manhood, being in his forty-fourth year, and the other but twenty-seven years of age; both were shortly to be married to young ladies then resident at York, General Brock to Miss Sophia Shaw, daughter of

Prevost's armistice destroys his plans.

Major-General Aeneas Shaw, Adjutant-General of Militia, and amongst the many congratulations and felicitations which were showered upon him there were those from one especially which would necessarily and naturally be essentially dear and welcome to him. It was the fate of both these brave and ardent men, however,

"To change love's bridal wreath,
For laurels from the hand of death."

His intention was to proceed forthwith to Kingston and from thence to attack and destroy the American naval arsenal at Sackett's Harbour on Lake Ontario, and that accomplished, to sweep the whole American frontier from Sandusky at the head of Lake Erie to St. Regis on the River St. Lawrence. But when crossing Lake Erie, he was met with the astounding and most distasteful and unwelcome news that Sir George Prevost had entered into an armistice with the American General, Dearborn. His mortification at this intelligence, which paralyzed all his plans, and went far to nullify all the advantages which his energy and enterprise had already accomplished, can easily be conceived. To make matters worse, General Sheaffe, in command at Fort George while Brock was in the west, had acceded to General Dearborn's demand that the freedom of the lakes and rivers should be extended to the United States Government during the armistice, an opportunity of which the Americans did not fail to avail themselves to bring up reinforcements, provisions and all the necessary munitions of war, together with 400 boats and batteaux from Ogdensburg and other points to Lewiston, with a view to their contemplated attack on the Niagara frontier, which shortly took place at Queenston. General Sheaffe's extraordinary conduct on this occasion was again to be repeated on the very afternoon when they were there defeated; instead of following up the victory which Brock's wise precautions and glorious example had made possible, he agreed to another armistice.

Had the destruction of Sackett's Harbour, as Brock had determined upon, been then accomplished, the Americans could not have built and equipped the fleet which subsequently gave them the ascendancy on Lake Ontario, and enabled them twice in 1813 to capture the capital of Upper Canada. The project, however, had to be relinquished by express orders from the Commander-in-Chief. Prevost, indeed, in the following year, endeavored himself to accomplish what he had forbidden to Brock, and his ignoble fiasco at Sackett's Harbour was only to be equalled, even outdone, by his disgraceful failure at Plattsburg, where brave men broke their swords in the anguish of defeat, and for which he was called upon eventually to face court-martial, which he only escaped by the fortunate intervention of death occurring on the very eve of the assembly of the court which was to meet to try the charges Sir James Yeo had preferred against him. When we contrast the methods and the character and the fate of Sir Isaac Brock and Sir George Prevost we are perforce driven to a realization of the fact that men " are cast in different moulds, if not made of different clay."

But we are nearing the end of Brock's career—one more fight and we have done.

Battle of Queenston Heights. Death of Brock.

By the middle of October, the Americans had assembled on the Niagara frontier an army of 6,300 men, of which force 3,170 were at Lewiston under the command of General Van Rensselaer—with them he modestly announced to his government his intention " to cross the river in the rear of Fort George, take it by storm, carry the heights of Queenston, destroy the British ships at the mouth of the Niagara River, leave Brock no rallying point, appal the minds of the Canadians, and wipe away the past disgrace."

To oppose this somewhat extensive programme General Brock had part of the 41st and 49th Regiments, a few companies of militia and about 300 Indians, in all about 1,500 men, dispersed, however, at various points between Fort Erie and Fort George, so that only a small number was quickly available at any one point.

He knew that the attack was imminent, and with unwearied diligence he watched the movements of the enemy. During the night of the 12th October their troops were concentrated and embarked from Lewiston under cover of a battery which completely commanded the opposite shore. Suspecting the invasion, though not, of course, knowing the exact point at which it would take place, General Brock had that evening called together his staff officers and given to each the necessary and final instructions. Before the break of day on the fatal 13th, hearing the cannonade which announced their landing on Canadian soil, he hastily dressed himself, and calling for his charger "Alfred," he galloped off, followed closely by Colonel Macdonell and Captain Glegg, his aides-de-camp.

His first impression is said to have been that the attack indicated by the firing was only a feint to draw the garrison from Fort George, and that an American force lay concealed in boats around the point on which Fort Niagara stands, ready to cross over as soon as they had succeeded. He, therefore, determined to ascertain personally the nature and extent of the attack ere he withdrew the garrison, and with this in view he galloped eagerly to the scene of action, stopping for a moment only, and without dismounting, at the residence of Captain John Powell, to take a cup of coffee, which was brought to him by Miss Sophia Shaw, his fiancee, who never again was to see the gallant man who loved her. Hastily pushing on, he was met by Lieut. S. P. Jarvis, of the York Militia, who was riding so furiously that he could not check his horse, but shouted as he flew by, "The Americans are crossing the river in force, sir." Jarvis wheeled and overtook the General, who, without reining up, slackened his speed sufficiently to tell the rider to hurry on to Fort George and order General Sheaffe to bring up his entire reserve, including Brant's Indians, leaving Brigade-Major Evans with sufficient artillery to batter Fort Niagara. He passed with his two aides up the hill at full speed in front of the light company, under a heavy fire of artillery and musketry from the American shore. On reaching the 18-pounder battery at the top of the hill they dismounted and took a view of passing events, but in a few minutes firing was heard which proceeded from a strong detachment of American regulars under Captain Wool, who had succeeded in gaining the crest of the heights in rear of the battery, by a fisherman's path up the precipitous rocks, which having been reported as impassable, was not guarded. These men charged down upon them, and Brock, with his aides, and the twelve men stationed in the battery, after spiking the gun, were obliged hastily to retire. On regaining the bottom of the slope he sent Captain Derenzy, of the 41st, with an urgent message to General Sheaffe to hasten the advance of the battalion companies of the 41st and the flank companies of the militia and to join him without delay. Mounting his horse he galloped to the far end of the village where he held a hurried conversation with the few officers present, and despatched Macdonell to Vrooman's to bring up Heward's company of the York Militia, sending Captain Glegg to order Captain Dennis with the light company of the 49th, and Chisholm's company of the York Militia, and Captain Williams with his detachment to join him. When they arrived he took command with a view to the re-taking of the redan, satisfied that to wait for the arrival of the reinforcements under Sheaffe would but make the task more difficult, as it would enable the enemy to establish themselves in force, drill out the spiked gun and turn it upon his men. Under a heavy fire of musketry which did considerable execution they breasted the heights, Brock dismounting, and handing his horse to an orderly, placed himself at the head of his men, who, with the support which Macdonell brought up, numbered less than 190, with which he had to dislodge an enemy strongly entrenched and numbering upwards of 500, of whom 300 were regulars. As they advanced in this charge up the hill, Brock, conspicuous from his dress, his towering height, his position at the head of his men and the enthusiasm with which he animated his little band, was soon singled out by the American riflemen; a deflected bullet struck the wrist of his sword-arm, but he paid no attention to it, still urging on his men. They were now within fifty yards of the redan above them. He was calling to those nearest him to hold their fire for a moment, to prepare to rush the enemy and use their bayonets, when from a thorn thicket, an Ohio scout, Wilklow by name, singled him out, and taking deliberate aim, fired at him. The bullet entered his right breast, tore through his body, leaving a gaping wound. As he sank to the ground he begged that his fall might not be noticed, as it would disorganize his men, and thus he nobly died, with his face to the foe.

Death of General Brock.

Perhaps it is better that I should now give Mr. Walter Nursey's account of what immediately followed, rather than my own:

"After he fell the handful of men who were with him, overcome by his tragic end, overwhelmed by superior numbers and a hurricane of bullets and buckshot, wavered and then fell back and retreated to Queenston Village. Here, about two hours after, Colonel Macdonell collected and re-formed the scattered units, and made another bold dash to re-scale the heights and take the redan. With the cry of 'Revenge the General!' from the men of his old regiment, the 49th, Macdonell on Brock's charger, 'Alfred,' led the forlorn attack, supported by Dennis. At the same moment, Williams, with his detachment, emerged from the thicket; the two detachments then combined, and Macdonell ordering a general advance, they once more breasted the ascent. The enemy, over 400 strong, but without proper formation, fired an independent volley at the British as they approached to within thirty yards of the redoubt. This was responded to with vigour, and grenadiers and volunteers in response to Macdonell's repeated calls, charged fiercely on Wool's men, now huddled in disorder around the 18-pounder. Some of them started to run toward the river bank. One American officer, Ogilvie by name, of the 13th Regiment, thinking the situation hopeless, raised his handkerchief on his sword-point in token of surrender, when Wool, a brave soldier, tore it down, and a company of United States infantry coming up at that moment to his assistance he rallied his men.

"The momentary advantage gained by Macdonell's small band of heroes was lost, and in the exchange of shots that followed, Macdonell's horse, Brock's charger, 'Alfred,' was killed under him, while he—his uniform torn with bullets—was thrown from the saddle as the animal plunged in its death struggle, receiving several ghastly bullet wounds from which he died the following day, after enduring much agony. Williams, a moment later, fell, desperately wounded. Dennis, suffering from a severe wound in the head, at first refused to quit the field, but Cameron, having removed the sorely-stricken Macdonell, and Williams having recovered consciousness, the dispirited men fell back and, retreating down the mountain, retired upon Vrooman's battery. Here they waited unmolested, until two in the afternoon, for reinforcements from Fort George. The fight, though short, had been furious and deadly; Americans and British alike were glad to take breath.

"Meanwhile, unobserved, young Brant, with 120 Mohawk Indians, had scaled the mountain east of St. Davids, outflanking the Americans, and hemmed them in until Captain Derenzy, of the 41st, and Holcroft, of the artillery, arrived with the car brigade from Fort George, and trained two field-pieces and a Howitzer upon the landing. Merritt, with a troop of mounted infantry at the same time reached the village by the Queenston road. This movement, which was a ruse, deceived the enemy, who at once disposed his troops in readiness for an attack from this quarter. *[Indians scale the mountain east of St. Davids.]*

"The American commander was ignorant of the fact that General Sheaffe, with four companies of the 41st, 300 strong, the same number of militia and a company of negro troops from Niagara, refugee slaves from the United States, was at that moment approaching in rear of the Indians. The British advanced in crescent shaped formation, hidden by mountain and bush, and were shortly joined by a few more regulars and by two flank companies of the 2nd Regiment of militia from Chippewa—indeed many persons of all ranks of life, even veterans exempt by age, seized their muskets and joined the column to repel the invaders. The British of all ranks numbered less than 1,000 men. *[Arrival of General Sheaffe as instructed by Brock.]*

"The United States troops, which had been heavily reinforced, consisted of about 1,000 fighting men, on and about the mountain. Their number was supplemented from time to time, by fresh arrivals from Lewiston, encouraged when they saw the American flag planted on the redan; nearly all the new arrivals were regulars. Colonel Winfield Scott, of Mexican fame, a tried soldier, six foot four in his stockings, was now in command, supported by a second field officer, and many sharpshooters. Van Rensselaer, narrowly escaping capture, had retreated by boat to Lewiston, nominally to bring over more troops. Finding the conditions unfavourable, he did not do so, but sent over General Wadsworth, as a vicarious sacrifice, to take command. The gun in the redan had been unspiked and the summit strongly entrenched, but as Scott's men betrayed strange lukewarmness, orders were given 'to shoot any man leaving his post.'

"Sheaffe's men, having rested after the forced tramp, a few spherical case shot by Holcroft drove out the American riflemen. His gunners had at last silenced the Lewiston batteries, and finding the range, sunk almost every boat that attempted to cross. The Indians were now ordered to drive in the enemy's pickets slowly. Scouting the woods, they routed the outposts.

"About 4 p.m., Captain Bullock, with two flank companies of militia and 150 men of the 41st, advanced, charging the enemy's right, which broke in great confusion. A general advance was ordered, and with wild warwhoops from the Indians and cheers by the soldiers, the heights were rushed. Wadsworth's veterans were stampeded, the redan retaken at the point of the bayonet, and Scott's command forced to the scarp of the hill overhanging the river. The Americans now 'fled like sheep,' to quote their own historians, and scattered off in all directions. Some raced headlong down the main road, seeking shelter under the muzzles of Holcroft's guns; some sought refuge in the houses, others raced to the landing, only to find their boats no longer there—not a few, hot pressed by Brant's avenging Mohawks, threw themselves over the precipice, preferring death in that shape to the fate which otherwise awaited them, while others plunged into the Niagara, essaying to swim its irresistible eddies, only to be blown out of the green water by Holcroft's grapeshot, or sucked down by the river's silent whirlpools. One boat, with 50 struggling refugees, sank with its entire crew. Two others similarly laden were beached below the village, with only twelve out of one hundred souls still living. The river presented a shocking scene. On the surface of the water, many, maimed and wounded, fought and struggled for survival. This pitiable spectacle was actually taking place under the eyes of several thousand American soldiers on the Lewiston bank, who, almost impossible to believe, and to their lasting disgrace, refused even to attempt to succour their comrades.

Flight of the Americans.

Losses sustained by both sides.

"In all 958 American soldiers were taken prisoners by the British, 'captured by a force,' as Colonel Van Rensselaer stated in an official despatch after the battle, 'amounting to only about one-third of the number of American troops.'

Captain Gist, of the United States army, placed their killed at 400.

"General Van Rensselaer's defeat was complete and overwhelming. His chagrin at his failure 'to appal the minds of the Canadians' was so great that ten days later he resigned his command.

"The account as between Canada and the United States at sundown on that day stood as follows:

Total American force engaged	1,600
Killed, wounded and prisoners	1,425
The total British force engaged (of whom 800 men were regulars and militia, and 200 Indians) was	1,000
Killed, including Major-General Brock and Colonel Macdonell	14
Wounded and missing	96
Total American loss	1,425
Total British loss	110

"The next day, General Sheaffe, Isaac Brock's successor, signed another armistice. The second armistice within a period of nine weeks!"

Sheaffe signs another armistice!

Brock's lifeless corpse lay for a time where he had fallen, about one hundred yards west of the road that leads through Queenston, and after the battle was borne by a few of his old Regiment to a house in the village occupied by Laura Secord; later in the day Captain Glegg, Brock's brave aide—Macdonell, the other aide-de-camp, lay dying of his wounds—hastened to the spot, and had it conveyed to Niagara. On the 16th of October, the bodies of Major-General Sir Isaac Brock and Lieutenant-Colonel Macdonell were interred at Fort George. It is a tribute to the magnanimity of the Americans that during the funeral procession, minute guns were fired at every post on their side of the river, as their general orders stated, " as a mark of respect to a brave enemy."

Funeral of Gen. Brock and Col. Macdonell.

Thus we have seen the last of Sir Isaac Brock, a fitting culmination to his career and a life devoted to the service of his King and country.

* * *

Amidst the lamentations of his comrades in arms, the respectful salute of his opponents, the tears and blessings of the Canadian people, with the posthumous honours of his Sovereign awaiting him and the gratitude of future generations of Canadians for all time attending him, in his soldier's grave, first at Fort George, and now under the monument on Queenston Heights erected to commemorate his fame, there let us leave him.

" Sound, sound the clarion, fill the fife,
To all the sensual world proclaim
One crowded hour of glorious life
Is worth an age without a name."

II.

ROMANTIC ELEMENTS IN THE HISTORY OF THE MISSISSIPPI VALLEY.*

By Reuben Gold Thwaites, LL.D.,
Superintendent of Wisconsin State Historical Society.

Perhaps to some of my auditors it may at first seem a far cry from the field of Ontario history to that of the Mississippi Valley—from a consideration of Sir Isaac Brock, a master of modern warfare in this highly-developed centre of civilization, to those rude pioneers who, but improving the methods of savagery, rudely opened to civilization the vast wilderness of the trans-Alleghany. But the association of the annals of Ontario with those of our own Middle West is surely intimate enough to warrant this shifting of the scene.

With you, the roots of our history are deeply planted in the soil of New France. In this respect, at least, your history is warp and woof with our own—whether it be Minnesota, which once knew Du l'Hut and Hennepin; Wisconsin, claiming Jean Nicolet as her discoverer; Michigan, proud of her Cadillac; Indiana, having within her bounds the portage paths of La Salle; Ohio, with her memories of Céleron; Pennsylvania, where Washington met the French advance southward; New York, wherein Champlain slaughtered the raging Iroquois, and Jogues met retributive martyrdom; New England, with her century and a half of border turmoil by land and sea, long remembered with bitterness, but at this distance viewed with philosophic calm; or Louisiana, founded by Iberville and Bienville. Wherever French habitant leisurely toiled in sweet contentment, French explorer feverishly extended the bound of empire, French fur-trader wandered, cassocked priest said mass, white-frocked soldier kept watch and ward over the interest of the great Louis, ambitious miner found veins of copper and coloured earths, or English and French and Indian met in mortal combat on the frontiers of civilization, the history of New France (of which Ontario was once so important a part) is taught as the local tradition of every northern state of the Union, east of the River Missouri.

*Read at the meeting of the Ontario Historical Society at Napanee, Ont., 1912.

I feel, therefore, that you will think it not incongruous if at this gathering, whose programme * is at least grimly suggestive of an international conference, I very briefly recite a few of the romantic elements (French and British, as well as American) in the historical drama, nearly three centuries in the acting, which has found its stage in the Valley of the Mississippi. From these elements of romance are to be fashioned those novels and poems of the future that shall give to this period and to this region that charm of literary association without which no annals can long endure in the heart and imagination of the people.

The advent of the Spanish explorers in our valley was meteoric in brilliancy and in suddenness of departure. But he who seeks rich color, will doubtless find the French régime the more entertaining. Entrenched with apparent security on the rock of Quebec, New France early despatched her explorers westward through the majestic trough of the St. Lawrence. With rare enterprise and bravery they gradually pushed their way up toilsome rivers, along westering portage paths, and far over into the vast-stretching wilderness of the continental interior lying to the west and south of Canada.

Where are there finer examples of dramatic adventure than the great journey of Nicolet, sent by Champlain into Darkest America to discover a short route to China? Donning his diplomatic garb of figured damask, to meet supposititious mandarins, he encountered only naked Winnebago savages on the inland waters of Wisconsin. What more stirring incident in history than the famous expedition of Joliet and Marquette to discover the far-away Mississippi, which in stately curves glides unceasingly and with awesome power past eroded bluffs and through sombre forests southward toward tropic seas? Or, the far-distant rovings of those masterful fur-trade adventurers, Radisson, La Salle, Tonty, Perrot, Du l'Hut, and a host of kindred spirits? Is there anywhere a nobler instance of self-sacrifice than the splendid martyrdom of the Jesuit missionaries, who, imbued with the proselyting zeal of mediæval saints, in their quest for souls often suffered the horrors of the damned?

Annual trading fleets of Indian canoes and batteaux from the far-distant regions of the Mississippi and the Upper Lakes, laboriously journeyed over a thousand miles to Montreal and to Quebec, to barter rich furs for colored beads and glittering trinkets fashioned in the

*The majority of the papers presented had reference to the War of 1812.

shops of Brittany and Paris. Piled high with bales of peltries, and propelled by gaily-appareled savages and voyageurs, the flotillas swept eastward down the broad rivers in rude procession, paddles flashing in the sun, the air rent with barbaric yells and the roaring quaver of merry boating songs.

We can hear and see the boisterous welcome from the garrisons of Lower Canada; the succeeding weeks of trade and mad carousal on the strand of Quebec or Montreal; and then the return of the copper-skinned visitors to the "Upper Country," tricked out in gaudy finery, bearing into the wilderness fresh stores of gew-gaws, and accompanied by another contingent of traders and explorers—often, also, by Jesuit missionaries bent on showing them, even against their will, the path to the White man's Manitou.

Away off in the then mysterious land of the Far West, were insignificant military outposts, bulwarks of the authority of New France— Detroit, Mackinac, Green Bay, Chequamegon Bay, Vincennes; and, ranged along the Mississippi, lay Kaskaskia, Cahokia, Chartres, and many another rude bankside fort or stockade, all the way from Lake Pepin to Natchez.

Around each of these little forest strongholds—of logs or of stone, as materials came best to hand—was clustered a tiny hamlet of habitants: boatmen, tillers of the soil, mechanics, according to bent or to necessity. At the head of society in this rude settlement was the military commandant. Next in social precedence was the Jesuit Father, whose scanty chapel lay just within the gate; perhaps of noble birth and training, inevitably a scholar, but bound by unalterable vows to a life of toilsome self-sacrifice for the winning of savage souls in these inhospitable wilds. Ever was the black-robe coming and going upon long and wearisome journeys among the tribesmen, his life often embittered by the jealousy of the commandant.

Frequent visitors at the frontier fort were wandering traders, each at the head of a band of rollicking voyageurs, jauntily clad in fringed buckskins and showy caps and scarfs, with a semi-savage display of bracelets, dangling earrings, and necklaces of beads. The coureur de bois, or unlicensed trader, accompanied by a sprightly party of devil-may-care retainers, occasionally called, upon unheralded expeditions here and there through the dark woodlands and along sparkling waters. He was in his day the most daring spirit and the widest traveller in North America.

Freely mingling with this varied and variegated company were bands of half-naked, long-haired savages and halfbreeds, glistening with oils, and tricked out with paint and feathers. For the most part the boon companions of the French, now and then would they smite their white allies with cruel treachery, suddenly converting into a charnel-house many a self-confident outpost of the far-stretching realm of the great Louis.

Upon this inviting amphitheatre of New France, we find a heterogeneous semi-feudal society, with many feudal manners and customs, and a never-ending variety of connections with the Old World. Social, political, and mercantile complications were multiplied by the adventurous and diversified aims and pursuits of the colonists, scattered as they were through thousands of miles of savage wilderness.

At last, one fateful summer, the men of the hamlets and wilderness stations, seigneurs and tenants, traders and voyageurs, commandants and soldiery, were summoned by Indian runners to hasten to the Lower St. Lawrence, to free New France from the English invaders, whose very existence was to not a few of these forest exiles virtually unknown. On the Plains of Abraham many a brave fellow from the Upper Lakes and the Mississippi Valley gave up his life for the *fleur de lis*. But all in vain, for the time had come to ring down the curtain on this gallant drama. New France was no more.

The English, however, won only that portion of the great valley lying eastward of the river; upon Spain, France by secret treaty bestowed New Orleans and the trans-Mississippi. But for a full century, English explorers, fur-traders, and settlers from Pennsylvania, Virginia and the Carolinas had been trespassing on French preserves to the west of the Appalachians, and tampering with the Indian allies of the Bourbons. The temerity of these fearless over-mountain adventurers had directly incited the French and Indian War, which resulted in the downfall of New France.

Contemporaneously with the uprising of the American colonies against the Mother Land, there began a great transmontane irruption into our valley—buckskin-clad borderers (largely Scotch-Irishmen) laboriously crossing from the Atlantic uplands into Kentucky, whither Finley, Boone, the Long Hunters, and their several predecessors had led the way. This Arcadia of forests and glades and winding streams and incomparable game was won from savagery only after long years of sturdy warfare. The story of that winning is filled to the brim with picturesque and tragic incidents. Cherokee, Catawba, and Shawnee, moved to vengeance by persistent pressure upon their hunting grounds, fought, after their own wild standards, and fought well, for what they held most dear; they would have been cravens not to have made a stand. The white man, pouring his ceaseless caravans through Cumberland Gap and down the broad current of the Ohio, brooked no opposition from an inferior race, for white man's might makes right, and struck back with a fury often augmented by fear. Such is the bloodstained story of our method of conquering the American wilderness.

To save backwoods Kentucky from devastating forays by the Indian allies of the British forces in Canada, George Rogers Clark, at the head of that now famous band of Virginia frontiersmen, many of whom were garbed in an airy costume combining that of the Highlander with that of the savage, undertook his hazardous but successful expedition against Kaskaskia and Vincennes; an event abounding in dramatic scenes that will doubtless live long in the history of the United States.

Kentucky, having at last quieted the aborigine by crushing him, now entered on a period of relative prosperity. Down the swift-rolling Ohio, through several decades descended a curious medley of oar and sail-driven craft, fashioned in the boatyards of the Allegheny, Youghiogheny, and Monongahela—rafts, arks, broad-horns, flat and keel-boats, barges, piroques, and schooners of every design conceivable to fertile brain. These singular river fleets bore emigrants eager to found new commonwealths in the bounding West. Hailing from a thousand neighborhoods in the Eastern States and from many countries of Europe, they came with their children, their tools, their cattle, their household gods—lusty, pushing, square-jawed, unconquerable folk, suffering on the way and in the early years of their settlement privations seldom if ever surpassed among the tales of the border.

And now Kentucky's crops had become larger than her population could consume. She needed to convey them to the markets of the world, to barter them for the goods and products of other communities. But Spain held firm control of the mouth of the Mississippi, and of the rich lands beyond the broad river, and upon these lands our Westerners were beginning to look with hungry eyes. The federal authorities of that day were slow to realize that the free navigation of the Mississippi was a vital factor in the development of the West. Consequently there was active discontent among the leaders of Kentucky. Political uneasiness was fomented first by Spanish intrigues, and next by French—

for France was at last beginning to display some jealousy of the young republic whom she had assisted into life, and apparently she would fain have unofficially rejoiced both in Western secession and in the utilization of trans-Allegheny Americans in filibustering expeditions against Spanish Louisiana. Thus was the West, through twenty years of its formative period, in a state of secret ferment. The full story of this plotting is even yet unrevealed; but gradually the facts are being brought to light, and furnish fit material for historical romance.

Spain, fearing that an assault might be made on her trans-Mississippi possessions from British Canada, made flattering offers of land grants west of the river to American pioneers who should colonize her territory in that region and cast their fortunes with her people. Many discontented Kentuckians accepted these terms and moved on to Missouri, among them the wandering Boones, who, now that they might see from the nearest hill-top the fire-place smoke from neighboring cabins, were already sighing for "more elbow room"; glad enough were they to be rid of the crowds now coming to Kentucky, to get new and cheap lands in the farther West, to avoid taxes, to hunt big game, and once more to live an Arcadian life. I love to picture the great Daniel, transplanted in his old age to these fresh wilds westward of the great Mississippi, seated at the door of his little log cabin on Femme Osage Creek, dispensing justice at a Spanish syndic, by methods as primitive and arbitrary as those of an Oriental pasha. Caring little for rules of evidence as laid down in the books, saying he but wished to know the truth, the once mighty hunter oftentimes compelled both parties to a suit to divide the costs between them and begone.

By now, an incipient American empire had become established in the trans-Allegheny. Settlement had advanced slowly down the great eastern affluents of the Mississippi, as along the fingers of the hand— the broad and rich valley bottoms being occupied by a crude but hard-headed border folk, while the intervening highlands were as yet left untouched, save as farmer-hunters here roved for game to stock their larders.

The great Napoleon had meanwhile risen to power. Reflecting on the tragic story of the ousting of France from North America, he deemed it possible to rehabilitate New France to the west of the Mississippi, and at the same time to check the United States in its westward growth. He therefore coerced Spain into retroceding the far-stretching Province of Louisiana to its original European owner.

Now came another fateful move upon the political chess-board. Three years later, Napoleon was facing a probable war with Great Britain. He feared that his arch enemy might, in the course of the struggle, seize this far-away possession, he needed money with which to replenish his treasury, and at the same time he thought to checkmate England by allowing her growing American rival at last to expand her bounds. He therefore sold Louisiana to the United States—an event lacking but a year of two centuries after the first successful settlement of the French in Canada. Nine years ago, with joyous acclaim, we of the United States celebrated the hundredth anniversary of this epoch-making purchase that has helped to make the Union one of the mightiest nations of the earth. The history of the transaction is to-day, in our land, as household words.

But even had not the Louisiana Purchase been made just when it was, American acquisition of the trans-Mississippi was sure to have come. A river is no adequate boundary between nations, if on one bank be a people like the Kentuckians, feverish to cross, and on the other a lethargic folk, like the Spanish-French of Louisiana Province. The Valley itself is a geographical unit. Tens of thousands of Americans had by this time descended the eastern slope of the basin, and many had not even waited by the eastern riverside for a change in the political ownership of the western. Before the Purchase, Kentuckians had, uninvited as well as invited, settled on Spanish lands along the lower reaches of the Missouri River. The chief increase in the population of Upper Louisiana had, during the last two decades of the 18th century, been American borderers. They had settled on French lands near New Orleans; and there was a dense American centre at Natchez. The great Purchase only hastened and facilitated the national progress of the Americans.

The ever-fascinating and thrilling tale of Lewis and Clark, as under President Jefferson's masterly direction they broke the path for civilization all the long rugged way from the mouth of the Missouri to the estuary of the Columbia, is still ringing afresh in American ears, because of recent centennial observances.

While still the great expedition was upon its route, other official explorers were searching the valleys of the Red, the Arkansas, and the Republican, reaching out to Spanish New Mexico, and pushing on over the rich grazing plains of Nebraska and Kansas to the snow-capped peaks of the eastern Rockies. The golden age of American exploration through the newly-acquired Territory of Louisiana, forms a splendid chapter in the annals of the Anglo-Saxon race. The names of Pike, Long, Frémont, Carson, recall many a rare adventure in the cause of scientific research. The records of the great rival fur-trading companies operating in the trans-Mississippi, with their picturesque annual caravans over the Santa Fé and Oregon trails, and the stories of roving bands of trappers and scouts who in following the buffalo discovered mountain passes that are to-day highways of the world's commerce, furnish thrilling scenes to grace the pages of a thousand romances.

In due time, the narrow paths of fur-traders, trappers, and explorers were broadened by emigrants, who throughout the nation's history have ever crowded toward our Farthest West. The great migration to Oregon in the forties of the last century was an event of supreme significance, and in some measure it is part and parcel of Canadian history also. Bold and restless pioneers set forth from the older settlements in wagons and on foot, with their women and children, with herds of cattle and horses, and after slowly traversing the broad plains, painfully crept over the mountain barrier and spread themselves into the verdant valleys of the Willamette and the Columbia.

Soon came the news that gold was discovered in California. Then followed another mighty westward rush over the transcontinental trails —within three years a hundred thousand men and women from both hemispheres crossed the Mississippi in their mad struggle to reach the El Dorado of Pacific tidewater. Ten years later, the Colorado hills also revealed the story of their hidden wealth. Up the long valleys of the Platte, the Smoky Hill, and the Arkansas, singly and in caravans, wearily toiled tens of thousands from all the corners of the earth, many falling by the way from fatigue, starvation, and the wounds of Indian arrows. Yet their experience in no wise checked the human tide that had set in the direction of the everlasting hills.

Overland stages and "prairie schooners" were quickly withdrawn upon the advance of the Pacific railways. The buffalo and grizzly soon disappeared from our Western plains. The Indian, stoutly standing for his birthright, was subdued at last. The cowboy succeeded the explorer and the trapper. Upon our great rivers—the Ohio, the Mississippi, and the Missouri—the introduction of steamboats, and later the bankside railways, wrought a like transformation. The old river life with its picturesque but rowdy boatmen, its unwieldy produce-laden flats and keels and arks, began gradually to pass away, and water traffic to approach the prosaic stage.

Prosaic, perhaps, because nearer our present vision. But in America, at least, we are ever in a period of transition. For example, now that the great northern forests in the Mississippi Valley have nearly been obliterated, and the day of the lumber raft is for us fast fading, and the " lumberjack " in in his parti-colored Mackinac blouse is about shifting his career to new fields of activity in our South and in your Northwest, we can realize that he, too, has been a striking figure on our stage—worthy of a place beside the coureur de bois, the voyageur, the habitant, the buckskin-clad Scotch-Irishman of the Wilderness Trail, the flat-boat man, the scout of the plains, the Rocky Mountain trapper, the Oregon pilgrim, the California " forty-niner," and the cowboy.

In our story of the American West, also, we must leave many a page for the stout flood of agricultural settlement that poured into the trans-Allegheny during the quarter of a century just previous to the War between the States. New England and New York, and almost every hamlet of western and northern Europe, sent the choicest of their people. By thousands they came to found new fortunes on lands recently acquired by purchase from the tribesmen. Our local history is rich in stirring details of their migration, and in particulars of their privations and their hardihood. The pioneers have, in the order of nature, now all but left us, in the United States; we no longer possess a Western frontier; and we are just beginning to understand that the story of these frontiersmen is a splendid epic still waiting to be sung.

What may we not say, too, of the part our great Valley played in the war for the preservation of our Union? As in the earlier days of the giant struggle between France and England for supremacy in North America, control of this vast drainage system was hotly contested. Whatever might have been the result of operations on the Atlantic Coast, the power holding the interior valley must, in the end, surely have won. From the population to the west of the Appalachians came the great bulk of both Northern and Southern armies; nowhere was the struggle more nearly brought home to the people. Song and story will always find abundant theme in our local annals of the war.

Equally important has been the Valley's share in the subsequent development of our nation—the social, economic, political, industrial, intellectual forces of the interior are to-day dominating us as a people.

Such are some of the elements that lend to the annals of the Mississippi Valley dignity and national significance. Until the close of the Revolutionary War, they are in considerable measure, also, the annals of Canada. You Canadian historians will, I am sure, rejoice with us in their picturesque vitality, in the stirring visions which they bring, and will with us, in the spirit of that reciprocity that should everywhere exist between students of local history in North America, anticipate the time when the poet and the novelist shall find in them material for their art; for after all (to return, in conclusion, to my text), those annals that may live long in the minds of the people are only such as shall be interpreted to them by the masters of romance.

III.

COLLECTIONS OF HISTORICAL MATERIAL RELATING TO THE WAR OF 1812.*

By Frank H. Severance, L.H.D., Buffalo, N.Y.,
Corresponding Member of the Ontario Historical Society.

The subject assigned to me in your programme is "Collections of Historical Material Relating to the War of 1812."

Two constructions, I think, may fairly be put on the subject. It seems to call for an account of existing collections in public or private libraries relating to the War of 1812; it also may be treated with propriety by submitting an analysis of the material which makes up the literature of this subject. The first method of treatment would be brief; the second method, properly followed, would of necessity be long and elaborate. For our present purpose it appears best, first, merely to glance at the collections on this subject as contained in notable libraries, and secondly, to survey, so far as time permits, several phases presented in the general field of literature of this war.

I need hardly remind you that outside of books much "material" is to be found which has true educative value. Our historical museums are many of them rich in relics, pictures and other reminders of this war. This is specially true in communities which during that war were the scene of special activity. In New England, New York, throughout the seaboard States, especially at Baltimore and at New Orleans, are preserved many reminders of this conflict. The regions about Lake Champlain and the Great Lakes are peculiarly rich for the student, not only in relics preserved, but in associations. Buildings and battlefields are other sorts of "material" which teach, often more effectively than the document or the printed page. But it is not with this phase of the subject that I am to deal. My especial theme is the literature of the War of 1812.

I have made some effort to learn what is contained in great libraries on this subject. The replies from experienced librarians are those which all library workers would anticipate. I am told in effect by the Librarian of Congress, by Doctor Thwaites of the State Historical Society of Wisconsin, by the Librarian of Harvard University,

* Read at the meeting of the Ontario Historical Society at Napanee, Ont., 1912.

and by the custodians of other notable historical collections, that it is impossible to say with definiteness how much material they have on this subject. While every library has numerous works brought together under its classification system relating to the War of 1812, that same classification system refers to other headings and departments a vast amount of material bearing on the same subject. It is enough to remind you that all the general classifications of a large library, such as biography, individual or collected; periodicals; naval history; general military history; poetry, etc., would naturally embrace much material important to the student of the War of 1812 period. Hence it might follow that a library, the catalogue of which showed by title comparatively few books or pamphlets or papers on this subject, might still contain far larger and more important collections on the general subject than another library which had in its catalogue cards a larger list under the 1812 classification.

With this general reminder, it is hardly necessary to specify further along this line. Naturally the great libraries of our country are strongest in 1812 as in other collections. Perhaps first in any list should be named the Library of Congress, which is all-embracing. After that, and possibly the New York Public Library, the student of this subject would turn to the great New England depositories: the Carter Brown Library at Providence, the Library of Harvard University, the Boston Public, and the Antiquarian Society at Worcester. Other important regional literatures have been brought together by the Maryland Historical Society at Baltimore, and I believe by the Library of Tulane University at New Orleans. So far as I am aware, the best collection of periodical literature on this period is to be found at Madison.

It is a matter of record, to be mentioned now without comment or preachment, that two of the most notable collections on the subject, supposedly housed in secure depositories, were turned to smoke and ashes by the conflagrations in the Parliament Buildings at Toronto and the State Capitol at Albany. I had some acquaintance with these collections and am of the impression that both ranked high in value relating to the 1812 period.

There is in Buffalo a little library, not at all to be mentioned with the great book collections of America, in which is to be found an exceptionally comprehensive collection on the period we are considering. The Buffalo Historical Society had already a good representative collection on this subject when, a few years ago, there was turned over to it a larger collection, the formation of which had been for a long period one of my diversions. As a result, the Buffalo Historical Society now has what I believe to be one of the best collections on this subject. A card list which I prepared some time ago enumerates some nine hundred titles, not including perhaps twice as many entries of papers and studies of special phases of our subject contained in local histories, in periodical publications, and especially in the transactions of learned societies. While this does not tally accurately with the material in our possession, it is still fairly representative. As it is this collection I am best acquainted with, it seems appropriate for me to consider it in passing to the second phase of my subject.

Our collection, then, contains, as must any collection which aims to be comprehensive in the literature of the War of 1812, books and pamphlets which fall into the following classes: Events leading up to the war, especially the Embargo and non-intercourse; general naval histories of the United States and of Great Britain; general military histories; official gazettes, journals and like publications; periodicals, not official; special histories of the period of the war; biographies; memorials, including transactions of institutions relative to the erection of monuments and the observance of anniversaries; controversial publications, both political and personal, the latter as to the service of this or that officer, etc.; claims, either for Government promotion for service rendered, pensions, or for damages and losses sustained by non-combatants; sermons, in which political doctrines were promulgated in the guise of religious instruction; poetry, drama, fiction, juvenile literature, and, omitting much, modern philosophical studies in which it is explained how things might have been otherwise.

This list could still be considerably extended and classified. There are numerous works pertaining to our subject, which consider chiefly the financial aspect of the times. There are others dealing with special phases of the causes that led up to the war, as, for instance, the violation of neutral rights and the impressment of seamen. There is a considerable literature of wanderers' narratives, including some of the curiosities of our history; and there is also a considerable literature of brag and bluster, contributed to, perhaps, in equal proportions by all the contending parties.

That what is commonly referred to by American writers as "our second war with Great Britain" has enlisted the pens of able students is seen when we glance at the title pages of many of the best known works. To this period belong writings of Thomas Jefferson, James Madison, James Fenimore Cooper, George Bancroft, A. J. Dallas, Richard Hildreth, Alexander H. Stephens, General James Wilkinson, Governor Daniel D. Tompkins, Major-General George W. Cullum, Henry A. S. Dearborn, George Cary Eggleston, Benson J. Lossing.

J. C. Gilleland, Solomon Hale, J. T. Headley, T. W. Higginson, Robert McAfee, R. B. Mitfee, Charles J. Ingersoll, Major A. L. Latour, T. O'Connor, James Parton, Theodore Roosevelt. These among the Americans. Among the English authors, very notably, William James, John Symons, Frederick Brock Tupper, Major-General Sir Carmichael Smith, G. R. Gleig, the Marquis of Wellesley, and many others.

Of Canadian authors in this field, again omitting many of note, I may mention G. Auchinleck, Robert Christie, Ernest Cruikshank, Captain F. C. Denison, Colonel George T. Denison, William Kingsford, William Kirby, Captain W. H. Merritt, D. B. Read, Charles Roger, Thomas Rideout and Matilda Edgar, and especially Major John Richardson, whose "Narrative of the Operations of the Right Division of the Army of Upper Canada, during the American War of 1812," printed at Brockville in 1842, is one of the rarest of Canadiana.

The student of this period cannot neglect certain very able chapters in works of wide scope, such as C. D. Yonge's "History of the British Navy," Von Holst's "Constitutional and Political History of the United States," G. Bryce's "Short History of the Canadian People," and numerous other works of general character.

Let us glance briefly at some of the books which we have referred to some of these classes. The literature which may be entitled "Causes leading up to the war," is surprisingly large and important. I do not need to remind this audience that no period in history can be separated from what has gone before, or what follows, and ticketed off as complete. To embrace all of the causes of this second war thoroughly and conscientiously would mean to include much of the story of America. For library purposes, however, it is possible to draw the lines with fair satisfaction, so that they shall include such studies as Alexander Baring's "Inquiry into the causes and consequences of the orders in council, and an examination of the conduct of Great Britain towards the neutral commerce of America," published in London in 1808. For some years earlier even than that date these subjects occasioned many pamphlets and many discussions in Parliament. Of importance, too, for this period is James Stephen's "War in Disguise, or the Frauds of the Neutral Flags," a London publication of 1807. Many others of this character might be mentioned.

Then we have a surprisingly large contemporary literature that might be gathered about the single word "Embargo," ranging, to mention only American authorship, from William Cullen Bryant's juvenile work, "The Embargo," printed in 1808, to Thomas Jefferson's voluminous writings, ending with his life in 1826.

The personal phase of this period is picturesquely brought out in numerous narratives of impressment; such, for instance, as that by Joshua Davis, "who was pressed and served on board six ships of the British," etc.; or the harrowing tale of James McLean, who at Hartford, in 1814, published his "Seventeen years' history of Sufferings as an Impressed Seaman in British Service." There are numerous narratives of this character which, taken together, make up an exceedingly lively prelude to the war itself.

The political shelf of our 1812 library must contain, not only long series of debates in Parliament and speeches in Congress, but a number of important serial or periodical publications, some of them official, such as the London Gazette, which through many years contains in bulletin form precise data invaluable to the student; The Royal Military Calendar; Dodsley's Annual Register; and, in America, The United States Army Register; Nile's Register; The Portfolio; the periodical entitled "The War," and scores of others of varying value.

Of controversial works, especially pamphlets, there is no end, many of them illustrating, better than the fuller and more deliberate histories, the temper of the time. It was a period when for one reason or another anonymity was thought to be an essential of political discussion. Some of you no doubt can tell me who was the author of the letters of "Veritas," first published in the Montreal *Herald,* afterwards brought together and printed in Montreal in 1815, in which is given a narrative of the military administration of Sir George Prevost during his command in the Canadas, "Whereby it will appear manifest that the merit of preserving them from conquest belongs not to him." In the guise of "A New England Farmer," John Lowell, of Massachusetts, bombarded President Madison with numerous pamphlets. In earlier years, "Juriscola," in a series of fifteen letters, had done his best to annihilate Great Britain; and "Don Quixote," in a most remarkable publication, "Ichneumon," laboured as a patriot to settle internecine strife.

Perhaps better known are the papers of "Touchstone," who, it appears, was DeWitt Clinton. I could go on in this field at great length. It is a piquant and a tempting one to the bibliographer in its variety and its occasional discoveries.

I doubt if any period in our history has developed more literature that may be summed up as curios. Many of them are trifling in historical value, but our library must have them. Here, for instance, is the treatise entitled "The Beauties of Brother Bull-us, by his Loving Sister, Bull-a." Who would think of finding essays on the War of 1812 hidden under such a title as C. W. Hart chose for his work printed at Poughkeepsie in 1816, "Colloquy between two Deists, on the Immortality of the Soul"? Better known and more amusing is the work ascribed to Israel Mauduit, "Madison Agonistes, or the agonies of Mother Goose," a political burletta represented as to be acted on the American stage. Among the *dramatis personæ* are Randolpho and Adamo, Members of Congress, etc. I may also mention "The Federal Looking Glass," published in 1812, which pictures General Hull's "surrender to the Devil."

Surely to this class belongs "The Adventures of Uncle Sam in Search After his Lost Honour," by Frederick Augustus Fidfaddy, Esq., who announced himself as "member of the Legion of Honour, Scratchetary to Uncle Sam and Privy Counsellor to Himself." The title-page motto in "Merino Latin"—"*Taurem per caudem grabbo*"—sheds light on the serious character of the work.

More serious, but I think also more amusing, is the work entitled "An Affecting Narrative of Louisa Baker, a Native of Massachusetts who in Disguise Served Three Years as a Marine on board an American Frigate." This is a Boston imprint of 1815, but is not unique as a record of a woman disguised serving in this war, for we have still another work with the following title: "The Friendless Orphan. An affecting Narrative of the Trials and Afflictions of Sophia Johnson, the Early Victim of a Cruel Stepmother, whose Afflictions and Singular Adventures probably exceed those of any other American Female living, who has been doomed in early life to drink deep of the cup of sorrow," etc., etc. Sophia experienced her sorrows in part at Buffalo, Fort Erie and elsewhere on the frontier disguised as a man, and lost an arm at the Battle of Bridgewater, of which an extraordinary engraving is given. Sophia, *sans* arm, is also portrayed.

I will merely mention G. Proctor's "Lucubrations of Humphrey Ravelin, Esq., Late Major in the * * * Regiment of Infantry." This is a London publication, giving some account of military life and Indian warfare in Canada during the 1812 period. Another curious work is Gilbert J. Hunt's "Historical Reader," of which numerous editions were published. The narrative is a poor imitation of the style of Chronicles and other historical books of the Old Testament.

Perhaps rarest of these curios, at least in the original edition, is "The War of the Gulls, an Historical Romance in Three Chapters," reputed to be by Jacob Bigelow and Nathan Hale, published at the

Dramatic Repository, Shakespeare Gallery, New York, in 1812. This work has been recently reprinted, an honour which it quite deserves.

Among the curios, too, should have place sundry plays and dramas based on the war. I mention but two of them: one by Mordecai Manuel Noah, a Hebrew journalist of New York, who undertook to establish a modern Ararat and Refuge City for the Jews on Grand Island, in Niagara River, but whose contribution to this field of letters is entitled: "She Would be a Soldier, or the Plains of Chippewa; an Historical Drama in Three Acts." Major Noah's play was enacted for a time on the New York stage. Half a century later Clifton W. Tayleure produced another play of this period, "The Boy Martyrs of September 12th, 1814," which with little literary merit and seemingly less dramatic possibilities, was staged for a time in New York.

Under the heading of "Prisoners' Memoirs" there are numerous publications relating to the war, which fall into two classes. First, the narratives of men who shared in Western campaigns, usually American pioneers who were taken by British and Indians. An example is the narrative of William Atherton, entitled "Narrative of the Sufferings and Defeat of the Northwestern Army under Gen. Winchester; Massacre of the Prisoners; Sixteen Months' Imprisonment of the Writer and others with the Indians and British," etc., a prolix title, the work itself printed at Frankfort, Kentucky, in 1842. Still other chronicles of this character are to be gathered.

A wholly different field of experience was that of Americans who underwent imprisonment at Dartmoor in England. Perhaps the best known of these memoirs is the volume by Charles Andrews, "Containing a Complete and Impartial History of the Entire Captivity of the Americans in England from the Commencement of the Late War * * * until all prisoners were released by the Treaty of Ghent. Also a particular detail of all occurrences relative to that horrid massacre at Dartmoor, on the fatal evening of the 6th of April, 1815." Andrews' tale was printed in New York in 1815.

The next year, at Boston, Benjamin Waterhouse published "A Journal of a Young Man of Massachusetts, late a Surgeon on board an American privateer, who was captured at sea by the British, in May, 1813, and was confined, first at Melville Island, Halifax, then at Chatham, in England, and last at Dartmoor prison."

In 1841 appeared "A Green Hand's First Cruise, Roughed out from the Log Book of Memory of 25 years standing, together with a residence of five months in Dartmoor." This two-volume work, one of the scarcest books of the War of 1812, was published at Baltimore by "A. Younker," probably a pen-name.

As late as 1878 appeared still another contribution to this class of works: "The early life and later experiences and labours of Joseph Bates," who records that in early life he was a sailor, was captured by the English in the War of 1812 and confined in Dartmoor prison. In later life he became an anti-slavery agitator.

The phrase "Wanderers' Narratives" fairly describes numerous works which the student of our subject will encounter; books, for instance, like Richard J. Cleveland's "In the Forecastle; or Twenty-five Years a Sailor." His sailing days were from 1792 to 1817, and he saw much and records much of privateering during the War of 1812.

Another "wanderer" was Patrick Gass, whose "Life and Times," first published, I believe, at Wellsburg, Va., in 1859, has in recent years been reprinted. When he wrote his Memoirs, Gass claimed to be the sole survivor of the Lewis and Clark overland expedition to the Pacific of 1804 to 1806. He was also a soldier in the war with Great Britain, 1812 to 1815, and fought at Lundy's Lane. About fifty pages of his book relate to this war, mostly to events on the Niagara.

In this class may perhaps be mentioned a well-known work, Captain David Porter's "Journal of a Cruise made in the Pacific Ocean in the United States Frigate *Essex*, in the years 1812, '13 and '14."

Much less known is P. Finan's "Journal of a Voyage to Quebec in the Year 1825, with Recollections of Canada during the late American War, in the Years 1812, 1813." In the second part of his book Mr. Finan gives his personal experiences in the war. He was with his father, an officer, at the burning of Toronto, April 27th, 1813. As an eye-witness his record of that and other events is important.

I may dismiss this special phase of our subject with the mention of but one other work, "The Travels and Adventures of David C. Bunnell." After a life suspiciously full of romantic adventure, some none too creditable, Bunnell joined the American navy under Chauncey, served on Lake Ontario, 1812-13, and left Fort Niagara July 3, 1813, in Jesse Elliot's command, going from Buffalo to Put-in Bay in open boats. According to his narrative, he was on the *Lawrence* during the Battle of Lake Erie, and afterwards was put on the schooner *Chippewa*, as second in command, and ran her between Put-in Bay and Detroit "as a packet," being finally caught in a gale, blown the whole length of Lake Erie and driven ashore upon the beach about a quarter of a mile below Buffalo Creek. He landed safely, remaining in Buffalo until Perry and Barclay arrived and were given a public dinner, on which occasion, he says, " I managed a field piece and fired for the toasts." His account of his services and adventures on the lakes appears to be veracious, which is more than can be said of some portions of his romantic but highly entertaining chronicle. It may be noted that his book was issued in the same year and apparently from the same press as the rare first edition of the Book of Mormon, being printed at Palmyra, N.Y., by Grandin in 1831.

A considerable shelf, perhaps " five feet long," could be filled with stories of the War of 1812. My studies of American history have well-nigh convinced me that that war was fought, not to maintain American rights on the high seas, but to stimulate the development of American letters by supplying picturesque material for budding romancers. The only drawback to that theory is that the straightforward unadorned record of the old sea duels, like that of the *Constitution* and the *Guerrière,* has more thrills in it than the romancers can invent. But for well-nigh a century the novelists have hovered about this period, like bumble-bees in a field of clover. The war on the lakes and the Niagara frontier has had a share of their attention. There are boys' books with Perry for a hero—always with the introduction of things more or less impossible to the character. The events of 1812-14 on the Niagara have been much used by Canadian story-writers. There is " Hemlock," by Robert Sellars (Montreal, 1890), which follows many of the events of the war in our district and is none the less worthy of American readers because its point of view and sympathies are so notably Canadian. A work of greater merit is " Neville Trueman, the Pioneer Preacher, a Tale of 1812," by W. H. Withrow, published in Toronto in 1886. The fictitious characters mingle with the real, at Queenston Heights, Fort George, the burning of Niagara, Chippewa and Lundy's Lane. It is a simple tale, with no affectations; and it makes a record which we are glad to have of high character and worthy impulses. There were true patriots in Canada in those days, and it is wholesome to read of them, no matter on which side of the river one may live. In this class belongs Amy E. Blanchard's tale, " A Loyal Lass; a Story of the Niagara Campaign of 1814." The list might be much extended.

If this war has inspired the production of fiction, it has also proved, at least in the earlier years, an unfailing fount of inspiration for the poets. I do not know of much poetry produced in England on this account. The affair does not appear to have presented a poetic aspect to British authors. But to many an American, especially of the type easily fired to extravagant patriotic expression, it was provocative of wonderful results. Some worthy poets produced true poetry with this war as the theme. Some of the patriotic songs of Philip Freneau deserve the place they have held in American literature for a century. Samuel Woodworth's "Heroes of the Lake," a poem in two books, contains excellent lines. So long a production could hardly fail of being good at intervals. Many of Woodworth's poems, odes, songs, and other metrical effusions were based on incidents in this war. So was John Davis' "The American Mariners," vouched for on the title page as "A moral poem, to which are added Naval Annals," a delightful combination of the flight of Pegasus and the most uninspired of statistics. This work, first published at Salisbury, England, in 1822, has had at least two or more editions.

I can only mention such works as the "Court of Neptune and the Curse of Liberty," New York, 1817; the "Columbian Naval Songster," and other collections, containing numerous songs celebrating the exploits of Perry, McDonough and others; and "The Battle of the Thames," being an extract from the unpublished work, entitled "Tecumseh," the author veiling his identity as "A Young American."

Thomas Pierce's "The Muse of Hesperia, a Poetic Reverie," appeared in Cincinnati in 1823. A note in Thomson's Bibliography of Ohio says of this work, "For this poem the author was awarded a gold medal by the Philomathic Society of Cincinnati College, in November, 1821, but he never claimed the prize." It relates mainly to the events of the War of 1812 in the Northwest, and contains notes relating to persons and events mentioned in the text.

In Halifax, in 1815, there appeared "A Poetical Account of the American Campaigns of 1812 and '13, with some slight sketches relating to Party Politics which governed the United States during the War and at its Commencement," dedicated to the people of Canada by the publisher, said publisher being John Howe, Jr.

"The Year," a poem in three cantos, by William Leigh Pierce, was published in New York in 1813. Appended to the poem are seventy pages of historical notes, the whole production being intended as a poetical history of the times, including the War of 1812 so far as it had then progressed.

A poetical curio is "The Bladensburg Races," written shortly after the capture of Washington City, August 24, 1814. The poem ridicules the flight of President Madison and household to Bladensburg, and the erudite author adds an illuminating note: "Probably it is not generally known that the flight of Mahomet, the flight of John Gilpin and the flight of Bladensburg, all occurred on the 24th of August."

The local bibliophile or collector would wish me to mention "The Narrative of the Life, Travels and Adventures of Captain Israel Adams who Lived at Liverpool, Onondaga County, N.Y., the man who during the last War [1812] Surprised the British Lying in the Bay of Quoenti; Who Took by Strategem the Brig *Toronto* and Took Her to Sackett's Harbor, and for whom the British offered a Reward of $500."

Of peculiar local interest to those of us who live on the Niagara is David Thompson's "History of the Late War," etc., published at Niagara, Upper Canada, in 1832; one of the earliest of Upper Canada imprints and a better one, I venture to say, than old Niagara could turn out to-day. It is not a soothing book for a thin-skinned American to read. If it should fall into the hands of such a singular, not to say exceptional, individual, he could find balm, if not, indeed, a counter-irritant, in James Butler's "American Bravery Displayed in the Capture of 1,400 vessels of war and commerce since the Declaration of War by the President." This volume of 322 pages, published in 1816, did not have the unanimous endorsal of the British press.

As I survey the literature of this period I find no bolder utterance, no fiercer defiance of Great Britain's "Hordes," than in the sonorous stanzas of some of our gentle poets. Iambic defiance, unless kindled by a grand genius, is a poor sort of fireworks, even when it undertakes to combine patriotism and appreciation of natural scenery. Certainly something might be expected of a poet who sandwiches Niagara Falls in between bloody battles and gives us the magnificent in nature, the gallant in warfare and the loftiest patriotism in purpose, the three strains woven in a triple pæan of passion, ninety-four duodecimo pages in length. Such a work was offered to the world at Baltimore in 1818, with this title page: "Battle of Niagara, a Poem without Notes, and Goldau, or the Maniac Harper. Eagles and Stars and Rainbows. By Jehu O'Cataract, author of 'Keep Cool.'" I have never seen "Keep Cool," but it must be very different from the "Battle of Niagara," or it belies its name. The fiery Jehu O'Cataract was John Neal, or "Yankee Neal," as he was called.

The "Battle of Niagara," he informs the reader, was written when he was a prisoner; when he "felt the victories of his countrymen." The poem has a metrical introduction and four cantos, in which is told, none too lucidly, the story of the battle of Niagara, with such flights of eagles, scintillation of stars and breaking of rainbows, that no quotation can do it justice. In style it is now Miltonic, now reminiscent of Walter Scott. The opening canto is mainly an apostrophe to the

Bird, and a vision of glittering horsemen. Canto two is a dissertation on Lake Ontario, with word-pictures of the primitive Indian. The rest of the poem is devoted to the battle near the great cataract—and throughout all are sprinkled the eagles, stars and rainbows. Do not infer from this that the production is wholly bad; it is merely a good specimen of that early American poetry which was just bad enough to escape being good.

A still more ambitious work is "The Fredoniad, or Independence Preserved," an epic poem by Richard Emmons, a Kentuckian, afterwards a physician of Philadelphia. He worked on it for ten years, finally printed it in 1826, and in 1830 got it through a second edition, ostentatiously dedicated to Lafayette. "The Fredoniad" is a history of the War of 1812 in verse. It was published in four volumes; it has forty cantos, filling 1,404 duodecimo pages, or a total length of about 42,000 lines. The first and second cantos are devoted to Hell, the third to Heaven, and the fourth to Detroit. About one-third of the whole work is occupied with military operations on the Niagara frontier. Nothing from Fort Erie to Fort Niagara escapes this metre-machine. The Doctor's poetic feet stretch out to miles and leagues, but not a single verse do I find that prompts to quotation; though I am free to confess I have not read them all, and much doubt if anyone, save the infatuated author, and perhaps a long-suffering proof-reader, ever did read the whole of "The Fredoniad."

I have already mentioned several very rare books and pamphlets; but if asked to designate the rarest of all on the War of 1812, I should name a fifteen-page pamphlet, published without title-page at the Regimental Press, Bungalore, India, dealing with the relations between British agents and Indians in the Northwest after the Treaty of Ghent. But twenty copies were printed. It contains letters from Lieut.-Colonel McDowell to His Excellency Sir F. P. Robinson, Drummond Island, September 24th, 1815, and later dates; and an account of the proceedings of a court of inquiry held to investigate charges, preferred by the United States Government, that the Indians had been stimulated by the British agents to a continuance of hostilities since the Peace. This publication, issued three-quarters of a century or so after the event, from a regimental press in India, is an effort to show that the Indians were not so stimulated; all the stimulus they received from the British agents, it may be presumed, was of an entirely different kind.

The field of biography in its relation to our general subject is vast. Around such figures as Andrew Jackson and William Henry Harrison there has developed a mass of literature which, if thoroughly listed and analyzed, would constitute a considerable bibliography in itself. There are biographies and memoirs of most of the British admirals and other naval and military commanders in active service during this period. In our list must be included the life stories of Thomas Jefferson, James Madison, Lewis Cass, Joshua Barney, Commodore Bainbridge, Winfield Scott, Oliver Hazard Perry, Henry Clay, Josiah Quincy, John Quincy Adams, George Cabot, and many other makers of American history.

Of the British and Canadian officers we have admirable biographies, including those of General Brock, Admiral Broke, Admiral Sir Edward Codrington, and others.

The Treaty of Ghent is the subject of numerous publications. An excellent account of the proceedings of the commissioners, and especially of the difficulties met and overcome by the American representatives, is by Thomas Wilson, in the *Magazine of American History*, November, 1888. A most interesting work on this subject is the scarce quarto, published in London in 1850, entitled "*Mèmoires d'un Voyageur qui se repose.*" It is the private journal and correspondence of a diplomatist in the secret service of England. He is here designated by the pseudonym of "Miller," and appears to have been entrusted with four separate special missions to America, one of which, in 1814-15, was to exchange the ratifications of the Treaty of Ghent. The volume contains a mass of private information on diplomatic relations between Great Britain and the United States, including a journal of the signing of the Treaty of Ghent.

A noticeable, not to say notable, feature of much of this literature is its partisanship. Especially in statistical matters, such as the numerical strength of the contending forces, the number of guns or the weight of metal—matters which one would suppose would have been settled by the official reports—there has existed for a century, and still exists, utterly irreconcilable divergence. The unbiased student of this period, who seeks only to learn the facts, is still bewildered and in doubt when he compares American with Canadian or English accounts. If the bitterness and rancour of the old books has abated in these later days of courtesy and fair speech, the divergence of record, though perhaps dispassionately stated, still exists. An instance is the battle of Lundy's Lane, which at last accounts was still being fought.

It may not be a wholly whimsical proposition to suggest, as a feature of our centenary of peace, the establishment of an international commission—by this Society, say, on the one hand, and the American

Historical Association on the other—whose task should be, if possible, the production of a simply-told history of the War of 1812, which should meet with equal commendation as a truthful and unprejudiced chronicle on both sides of the border. But perhaps I suggest the impossible.

I could say much of the ever-lengthening list of modern studies of this or that phase of the war; such, for instance, as Nicholas Murray Butler's " Influence of the War of 1812 upon the Consolidation of the American Union," Captain A. T. Mahan's " Sea Power in its Relation to the War of 1812," and very many others, usually revealing a better grasp of the significance of events than the earlier works, and usually, too, written in a better temper. Not least among these modern studies is the notable group of papers which at this meeting we listen to with great satisfaction.

IV.

DESPATCH FROM COLONEL LETHBRIDGE TO MAJOR-GENERAL BROCK.

By Lieut.-Colonel Cole, Brockville, Ont.

Sir,— Kingston, August 10th, 1812.

My letter to Colonel Cartwright from Prescott will have apprised you of the reason of my sudden departure from this—and most grieviously mortified I was on my arrival below to find the Julia Schooner had the singular good fortune of effecting her escape. My decided purpose was, in the event of our vessels being detained at Brockville by a westerly wind till the return of Lieut. Fitzgibbons with the bateaux from Kingston, to have attempted the Capture of the Julia by an attack on Ogdensburg—with our vessels—aided by a detachment on land—but my instructions to the Captains were that in case a strong easterly wind sprang up in the interim they were then to proceed to Kingston, having, of course, in my mind your directions for the Earl Moira to proceed to Niagara. An easterly wind did spring up and the vessels proceeded for this place.

The enclosed report of the deposition of a deserter from the enemy will in some degree illustrate their situation at Ogdensburg and I am much inclined to credit the material parts of it from the manner in which it was related. I proceeded down the river to Williamstown in Glengarry looking at the different corps of militia as I passed. Of the Counties of Grenville, Dundas, Stormont and Glengarry, I feel sincere satisfaction in noticing their uniform zeal to exert their best endeavours for the defence of their country though as yet almost in the infancy of discipline, with the execution of the manual and platoon exercise—owing to the general want of instructors. But their wants and privations are many, but notwithstanding that, at Prescott they were not only without blankets but even straw was not to be procured. The alacrity of both officers and men to assist in erecting a stockaded fort with three embrasures at each of two angles was highly meritorious, and as no allowance had been made for their trouble in any shape and under the privations it was represented to me they were experiencing, I ventured to order an issue of rum of a pint per man. This issue I trust will meet with approbation under this singular case of His Excellency the Commander of the Forces and yourself. The Dundas and Stormont Militia are very desirous of having a troop of cavalry established and being persuaded of its utility, both as patroles and for the purpose of carrying dispatches along the communication, I am desirous of seconding their propositions. It seems a Mr. Forrester has been at York and made application on the subject, and was referred by you to Major General Shaw, who did not happen to extend his journey so far down. But though I should recommend Mr. Forrester for being one of the officers of the troop I do not feel encouraged by the accounts I hear of him (though no impeachment on his loyalty) to suggest his having the command of the troops.

The Dundas Militia are unhappily in a state of schism at least between the two field officers, Col. McDonnell and Major Mackay. The former certainly much advanced in years, the latter very shrewd and I believe extremely able and zealous, though inflexibly stern. I beg leave to propose my way of healing the breach,—the substitution of Colonel Thomas Fraser to the command of the Dundas Militia, an arrangement I have been assured would be agreeable to Col. McLean (?) and I dare say would not be ill taken by Major Mackay. The Cornwall Militia are very well attended to by Col.   *. He has been obliged to hire a store for the accommodation of his men at the moderate rate of 20 per annum, which by properly dividing by berth, is adequate to contain the whole of their present number embodied; more arms will be supplied to him when our means are more abundant. No blankets, but a supply of straw. He has been obliged to purchase some camp kettles. The flank companies of the Glengarry Militia partly assembled at McLaughlin's. Colonel McMillan has been under the indispensable necessity, from the situation being destitute of other resources, of contracting for shed to cover his men, to build ovens, and I authorized his having a supply of kettles, a surgeon to attend the sick, and I have sanctioned his having the assistance of Mr. Wilkinson, from Cornwall until your pleasure is ascertained. I do intend removing a part of the flank companies of the Glengarry to Cornwall as a point more material to be guarded than the mouth of the River Le Raisin. I have been obliged to order them some ketttles. There are four points in the river more vulnerable from musketry than others from five to eight hundred yards distant from the American shore between the Rapid Plat and Cornwall. The best defence for which would appear

*No name given.

to be two or three light pieces of flying artillery, which the inhabitants would undertake to furnish the horses for. But of this and the number of militia and the number of arms received, a more detailed report shall be forwarded to you at Niagara, to which place I apprehend you are now removed and will probably reach you before this. I confess I have had a most fatiguing week and request you will refer any inaccuracies in this to that cause.

I have the honor to transmit a plan of the proposed work at Point Henry which I am the more convinced of the utility of. You are, of course, apprised of the approach of some regular troops to those quarters which I shall permit to come on here in the first instance unless I receive any instructions from you to the contrary, I have no doubt that a proportion of those troops are intended for Prescott and I especially reported the necessity of a force there. The schooner Julia was lying very quietly in the secure harbor of Ogdensburg, and afforded not the least molestation to the large brigade of Batteaux under Lieut. Fitzgibbons on his return. Colonel McLean is erecting a block house on a point about twelve miles above Cornwall for accommodation for his men as a Centrical rendezvous for a part of them and an accommodation with all. The cost of which will be but trifling, it being done by the militiamen as far as labor is concerned.

There are, I am sorry to say, several exceptions to universal loyalty in the County of Leeds and I wish to be honored with your instructions in respect of men who have lived as peaceable inhabitants but who being called on refuse taking the oath of allegiance. To send them across the river is perhaps accomplishing the very object that they have at heart. I fell in with General Sheaffe at the mouth of the River Le Raisin and I returned here sooner, perhaps, than I should otherwise have done.

The Royal George is returned to this place; she had been some way down the river and very near cutting off the Three Durham Gun Boats. She will sail on the look-out to-morrow.

      I have the honour to be, &c.,
        Your most H. Servant,
          LETHBRIDGE, COLONEL.

To Major General Brock.

V.

MILITARY MOVEMENTS IN EASTERN ONTARIO DURING THE WAR OF 1812.*

BY LIEUT.-COLONEL W. S. BUELL, BROCKVILLE, ONT.

Although war was declared by the United States on 18th June, 1812, official notice was not received by Sir George Prevost, the Governor-General of Canada, until 7th July. Private messages from New York, however, arrived about 25th of June. On the 29th of June, eight schooners that were in Ogdensburg Harbor attempted to escape to Lake Ontario. Mr. Dunham Jones, who resided near Maitland, saw the movement, and fully appreciating the advantage which would result to the British interests if this fleet could be prevented from reaching Lake Ontario, gathered a company of volunteers and pursued them in rowboats, overtaking them at the foot of the islands just above Brockville, apparently about Big Island. Two of the vessels, the *Island Packet* and the *Sophia,* were captured; the crews were landed on an island and the vessels burned. The remainder of the fleet made their way back to Ogdensburg as fast as they could go.

At the opening of the war the American plan of campaign was to invade Canada with three great armies, viz., the Army of the West on the Detroit Frontier, the Army of the Centre on the Niagara Frontier, and the Army of the North from Lake Champlain.

The Army of the West under General Hull was captured at Detroit by General Brock; and the Army of the Centre, under General Van Rensselaer, was defeated at Queenston Heights. The Army of the North was the most pretentious of the three. It was composed of 10,000 troops and was commanded by General Dearborn, the Commander-in-Chief of the United States army. It mobilized at Lake Champlain with the evident intention of marching straight on Montreal. Nothing, however, was attempted further than a few unimportant and unsuccessful skirmishes and then it retired to safe winter quarters at Plattsburg.

Early in the winter of 1813 a detachment of the garrison of Ogdensburg, under Captain Forsythe, made a night attack upon Gananoque,

* Read at the annual meeting of the Ontario Historical Society at Brockville, Ont., 1910.

which at that time consisted of a country tavern and a sawmill, with an adjoining log house. The enemy wounded a lady and carried off a few pigs and poultry. Yet the event was represented as a gallant action.

On the night of the 6th of February, 1813, Captain Forsythe, with 200 of his command and some so-called gentlemen volunteers, made an attack on Brockville, coming across from Morristown on the ice. At that time Brockville was but a struggling village. It was considered of no consequence from a military standpoint and there was posted there but one company of the Leeds Militia. I am sorry to say that the captain, officers and men of this company, excepting one sentry, were sound asleep in their beds when the attack was made. Forsythe had a six-pounder about the centre of the river on the ice. The sentry was wounded, the officers and about 20 militiamen were captured as were also about thirty residents. The detachment and gentlemen volunteers proceeded to break into and plunder the houses in the village and to throw open the jail. They carried off provisions, horses, and cattle. Among the residents captured were several veterans of the American Revolutionary War, who according to the custom of the time had been given honorary military titles by their neighbors. Forsythe consequently reported having taken as his prisoners so many Majors, Captains, etc., and so many rifles, leading his readers to infer that he had captured a large military force. As a matter of fact the bulk of the rifles he took were securely boxed up en route to the force at Prescott, to which force most of the able-bodied men of the village were attached.

The force at Prescott was about 500 strong, under the command of Colonel Pearson. He sent Major Macdonell of the Glengarry Fencibles, Light Infantry (known as "Red George"), to proceed with a flag of truce to Ogdensburg to remonstrate against such expeditions. Macdonell was received by the officers at Ogdensburg with extreme discourtesy, with taunts and boasting. Forsythe, the officer in command, was no whit behind his subordinates in insolence, and suggested that the two forces should try their strength on the ice. Macdonell replied that in two days he, himself, would be in command at Prescott and that then he would be happy to accommodate them.

Two days later Macdonell succeeded to the command at Prescott, but on that same evening Sir George Prevost arrived there on his way from Quebec to Kingston. The British Government had not even by this time relinquished the idea that the United States did not really intend to fight with their own kith and kin and had impressed their views upon Prevost. Consequently, when Macdonell reported to him all that had taken place and asked authority to attack Ogdensburg, Prevost would not entertain his request, saying that he did not desire by any hostile acts to keep up a spirit of enmity.

Macdonell then tried another method, and a few hours later told Prevost that two men had deserted and gone over to Ogdensburg, and that in all probability Forsythe would by that time know of his, the Governor-General's, presence, in Prescott. He suggested that the Governor-General should at once start for Kingston with a small escort while he, Macdonell, would make a demonstration in force on the ice, to keep the enemy occupied. The Governor finally reluctantly consented and started at daybreak on 22nd February, 1813, for Kingston, and Major Macdonell at once commenced arrangements to meet Forsythe as promised.

Sir George Prevost evidently repented after leaving Prescott, for on arriving at Brockville he wrote a note (which he headed "Flint's Inn"), to Macdonell instructing him on no account to exceed his instructions and do anything of a hostile nature. This note he despatched by a galloper, who, fortunately, was too late. Macdonell received the note in Ogdensburg about eight o'clock a.m.

At Ogdensburg there was an old French Fort, once known as Fort Presentation. It was situated just south of where the lighthouse now stands. The village was on the east side of the Oswegatchie River, which flows into the St. Lawrence at that point, and protected by a battery of heavy field artillery stationed on an eminence near the shore. Forsythe had under his command at Ogdensburg between five hundred and one thousand men, His own report says five hundred, while Macdonell estimated them at one thousand.

Macdonell had a force of 480 officers and men. The composition of his force represented many portions of the Empire. Owing to the state of the ice, which is said to have been quite weak and dangerous for so many to cross at once, and owing also to the position of the enemy in the old Fort, the force was divided into two columns. The right, commanded by Captain Jenkins, of New Brunswick, was composed of a flank company of the Glengarry Light Infantry Fencibles, and 70 Canadian Militia. Captain Jenkins' orders were to check the enemy's left and intercept his retreat, while the left column under Colonel Macdonell himself (who was now Lieutenant-Colonel, in command of the Eastern District of Upper Canada), moved towards his position in the village. This left column was composed of 120 of the King's Regiment (Liverpool), some of the 41st (Welsh), 40 of the Royal Newfoundlanders, and about 200 Canadian militia, among whom were some French-Canadians.

When approaching the south side of the river the snow was found to be very deep, and the advance of both columns was retarded and both became exposed, particularly the right, to a heavy cross-fire from the batteries of the enemy for a longer period than anticipated. But pushing on rapidly, the left column gained the right bank of the river under the direct fire of the enemy's artillery and line of musketry and their right was turned by a detachement of the King's Regiment, their artillery was captured by a bayonet charge, and their infantry driven through the town. Some escaped across the Oswegatchie into the fort, others fled to the woods or sought refuge in the houses, from whence they kept up such a volume of fire that it became necessary to dislodge them with our guns, which now came up from the banks of the river where they had stuck in the deep snow.

Macdonell had now gained the high ground on the east side of the Oswegatchie (or Black River, as it was then called), and was in a position to assault the fort, but his men were exhausted by the rapid rush across the river, through the snow and up the bank. He gained a breathing spell for them by sending in under a flag of truce a demand for unconditional surrender. To this Forsythe replied that there must first be some more fighting.

During this time Captain Jenkins had led on his column and had encountered deep snow, when he became exposed to a heavy fire from seven guns, which he at once attempted to take with the bayonet, although they were covered by 200 of the enemy's best troops.

Advancing as rapidly as he could through the deep snow he ordered a charge and had not proceeded many paces before his left arm was shattered by a grape shot; but still he undauntedly ran on at the head of his men, when his right arm was shot; still he ran on cheering his men to the assault until exhausted by pain and loss of blood he fell. unable to move. His company gallantly continued the charge under Lieutenant McAulay, but had come to a standstill, stuck in the snow just at the moment when Macdonell's column came swarming over the Oswegatchie river headed by a Highland company of militia under Captain Eustace and rushed the fort. The enemy retreated rapidly by the opposite entrance and escaped into the woods, our right column being unable to intercept them.

Among others mentioned in the despatch of Colonel Macdonell besides Captains Jenkins and Eustace we find Colonel Fraser, who was in command of the militia, an ancestor of Colonel R. D. Fraser.

a former well-known officer of Brockville. The British losses were 8 killed and 52 wounded, among the latter being Colonel Macdonell himself.

The American losses were 20 killed and 150 wounded, while four officers and 70 privates were taken prisoners. Eleven guns were captured, among them being two twelve-pounders, surrendered by Burgoyne in 1777. There was also a large quantity of ordnance and military stores of all descriptions. Two barracks were burned, also two armed schooners, and two large gun-boats, which being frozen in the ice, could not be moved. The honor of this action was not tarnished by any looting in spite of the way the Americans had plundered Gananoque and Brockville. Macdonell would not let his followers help themselves to so much as a twist of tobacco; he even paid American teamsters four dollars a day for their labor in hauling the military stores across to Prescott.

During the following spring and summer success varied. The Americans captured York (now Toronto), then suffered humiliating defeat at Stoney Creek and Beaver Dams. Again the United States Navy were successful on Lake Erie and their army followed it up by beating Proctor in the Battle of the Thames, where Tecumseh, the great Indian chief, is supposed to have been killed. Then they drove our forces in the Niagara Peninsula back to Burlington Heights.

Things looked gloomy for Canada.

The Americans had still their Army of the North at Lake Champlain, now under General Hampton. It had for nearly a year been constantly drilled under Major-General Izard, who had served two campaigns in the French army. These troops were all well uniformed and equipped, and the most efficient regular army which the United States were able to send into the field during the war.

At this time another army of from ten to twelve thousand (American reports admit ten thousand), were assembled at Grenadier Island, eighteen miles below Sackett's Harbor, with a huge fleet of boats called the Invincible Armada of the St. Lawrence.

It was planned that with the aid of their navy in Lake Ontario, under Admiral Chauncey, they were to capture Kingston, then come down the river, as a mere matter of detail take Prescott en route, and uniting with Hampton's army near St. Regis, sweep on to Montreal and so wind up matters. There was to be a triumphal entry into Montreal where they would take up comfortable winter quarters.

Such was the plan, but the best laid plans of mice and men gang aft aglee.

First let us follow the fate of Hampton and his Army of the North. He was at Burlington, Vermont. His intentions were unknown to the British. It was supposed that they were to march up the valley of the Richelieu to Montreal. A corps of observation was sent out under Colonel de Salaberry with instructions to move parallel to the American army, breaking up and obstructing the roads in his front and molesting him in every possible way.

De Salaberry was a French-Canadian gentleman who had entered the British army at an early age and having served eleven years returned to Canada. He raised a regiment of Canadian Voltigeurs.

The Eastern Townships during the Old Régime remained an almost unbroken wilderness. During the "War of Independence" this wilderness proved an important barrier against invasion and in the War of 1812 materially retarded the operations of the hostile armies.

Colonel Macdonell (Red George), had lately been appointed to the command of a regiment of French-Canadian Fencibles, and was at Kingston organizing and drilling them. On October 20th, Sir George Prevost, then at Kingston, heard rumors of approaching activity on Hampton's part and determined to go down to the Beauharnois frontier to see how matters were. Just as he was about to start at noon he met Macdonell and asked him how soon he hoped to have his corps in shape for active service. "As soon as they have finished dinner, sir," was the reply, so Prevost ordered him to bring them down to the assistance of De Salaberry, telling him of the information which he had received; and Prevost started on his journey.

Macdonell promptly procured boats, embarked his regiment, ran down the river and rapids, crossed Lake St. Francis in a storm, then threaded twenty miles of forest in single file in the dead of night and arrived just in time to assist De Salaberry, having travelled 170 miles by water and twenty by land in sixty hours, actual travel, and not one man absent.

In the meantime Hampton had left Burlington and marched on and captured Odelltown in apparently a straight line towards Montreal, but instead of proceeding directly he turned partially back and then westerly until he arrived at Chateauguay Four Corners, just on the American side of the border. He arrived there on the 24th of September and awaited orders. Four roads converged at this point, running, one towards Lake Champlain, another westerly towards Ogdensburg, another followed the Chateauguay River northeasterly to the St. Lawrence at Chateauguay and another more easterly.

While Hampton remained at Four Corners, De Salaberry could not divine which route he was likely to take. Hampton received orders on 21st October to move towards the St. Lawrence. De Salaberry, in order to reconnoitre, attacked Hampton's outposts and evidently obtained reliable information that Hampton meant to advance along the Chateauguay. Accordingly he took up a position on the northern bank of the Chateauguay along which the road ran, his left resting on the river, his front and right guarded by a series of natural ditches or ravines strengthened by rough barricades. He constructed an outwork of fallen trees across the road about a mile in advance of the main defences, in order to give a first halt to the advancing enemy. The weak point of the position was that just below it there was a ford, by which, if not securely guarded, the Americans, if they came down the south bank, could cross and take the defenders in the rear. But he placed a company of his Voltigeurs in a hidden spot on this bank.

On the 23rd and 24th Hampton had succeeded in establishing a line of communication with Ogdensburg, and having brought up his artillery and stores, on the 25th he matured his scheme of attack. One column was to cross the Chateauguay, to advance along its southern bank, to seize the ford and recross in rear of the enemy; the main force was to advance on the northern bank through six or seven miles of open country into the woodland where De Salaberry was posted, and charge his position by a frontal attack. The column on the southern bank, 3,000 strong, under Colonel Purdy, started on the night of the 25th. On the morning of the 26th the main body of about 4,000, under General Izard, regarded as the ablest officer of the United States forces, moved slowly forward along the road on the northern bank of the river.

De Salaberry had under his immediate command 300 French-Canadians, composed of some of his Voltigeurs and some Beauharnois militia, and also fifty Indians under Captain Lamothe. In reserve he had Colonel Macdonell's Regiment of French-Canadian Fencibles, 600 strong. With the exception of Colonel Macdonell and Captains Ferguson and Daly there was not a person of British blood on the field.

De Salaberry was without artillery or cavalry at any time, while Hampton had 180 cavalry and ten field guns. Purdy's column was first engaged by a handful of Beauharnois militia, who were pushed back, and Purdy made for the ford, expecting to occupy it with little opposition, but a company of Colonel Macdonell's regiment under Captain Daly had been sent across the river and received him with a well-directed fire. It is stated that Macdonell had taught his men to shoot while kneeling—this was apparently something new in those days. On this occasion it appears to have worked well. Even so, however,

Daly had to retire before the Americans and was himself severely wounded. Immediately above the ford the river took a sharp bend towards the east, and it was just at this bend that De Salaberry had posted his company in hiding. Purdy was eagerly pressing Daly's company back when this company of Voltigeurs suddenly poured a volley into his flank. The surprise was perfect—his column stopped, and the firing on his front and flank became heavier; at the same moment many British bugles from many directions were heard blowing the advance, and loud Indian cries came floating across the river. He thought he was opposed by thousands, and believing it impossible to cross the ford against such opposition he ordered a retreat, but even when he got out of range of our forces the firing on his column did not cease, for an excited body of Americans on the other side of the river, mistaking their identity, fired several furious volleys into them before the mistake was apparent.

Meanwhile De Salaberry and his 300 Voltigeurs were out about a mile in advance to meet the main body of the enemy, and along they (the enemy) came with cavalry and artillery.

A small working party first met them and retired into a line of skirmishers; these made Izard deploy into line, and the working party then retired behind the abattis where De Salaberry was stationed. A heavy fire was opened on both sides. The Voltigeurs—300 of them against 4,000—at one time broke and started to bolt, all but one man and a boy. The man was De Salaberry, and the boy was a bugler whom De Salaberry had grabbed by the collar and forced to sound the advance. Macdonell, back in the reserve, heard the bugle, and, interpreting it as a demand for support, caused his own bugles to sound and his men to cheer; he sent the buglers through the woods with instructions to separate and to continue blowing; he also called upon the Indians to yell with all their strength, and he rushed forward with his Fencibles to De Salaberry's assistance, the Voltigeurs going back with him.

The opposition then put up against the United States force was so brisk that with the cries and bugle sounds they hesitated, then halted. In such a crisis to halt was to court defeat, and shortly afterwards they broke and retired, a vigorous fire following them. There was no attempt to reform or to return the attack. Hampton believed that he had been opposed by a force of 7,000. Upwards of ninety bodies and graves were found upon the right bank of the river, and also a considerable number of muskets, knapsacks, etc., showing the confusion with which Hampton's column retreated. Twenty prisoners were captured. The Canadian loss was two killed and sixteen wounded. Hampton retreated with his full force to Chateauguay Four Corners, harassed by the Canadians and Indians, 100 odd more of whom had arrived. On the 11th November Hampton retired to Plattsburg, and thus ended the invasion of Canada by the Army of the North.

Returning now to Grenadier Island, where Wilkinson had finally on 1st November mobilized his army of 10,000. He was in blissful ignorance of Hampton's defeat and was acting under the full belief that Hampton's army was advancing victoriously through Lower Canada to join him at St. Regis. Wilkinson had been greatly delayed by rough weather, which had for some time prevented some of his troops leaving Sackett's Harbor to join him at Grenadier Island.

On 1st November, while the United States fleet on Lake Ontario under Chauncey attempted to blockade the British squadron under Yeo at Kingston, Wilkinson moved his vanguard and artillery to French Creek, about twenty miles down the St. Lawrence on the south shore, where is now the town of Clayton. In spite of Chauncey's blockade, two sloops, two schooners and four gunboats got out of Kingston and attacked them at French Creek, doing much damage on the afternoon of the 1st and forenoon of the 2nd, when Chauncey's fleet arrived in force and the British boats drew off, eluded him and got safely away through the islands.

On 5th November Wilkinson started down the river with his Invincible Armada of the St. Lawrence. He had given up all idea of attacking Kingston, owing to his delay in starting, it is said, but perhaps also because of Chauncey's failure to keep the British boats bottled up in Kingston. Wilkinson had a force of 10,000, as shown by his own reports. He is said to have had eight Generals in his army. At any rate he had four Brigades, commanded by Generals Boyd, Brown, Covington and Swartout. He had upwards of three hundred boats and scows, as well as twelve heavy gunboats. He had two twenty-four-pounders mounted on scows, so that they could be fired in any direction, and he had all the St. Lawrence river pilots of the United States. It must have been a grand sight to one on the south shore, to see this enormous flotilla glide down our beautiful river, through the Thousand Islands, but it was not all peaceful gliding. Vigorous pursuit was at once instituted from Kingston. A force of 600 in eight gunboats with three field pieces eluded Chauncey's fleet and followed fast, under Captain Mulcaster, of the Navy. These boats were heavier and slower than Wilkinson's batteaux and Durham boats. One of the British gunboats, the *Nelson*, required eighty men to row her, forty on each side. She had mounted a thirty-two-pounder and a twenty-four-pounder. Whenever it could prove effective, artillery and musketry were discharged at the Armada. Wilkinson, late that first night, reached a point on the American shore seven miles above Ogdensburg. There he remained throughout the 6th, and issued an address to the inhabitants of Canada offering protection to those who remained quiet at home, whilst those taken in arms would be treated as enemies.

Because of the batteries at Prescott the troops were landed with the ammunition, and on the night of the 6th the boats with muffled oars dropped down along the American shore, and on the following morning were rejoined below Ogdensburg by the army, which had marched by Ogdensburg overland. That day a force of about 1,200 men was landed on the Canadian side to march down parallel with the boats and clear the way, for the river is narrower and much damage could be done from the shore. On the 8th a further body of cavalry was landed on the same shore, and the next day the whole expedition reached a point near the head of the Long Sault Rapids. At the head of the rapids Brown's Brigade of 2,500 men were landed, and the next day marched down towards Cornwall, being delayed by a small militia force under Captain Dennis, who broke the bridges and held the Americans in check. In the meantime the flotilla was waiting at the head of the rapids for intelligence that Brown had cleared the bank, and most of the remaining force had been landed under General Boyd to protect the rear from the British force in their wake, which numbered about 600 when it left Kingston. It was made up of the 89th, under strength, and a portion of the 49th, and was under command of Colonel Morrison, of the 89th. With him was Colonel Harvey, D.A.G., the hero of Stoney Creek. At Prescott they picked up two more companies of the 49th, some Canadian Fencibles and some militia, a small party of Indians and another six-pounder gun—numbering, altogether, something over 800. On the morning of the 11th, while Wilkinson, having heard from Brown, was giving orders for the American flotilla to run the rapids, the British gunboats opened fire, and at the same time Boyd reported that Morrison was pressing him on land. Wilkinson accordingly instructed him to turn about and beat them off, and in the middle of the day the battle of Chrysler's Farm took place. Boyd had about 2,500 men, including cavalry, and later in the fight was further reinforced. His cavalry was posted on the road on his left.

Morrison, probably under Harvey's advice, had chosen his ground well. He rested his right on the river, his left on a pine wood, both flanks being thus protected by nature. The intervening distance of open ground was about seven hundred yards. Next the river were three companies of the 89th, with one gun; away in front, athwart the road, were the flank companies of the 49th, with some Canadians and a gun, under Colonel Pearson; on the left and in echelon thrown back and reaching to the wood, was the remainder of the regiment, with the third gun. In the wood were the Canadian Voltigeurs and Indians, whose duty it was to skirmish in advance and draw the Americans on to the main British position.

The fight began by the skirmishers being driven in on the British left, which was followed by an attack in force upon that side of the position about 2.30 p.m. The Americans came within range before they deployed, and during deployment regular volleys by platoons were poured into them and beat them off in disorder. General Covington then came on the field with his brigade, and an attempt was made to outflank and crush our right nearest the river. During this attempt General Covington was killed. The British gunboats immediately afterwards succeeded in firing some shrapnel into the ranks of the enemy. The advanced party of the 49th made a counter charge for one of the enemy's guns, but was pulled up by a threatened American cavalry charge. The 89th nearest the river then rushed forward in support, and together they beat off the dragoons and took the gun. This decided the battle. The Americans after two hours' fighting retreated, and their infantry was taken on board the boats and down the river, while the cavalry and artillery followed on land.

The Canadian casualties were 3 officers and 21 men killed, 8 officers and 137 men wounded, and 12 missing, in all 181 out of 800. American official reports put their casualties at 102 killed and 253 wounded, which included General Covington amongst those killed; 180 prisoners were taken and one gun captured. Colonel Harvey, D.A.G., in a letter dated Chrysler's, 12th November, says there were at least 4,000 Americans engaged, and he ascribes our success to the steady countenance of our men and to superiority of fire, our regiments firing regularly in volleys by platoons and wings, while the Americans' fire was entirely irregular. He says the enemy left 180 dead on the field.

The next day Wilkinson learned of Hampton's defeat and retreat to Lake Champlain, and he decided to give up all idea of attacking Montreal. Accordingly he took his forces across the river and went into winter quarters at French Mills and Malone. In February the army was broken up. It had been always harassed by the Canadians. Thus failed the Invincible Armada of the St. Lawrence.

Before the end of the year, under General Gordon Drummond, who had taken command in Upper Canada, the Americans were driven out of the Niagara Peninsula, and Canada was free of them.

The next year Britain was able to spare more troops, and soon the seat of war was removed to the United States; and on 24th December, 1814, the Treaty of Ghent was signed.

VI.

DEFENCE OF ESSEX DURING THE WAR OF 1812.*

By Francis Cleary, Windsor, Ont.

The Essex Historical Society determined last year to place a tablet on the River Canard Bridge to record the engagements which took place there between the British and American troops during the above war. This tablet has recently been completed and placed in position. It is of bronze, with raised letters, and is 19 by 24½ inches in size, and bears the following inscription :—

> This marks the place
> of several engagements
> between
> British and United States
> troops in defence of
> the River Canard Bridge,
> where *First Blood* was
> shed during the War of
> 1812-14.
> July 24th, 1812.

At a meeting of the Essex Historical Society held at the Public Library here on May 3rd, 1911, a paper was read by one of the members, Mr. Gavin, containing a short account of the events which took place in and around this county during the war, part of which may be repeated here.

In the " Journal of an American Prisoner at Fort Malden and Quebec in the War of 1812," edited by G. M. Fairchild, Jr., and published at Quebec in 1909, after stating how the Journal came into his possession, in the preface or historical note he says: " Anticipating the formal declaration of war, President Madison during the winter of 1811-1812 commissioned Gov. Wm. Hull, of the Territory of Michigan, as a Brigadier General to command the Ohio and Michigan troops at Detroit, with the understanding that immediately upon the announcement of war he was

* Presented at the Annual Meeting of the Ontario Historical Society at Napanee, Ont., 1912.

to invade all that part of Canada contiguous to Detroit. On June 24th, 1812, General Hull, with several thousand troops, had arrived at Fort Findlay. Here he received despatches from Washington to hasten his forces to Detroit. When the troops arrived at the mouth of the Maumee River, Hull determined to relieve his tired men of as much baggage as possible by dispatching it by water. Accordingly a considerable portion of the stores, Hull's and his staff's personal baggage, and the trunk containing Hull's instructions and the muster rolls of the army, together with other valuable papers, and Lieut. Goodwin and Lieut. Dent, with thirty soldiers, were transferred to the *Cuyahoga* packet and an auxiliary schooner.

"On the morning of the 2nd July the *Cuyahoga* and the schooner entered the Detroit River, and while sailing past Fort Malden (Amherstburg), the British armed vessel *Hunter* went alongside the *Cuyahoga*, and vessel and cargo became a prize, while the crew, troops and passengers, forty-five in all, were declared prisoners of war. The schooner was also captured. Col. St. George, the commander at Fort Malden, had received the news of the declaration of war on the 30th of June, while General Hull received it only on the 2nd July, when he immediately sent an officer to the mouth of the River Raisin in Michigan to intercept the two vessels, but he arrived too late. In the capture of these two vessels, valuable stores and still more valuable information fell into the hands of the British."

On July 12th General Hull crossed with his army of 2,500 from Detroit and took possession of the Town of Sandwich, the few British troops stationed there retiring to Malden. It was at this time that General Hull pitched his tents on the Indian Reserve at Sandwich for his 2,500 soldiers, and remained there until shortly before the arrival of General Brock at Amherstburg, when he returned to the Fort at Detroit.

The Journal in question begins July 1st, 1812, and some of the events therein recorded, from such observations as were possible to a prisoner and from stray information, are worth mentioning in connection with what took place on this border at the time. The journey from Malden to Quebec is recounted almost day by day, until the prisoner with others was sent to Boston for exchange. Here are a few extracts (taking some liberties with the spelling and grammar).

"July 1st, 1812. After a long and tedious march, I, with the sick, went on board the *Cuyahoga* packet at Maumee. Doctor Edwards, Surgeon General of the North-Western Army, gave me charge of the hospital stores and sick to go by water to Detroit. We sailed about

4 p.m. At sunset we anchored for the night, and about 4 o'clock in the morning we weighed anchor and with a fair wind entered Lake Erie, thinking we should be at Detroit by 3 o'clock in the afternoon. To our surprise, as we were about to enter Detroit River, we saw a boat that hailed us and ordered our captain to lower sail. I thought it improper to make any resistance, as I had not been informed that war had been declared. Lieut. Goodwin, two other officers, three ladies and two soldiers' wives, making in all forty-five in number on board, it would have been imprudent in the highest degree to have attempted to resist a boat of eight well armed men and a captain, and another of five men who demanded us as prisoners of war when we were nearly under the cover of the guns of Fort Malden. We gave ourselves up, and were taken into Malden on July 4th. We were surrounded with savages singing and dancing their war dances through the town. O heavens! what a glory sun for independence! Can any person describe the feelings of a free born subject, to see the savages dancing their war dance and hooting about the town, and to be confined when we knew they were preparing to murder our fellow creatures.

"July 5th. Some gentlemen from our side came from Detroit with a flag of truce and brought news that our army had arrived there safe, and that the men were in tolerable health and spirits."

This no doubt refers to the fact that Col. Cass was sent to Malden with a flag of truce to demand the baggage and prisoners taken from the schooner. The demand was unheeded, and he returned to camp with Captain Burbanks of the British army.

"July 12th, Sunday. The American troops crossed the river into Sandwich and divested the people of their arms and sent them to their farms.

"July 16th. Captain Brown came to town with a flag of truce, on what express news we knew not, but could judge by the movements. Two top-sail vessels were sent out of the river and the people were moving out of the town at night.

"July 17th. The Indians were flocking into town all morning. It appeared by 10 o'clock that almost every person had left the town." Mr. Fairchild's footnote to this is to the effect that on the 16th Col. Cass of the American army, with a force of about 280 men, pushed forward to the Ta-ron-tee, or Riviere Aux Canards, about four miles above Malden, and engaged the British outposts guarding the bridge across the river. The British and Indians retreated. Hull retired the force to Sandwich, as he said the position was untenable with so small a force.

"July 19th, Sunday. There was considerable movement to-day; the Indians again passed armed, and about 2 p.m. we heard firing towards Sandwich."
The footnotes to this are as follows: "On the 18th July Gen. Hull issued an order for a general movement on Fort Malden. Col. McArthur, with a detachment of his regiment, joined Captain Snelling on the 19th at Petite Cote, about a mile from Aux Canards Bridge. A general skirmish ensued with the Indians under command of Tecumseh, and McArthur was compelled to fall back. He sent for reinforcements, and Col. Cass hastened to his aid with a six-pounder, but after another short engagement with the Indians and the British supports that had been hastened to their assistance, the American forces returned to Sandwich.

"Another engagement took place July 24th, When Major Denny and a considerable force of Americans were engaged with some Indians, and retreated in considerable confusion pursued by the Indians. Denny lost six killed and two wounded. This was the first blood shed in the war.

"August 2nd, Sunday. Nothing extra. The Indians commence to cross to Brownstown (now Trenton, Mich.), with British and officers." This is followed with short notes of what took place up to the following Sunday, viz.: "On 3rd soldiers and Indians crossed to Brownstown, twelve boats loaded; I should judge about 400 in numbers. On 4th the troops crossed the river as they did yesterday, and returned about 8 o'clock in the evening. 5th. The Indians crossed the river about 11 o'clock, and people appeared very much alarmed. A party of them returned about sunset, but the boats had few in them." Col. Proctor, who was then in command at Amherstburg, detached the Indians under Tecumseh across the river to intercept a convoy that Major Van Horne and a force of Americans had been sent to safely conduct within the American lines, and on the 5th August Tecumseh badly defeated Van Horne's force of Americans near Brownstown. This victory, however, was reversed on Sunday, 9th, at the battle of Magagua, where Col. Miller, in command of the Americans, defeated the British and Indians, and drove them to their boats, when they returned to Malden.

The Journal entries under dates of August 14th, 15th and 16th are shortly as follows: "Friday, 14th. There were five boats came up loaded with soldiers and five more this morning with from 15 to 20 men in each, making in all about 170 men; another boat arrived about 11 o'clock with 20 men; the new soldiers all appeared to leave town about sunset.

"Saturday, 15th. Foggy; the drums beat to arms about sunrise and the troops were all in motion. The citizens all entered boats for Detroit, as I am told. The Indians went by boats, by land 300. About sunset the cannons began to roar at Sandwich.

"Sunday, 16th. Pleasant weather but unpleasant news. We heard about noon that Hull had given up Detroit and the whole territory of Michigan. The Indians began to return about sunset, well mounted and some with horses."

This news was soon confirmed. As a matter of history it is known that Gen. Brock had left Niagara shortly before this date and joined Col. Proctor at Fort Malden on the night of the 13th August with 300 militia and a few regulars, and had marched the following day with the forces under his command and taken possession of Sandwich, which had been abandoned by the Americans. About 4 o'clock on the afternoon of the 15th a general cannonading began between the British at Sandwich and the Americans at Detroit. Considerable damage was done by the British artillery, and several American officers were killed. Two guns on the British side were silenced by the American artillery. During the night the British crossed to the Detroit side of the river and prepared for an assault on the town. The guns at Sandwich opened a heavy cannonading and their range was so accurate that many were slain. The capitulation of Gen. Hull early followed; by the terms of surrender the American militia were paroled and allowed to return to their homes, but the regulars were declared to be prisoners of war and were sent on board the prison ships.

The American prisoner continues his narrative, giving a detailed account of the journey of the prisoners of war by sea and by land until they reached Quebec on the evening of the 11th September.

The next issue of the Quebec *Gazette* newspaper contains the following item: "The officers and regular troops of the American army taken at Detroit and which have no permission to return to their parole, arrived at Anse des Meres Friday afternoon, escorted by a detachment of the Regiment of Three Rivers. The prisoners, with the exception of the officers, were immediately embarked in boats for the transports. The officers were lodged in the city for the night, and the following day were conducted to Charlesbourg, where they will be domiciled on parole."

And the Quebec *Mercury* of the 28th October, 1812, contains the following: "The prisoners taken at Detroit and brought down to Quebec are on the point of embarking for Boston for the purpose of being exchanged. Five cannon are now lying at the Chateau Court taken at Detroit."

DEFENCE OF ESSEX DURING WAR OF 1812. 77

In the diary of Wm. McCaw, a militiaman from Niagara, and who was with Gen. Brock at the taking of Detroit, Aug. 16, 1812, many of the items in the American Prisoner's Journal are corroborated.

In going through the Fort at Detroit after the capitulation he says he saw several of the soldiers who had been killed and a number of the wounded.

It is worthy of mention here that Captain Frederick Rolette played an important part in the capture of the *Cuyahoga* packet already mentioned, and also in many of the important events of this war which took place subsequently. Frederick Rolette was educated at the Quebec Seminary, and when a mere lad entered the Royal Navy. He saw much active service, and received no less than five wounds at the battles of Aboukir and Trafalgar. He returned to Canada in 1807, and shortly afterwards was appointed to the Provincial Marine. By commission of October 4th, 1808, he was nominated second lieutenant in His Majesty's Provincial Marine. In 1812 he received promotion to the rank of first lieutenant in H. M. Provincial Marine, and was given command of the brig *General Hunter*, commissioned to cruise on Lake Erie. During the early days of Hull's invasion of Upper Canada in 1812, the *General Hunter* was in Amherstburg harbor, when Rolette espied a United States vessel approach, and put out towards her in a boat with eight armed men. Boarding the stranger, he was surprised, but not alarmed, apparently, to find himself on the deck of a Government vessel, the *Cuyahoga* packet, with four officers and forty men of the United States army on board, besides her own crew.

His pluck and presence of mind did not desert him. Placing one of his sailors as a sentry over the arm-chest and others at the companion-way, he issued orders in a loud voice to shoot down the first man who showed any disposition to resist. For a time his boldness had the desired effect, but before long some of the United States officers, chagrined at their position, began to make menacing demonstration. At this time the prize was approaching Fort Malden. Rolette, in a menacing voice, ordered the *Cuyahoga* to be run in under the guns of the battery. This quelled all idea of an uprising on the part of the Americans, and reinforcements conveniently arriving, the prize, which proved to be of great value, was secured.

Rolette served ashore with distinction under Brock at the capture of Detroit, and in the operations with Proctor on the River Raisin, being seriously wounded while commanding a naval gun detachment at Frenchtown. During the war he served successively on the schooner *Chippewa*, the sloop *Little Bell*, and the nineteen-gun ship, *De-*

troit. In the action on Lake Erie at Put-in Bay, Sept. 10th, 1813, he assumed command, though wounded, of the *Lady Prevost,* after her captain was killed, and was again very dangerously wounded when the magazines blew up. He was taken prisoner of war and held in captivity for several months. Upon his return to Canada he was presented with a sword of honor by his classmates of the Quebec Seminary.

It is fitting that something should be said here of the services rendered to the British by Tecumseh, the brave Shawnee chief, in repelling the attacks made by the Americans on those defending the Essex frontier during this war. He was with the British with his Indian allies in many of the engagements, including the capture of Detroit. It was much against his will that he joined in the retreat with Proctor from Detroit in October, 1813. The particulars of the battle at Moraviantown, where he gave up his life, are too well known to be repeated here.

Surely something should be done to erect a monument or other suitable memorial in testimony of his services. The question of where this should be erected has been much discussed. Various suggestions have been made. We would respectfully submit that it should be at or near Thamesville, where he gave up his life in the defence of his country, or at the Town of Amherstburg, where he was an active participator in the many stirring events in and around its vicinity.

VII.

THE ECONOMIC EFFECT OF THE WAR OF 1812 ON UPPER CANADA.*

By Adam Shortt, C.M.G., M.A., F.R.S.C., Ottawa, Ont.

In considering the economic conditions of any country, and especially of a new country, many considerations have to be taken into account besides a mere survey of prices, rates of profit, or volume of trade. Only when we know the social and economic atmosphere of the various districts, the conditions of transportation, labor, local production, etc., can we come to any rational conclusions. Thus, in dealing with the economic condition of Upper Canada before, during, and after the War of 1812, we require to know not only the isolated facts as to prices and values, but the general setting of the country, geographical, social and commercial.

In its early days there were two or three important general conditions which vitally affected the economic development of the Province of Upper Canada. In the first place, the frontier settlements of Ontario were planted much earlier than the corresponding regions of the adjoining states to the south of the lakes. The first settlers, being for the most part United Empire Loyalists, enjoyed the benefit of having been especially outfitted by the British Government and partially supported at its expense for several years. For various reasons, partly accidental and partly of an international nature, the Government established strong garrisons along the Canadian frontier, contributed largely to the support of the civil government, and undertook certain public works. The requirements of these establishments created very profitable local markets for the limited produce of the early settlers, much of which could not support the expense of shipment from the country. They furnished also a strong market for labor, so that during the first ten years of Upper Canada's existence as a separate province, the economic condition of the country was, on the whole, very satisfactory, especially along the frontier settlements, where the people had access to both local and central markets. The most important trade of the province in both exports and imports was conducted for a considerable time by Messrs.

* Presented at the Annual Meeting of the Ontario Historical Society at Napanee, Ont., 1912.

Cartwright and Hamilton, who were originally partners and always close business associates. In various capacities, the Honorable Richard Cartwright was associated with practically all the business of Upper Canada. These varied interests are fully represented in his commercial and general letter-books, which constitute the most extensive and accurate sources of information as to the more important affairs of Upper Canada, between the first settlement of the province in 1785 and the close of the War of 1812. This information is supplemented and confirmed by many special papers in the Canadian Archives, and by more fragmentary letters and records drawn from various private sources.

From these various sources we find that the early settlers of Upper Canada were by no means dependent upon their own resources for the establishment and development of the province. In other words, they were not compelled to pay for what they imported by furnishing exports to be disposed of in distant markets. Otherwise, their struggle for existence would have been much harder than it was, for few of them had much capital and not many of them had much experience in making their way in the wilderness. The most successful element from the point of view of individual resources, with a knowledge of agricultural conditions in a new country, were the subsequent American immigrants, such as the Quakers and others, who settled in Prince Edward County, and in other districts along the Bay of Quinte, the Niagara region, and at various points along the north shores of Lakes Ontario and Erie.

When the American settlers began to develop along the south shore of the lakes, they naturally depended upon the Canadians for the larger part of their food supplies, as well as for much of their imported European goods. These settlements proved to be very valuable and high-priced markets for Canadian produce. Thus it was, that, except for an odd year now and again, the greater part of the Upper Canadian agricultural produce found local markets. In such cases the price of agricultural produce in western Canada, instead of being determined by the price in Britain less the cost of transportation, insurance, commission and duty, expressed a local demand only, the limit of which was the price in Britain plus these items; because in those days, and occasionally in the future, Canada found it necessary to import food supplies from Europe.

It is a common mistake to suppose that since the forests have been largely cleared from the basin of the Great Lakes, the rainfall has been lessened and drouth is more common. The fact is that drouth was at least as common and the rise and fall of the lakes was as much commented upon over a hundred years ago as to-day. The period from 1794 to 1797 was an exceptionally dry one, and the people, with little past experience, were alarmed at the prospect of the permanent lowering of the Great Lakes. Crops suffered severely from drouth, as also from the ravages of the Hessian fly. In consequence, the harvests were light and prices high. At this time flour sold in Upper Canada at $4.00 to $4.50 per cwt., and on the American side of the lakes at even higher prices. Peas brought $1.00 per bushel, and very inferior grades of salt pork cost $26.00 per barrel. At the same time, the Government was importing food supplies from Europe to feed the troops in Lower Canada. When it is remembered that the cost of transporting a barrel of flour from Upper Canada to Montreal, up to 1802, had not been reduced below 80 cents, even when taken on rafts and scows, one can understand what difference it would make when the cost of transport was deducted from the price of provisions in Upper Canada. Cartwright summed up the situation very well when he said, " As long as the British Government shall think proper to hire people to come over to eat our flour we shall go on very well, and continue to make a figure, but when once we come to export our produce, the disadvantages of our remote inland situation will operate in their full force, and the very large portion of the price of our produce that must be absorbed by the expense of transporting it to the place of export, and the enhanced value which the same cost must add to every article of European manufacture, will give an effective check to the improvement of the country beyond a certain extent."

A few good harvests in the early part of the nineteenth century, and the rapidity with which the Americans brought their side of the lakes under cultivation, greatly changed the situation in Upper Canada. The price of wheat fell in the Upper Province because it had now to bear the cost of transportation to the Lower Province, and sometimes to England. It was estimated that between 1800 and 1810 the normal difference in the price of a barrel of flour as between Kingston and Montreal, including commission and freight, would range from $1.00 to $1.50. When, therefore, the price of grain fell, the people of Upper Canada turned their attention to the lumber and timber trade, and to the production of staves and potash. The timber, in particular, could be cheaply transported down the St. Lawrence.

The era of the Orders in Council, after 1808, and the increasing trouble with the United States before the outbreak of the war, coupled with returning short harvests, led to a revival of prices, between 1808 and 1811. Having regard to the price of wheat alone, one would infer that the province must have been increasingly prosperous during this period, but such was not the case. Prices, it is true, in Upper Canada were practically the same as in Lower Canada, because there was little to export, the wheat crop having been particularly poor during 1810. Moreover, as indicated, agriculture had suffered considerably for the past few years on account of the settlers going in for lumber and staves, but now there was a severe fall in the prices of these articles, as also of potash. The high price of staves during the years 1808 and 1809 had induced many settlers to go into that line very extensively, but in 1810 prices fell from forty to sixty per cent.

Owing to the slowness and uncertainty of transport, and the closing of the Canadian ports in winter, merchants required to order their supplies of goods considerably in advance. The result was that in 1810 the merchants found themselves overstocked with European goods, which the public were unable to purchase, or for which the merchants could not secure returns. The commercial distress first manifested itself at Montreal, but spread more or less rapidly to the outlying districts dependent upon it, and especially to Upper Canada. As Cartwright put it, " The large returns heretofore made in lumber have occasioned an immense quantity of goods to be brought into this country, and sudden depression in the price of that article would occasion great deficiency in remittances." The reaction caused even the price of food to drop. Flour, which had been $11 and $12 per barrel in April, fell to $8.40 in Montreal and $7.50 in the Kingston district. As a natural consequence of the depression, specie became very scarce, while merchant bills were a drug on the market. For lack of a better medium of exchange, notes of hand were in circulation in local centres. Towards the latter part of 1811 things were looking very blue indeed in all parts of Canada. Montreal merchants could not collect their debts from their western correspondents, because they in turn could not collect from their debtors. Bills of exchange, accepted by the merchants, were not met when due, and the cost of protesting them was heavy. Early in 1812 Cartwright was offered pork at $18.00 per barrel and flour at $9.00. In June it could be had at $8.00 delivered in Montreal. Early in July, however, it was learned that war had been declared and prices immediately took an upward turn. As the summer advanced, supplies of every description rapidly rose in price. In September flour had risen to $12.00 per barrel and in November to $13.00. In the spring of 1813 shipments of provisions down the St. Lawrence had quite ceased, everything available being in demand for the supply of the troops and others in the service of the Government. When the army bills went into circulation in August, 1812, they furnished an easy and safe means of meeting the immediate obligations of the British Government without the danger of shipping specie to Canada, while their being convertible into bills of exchange enabled the merchants to meet their obligations in Britain without expense. Towards the close of 1812, we find Cartwright beginning to receive quite a stream of payments from all parts of the province in commissariat bills and army bills, which he, in turn, was sending down to Montreal to pay off his indebtedness there.

From the beginning of 1813 to the close of the war, there was little or nothing going down the river beyond furs from the west and an ever increasing stream of bills of exchange and army bills. The whole movement of commerce was up the river, and the rates of freight were correspondingly high. In 1814 freight from Montreal to Kingston amounted to $12.50 per barrel of miscellaneous goods. The conditions referred to by Cartwright in the early nineties were reproduced in an exaggerated form. The British Government had sent large contingents of troops and marines to Canada, including Upper Canada. It was also employing men and horses wherever available from Cornwall to Detroit. It paid famine prices for all kinds of produce and hired men to consume it in the province. Owing to the great volume of exchanges drawn against Britain, the very unusual experience was realized, from the beginning of 1814, of Government exchange on Britain being at a discount. Thus we find Cartwright, in July, 1814, buying a bill of exchange on England for £61 2s. 2d. sterling for which he paid only £55 currency, a pound currency being rated at $4.00. Real estate and other property in the frontier towns had gone up enormously in value.

As supplies on the Canadian side began to grow scarce during the last two years of the war, those who had to furnish provisions for the troops, particularly in the lines of flour and meat, found it necessary to devise means of obtaining supplies from the adjoining districts of the United States. This was accomplished, as a rule, by the connivance of people of influence, military and other, on both sides of the line. This trade, once established, continued very briskly for nearly a couple of years after the war; the Province of Upper Canada in particular having been practically stripped of everything saleable in the food line.

During the war, certain permanent changes were made in the methods of conducting business. Money being very plentiful in all parts of the province, trade brisk, and the returns rapid, the old system of long credits, extending to at least a year and over, were gradually abolished, and at the close of the war the business of the province was pretty well established on a cash basis. On this basis the purely commercial business of the country remained, though in some of the newer sections and in minor retail trade, longer and more irregular credits once more prevailed. Again, in consequence of the universal employment of the army bills and the facilities which they afforded for effective exchange, the people had grown accustomed to the use of an efficient and reliable paper currency. Hence, when the war terminated and the army bills were withdrawn, the people were in a proper frame of mind for the establishment of banks. Thus, the Bank of Montreal appeared in 1817, and in the following year the Quebec Bank, the Bank of Canada at Montreal and the Bank of Upper Canada at Kingston.

On the other hand, there were certain unfortunate consequences which, if they did not originate from the exceptional prosperity of the war period, were at least greatly fostered by it. Merchants, wholesale and retail, transporters, laborers and farmers had all alike grown accustomed to obtaining large profits, good wages, and high prices, and all without any special enterprise, foresight, or industry on their part. When the fertilizing stream of British expenditure, all of it extracted from the pockets of the British taxpayer, had ceased to flow, the people could not believe that the prosperity which they had enjoyed must cease, and that they must henceforth largely depend upon their own exertions and enterprise for such wealth as they might acquire. Many people who had cultivated expensive tastes and who found it difficult to severely prune their expenditure, fell into financial difficulties and were ultimately ruined. Much wealth was, of course, left in the country when the war ceased, and so long as it lasted prices declined but slowly. Upper Canadian markets were therefore especially attractive to enterprising American producers. For fully three years the upper province imported quite abnormal amounts of American goods. Lastly, the war had not improved the social condition of the people. The lack of means to gratify their tastes accounted for the relative sobriety of a considerable element in the population during the early years of provincial history. Many of these persons, however, were quite unable to stand prosperity, hence drunkenness and other forms of vice flourished throughout the province in proportion to the diffusion of British wealth. Naturally, the later state of these people was much worse than the first, and the existence of a regular pauperized class dates from the close of the war.

It is difficult to determine whether Canada was, on the whole, benefited or the reverse by the exceptional period of prosperity which the war had brought to her doors. It may be said, however, that the more thrifty elements of the population and those who had not lost their heads through sudden wealth, utilized their savings for the establishment of permanent enterprises, while for the more unbalanced and incapable the war period had proved their undoing. A great change, therefore, was observable in the personnel of the leaders in economic and social life after the war, as compared with the period before it. On one point, however, there is no doubt whatever, namely, that the War of 1812, instead of being the occasion of loss and suffering to Upper Canada as a whole, was the occasion of the greatest era of prosperity which it had heretofore enjoyed, or which it was yet to experience before the Crimean War and the American Civil War again occasioned quite abnormal demands for its produce at exceptionally high prices.

www.ingramcontent.com/pod-product-compliance
Lightning Source LLC
Chambersburg PA
CBHW032106220426
43664CB00008B/1151